WHO'S
WHO
IN
GOLF

Who's Who in Golf

Len Elliott
Barbara Kelly

ARLINGTON HOUSE·PUBLISHERS
NEW ROCHELLE, NEW YORK

Library of Congress Cataloging in Publication Data

Elliott, Len, 1902-
  Who's who in golf.

  Includes index.
    1. Golf—Biography. I. Kelley, Barbara, 1945-   joint author. II. Title.
GV964.A1E44   796.352′092′2[B]   76-21059
ISBN 0-87000-225-2

EDITOR'S NOTE

The records of any sport are sometimes in dispute, and human error can play a role in the compilation of any work. For these reasons the authors would appreciate it if every reader would pass along any corrections. Beyond that, if the reader can think of any significant omissions, the authors would like to hear your opinions.

This volume is likely to become one of the established sources on the subject of golf. If you have any suggestions or corrections, please write to the authors in care of Arlington House Publishers, New Rochelle, N.Y. 10801. Everyone who helps will be making a significant contribution to sports research. Those whose suggestions, or corrections, are used will be given a credit line in the revised, enlarged, and updated edition we hope to bring out in the late 1970s.

PREFACE

This book, as its name might imply, is an honor roll of golf's outstanding players—men and women, amateurs and pros, living and dead, mostly American—as well as those others who have had a measurable impact on the game. The latter category includes several presidents of the ruling associations, top administrators and promoters, course architects, inventors, teachers, and writers who have added so much to the lore and enjoyment of the game. And there are a few others included who defy any category.

This is not to be confused with a record book. It is, rather, a register of the people who have made and who are still making significant contributions to golf. Including as it does the outstanding figures in Great Britain, Ireland, Canada, South Africa, and South America, it exceeds in volume and detail anything previously attempted in this country. We believe it will be invaluable as a research work as well as a book for casual browsing.

Before starting this book, the authors had to lay down a framework for inclusion, certain ground rules to work by. Otherwise where and when would we stop? This framework had to be arbitrary. It included, for the players, all those Americans who had won a national championship, amateur or professional, including seniors', but not juniors' or junior girls'. For the professionals, it included all those who had won at least one tournament on the major Professional Golfers' Association tour and, of course, all those who had made the Ryder Cup team. For the amateurs, who have no formal tour like the pros, it included, generally, those who had been selected for two or more Walker Cup teams or a World Cup team. Women pros were

7

limited to those who had won at least once on the Ladies' PGA tour, and the women amateurs to those with two or more Curtis Cup team memberships or one World Cup team membership. The non-players were our own choices, guided by the advice of knowledgeable people with long experience in their respective fields.

Readers will notice that heights and weights are carried for many professionals, both men and women, but not for others. This is because the PGA did not list these figures until about 1960 and the Ladies' PGA until later and not on all the women then. No figures ever were kept on the amateurs of either sex. To run them down individually would have taken much more time than we had at our disposal. We did, however, get the heights and weights of the outstanding men of an earlier era—Vardon, Ouimet, Evans, Jones, Hagen, Sarazen, Nelson, Hogan, Cooper, Diegel, and some others. These were giants of the game, and we felt that their vital statistics not only would be interesting but should be recorded before being lost for all time. Incidentally, Sarazen is listed at 160 pounds, which was what he weighed when he won the British and U.S. Opens in 1932. When he won the U.S. Open and the PGA in 1922, he weighed only 135.

In the process of digging and tracing, which often made us feel like a self-appointed missing persons bureau, we omitted a few players. Among them were: Women's champions Ruth Underhill (later Mrs. Harold T. White), the winner in 1899, and Pauline Mackey, the winner in 1905; Walker Cuppers Roland MacKenzie, Jimmy McHale, Gus Moreland, and Reynolds Smith; and Curtis Cuppers Claire Doran and Dorothy Kielty. We could not find them or their surviving relatives, as the case might be. We hope anyone with information of their whereabouts or relatives will write to us through the publisher, so that these players can be included in a revised edition of this book.

Many people helped us in our research, and we are more than happy to acknowledge their aid. Foremost among them were Janet Seagle and Bob Sommers of the USGA, Bud Harvey of the PGA, and Joseph C. Dey, former executive director of the USGA and later commissioner of the Tournament Players' Division of the PGA. Dey's background and memory were invaluable. Others were Carol McCue of the Chicago District Golf Association, Mrs. Herbert F. Larson of the Women's Metropolitan Golf Association, Charlotte Ivey of the Ladies' PGA, Desmond Sullivan, Robert L. Hollins, Violet Diegel, Mortie Dutra, Robert Bruce Herd, Herbert Warren Wind, Bailey Scott, the Ladies' Golf Union of Great Britain, and the Royal Canadian Golf Association. For the use of their facilities, we are also indebted to the New York Public Library, the Bloomfield and Montclair libraries in New Jersey, the Westport and Bridgeport libraries in Connecticut, the personal library of Ken Bowden, and the extensive archives of the United States Golf Association, which Miss Seagle oversees with such care.

March 1976

LEN ELLIOTT
BARBARA KELLY

AARON, THOMAS D. B. 2/22/37, Gainesville, Ga. 6'1", 180. The highlight of his career was his victory in the Masters in 1973. He was an outstanding amateur, reaching the U.S. Amateur final in 1958, losing to Charley Coe. He turned pro in 1960 and finished second so many times that he gained the appellation of "always a bridesmaid but never a bride." He finally won his first tournament in 1969, taking the Canadian Open. His first PGA tour victory followed in 1970 in the Atlanta Classic. Then came his triumph in the Masters, which he won with 283, playing steadily down the stretch. He attended the University of Florida. He has one of the most graceful swings in golf, long and rhythmic, and a little looser at the top than most of his fellow pros. Tommy has made it pay off to the tune of about three-quarters of a million dollars, official PGA career winnings.

ABBOTT, B. PATRICK B. 1/18/12, Pasadena, Cal. 5'11", 140. Abbott came all the way from Pasadena to Long Island to win the USGA Public Links Championship in 1936, defeating Claude Rippy in the final, 4 and 3. Two years later he reached the final of the USGA Amateur and was beaten by Willie Turnesa. In 1941 Abbott again reached the final, this time bowing to Bud Ward. In 1942 Pat won the Western Amateur. He turned pro after World War II, settling at the Memphis C.C. and has been there since. During this period he has been prominent in regional circles, winning the Gulfport, Miss., Open twice, the Southeastern PGA, and four Tennessee Open titles. In the 1941 Amateur final at Omaha, Neb., the gallery was so strongly behind Abbott that at the final putt it rushed in and lifted him, the loser, to its shoulders. An actor from his youth, Pat is still active on the stage with the Theater Memphis Group.

ABBOTT, LORRAINE B. 12/9/37, Toledo, O. Director of educational services for the National Golf Foundation since 1971. Lorraine Abbott taught physical education from 1962-66; as Class A, LPGA teaching-division pro,

9

she conducted 150 golf clinics and workshops between 1966-71. She has written golf instruction publications and film loops for the National Golf Foundation. She has won tournaments in Ohio and has competed in major amateur and LPGA events.

ADAMS, SAM B. 5/9/46, Boone, N.C. 5'7", 150. Adams is only the second left-hander to win on the PGA tour. This occurred in 1973 when he won the Quad Cities Open, firing 64s on his second and third rounds, the best back-to-back scores in recent history. Adams led the Appalachian State University golf team in 1968, turned pro the following year, and went on the tour in 1972.

AHERN, KATHLEEN B. 5/7/49, Pittsburgh, Pa. Kathy had a brilliant amateur record, starting when she won the Texas Public Links when she was only 15. The next year, 1965, she won the state amateur and state junior titles. In 1966 she was medalist and runner-up in the USGA Junior. She turned pro in 1967 and had rough going until she won the Southgate Open in 1970. Kathy was second in the Eve-LPGA the following year and had her best campaign in 1972, when she won the George Washington and the Eve-LPGA. She won over $38,000 and added almost another $16,000 in 1973, although she did not win.

ALCOTT, AMY B. 2/22/56, Santa Monica, Cal. After winning the USGA Junior Girls' Championship in 1973 and finishing as runner-up in the Canadian Women's Amateur in 1974, Miss Alcott turned pro. Only five weeks after passing the qualifying test for the LPGA tour, she celebrated her 19th birthday by winning the Orange Blossom Classic. She had a 1 handicap when she quit the amateur ranks and was president of the California Junior Girls' Golf Association. Amy holds the women's course record at Pebble Beach with a 70. She won her second tour victory in May 1976, taking the Trenton Classic.

ALEXANDER, STEWART (Skip) B. 8/6/18, Philadelphia, Pa. As captain of the Duke University golf team, Alexander won the Southern Conference Championship twice—in 1939 and 1940. He won the North and South Amateur in 1941, then a tournament of prestige, and during the same year was the medalist in the USGA Amateur. After World War II he turned pro and won the Gainesville Open in 1946 and the Tucson and Capital City Opens in 1948.

ALLEN, DONALD C. B. 5/19/38, Granville, N.Y. 5'8", 150. Twice a member of the Walker Cup and Americas Cup teams, both in 1965, 67, Allen was a consistent player in both match and stroke play. He reached the quarterfinal of the USGA Amateur in 1964, the year before the governing body switched to stroke play, and then tied for third the next year, 2 shots behind winner Bob Murphy. In 1966 he tied for sixth, again only 2 strokes behind Gary Cowan and Deane Beman. He was first alternate for the U.S. World Cup team that year but did not play. Allen was second low amateur in the Masters in 1965 and runner-up in the North and South that year. In his own area, Allen has been hard to handle for a long time, having won the New York State Amateur in 1961, 63, 64, 70, 72, 73.

ALLIN, BRIAN B. 10/13/44, Bremerton, Wash. 5'9", 133. Allin's amateur career at Brigham Young University (with Johnny Miller) gave little indication of later success. After graduation he spent 16 months in Vietnam as an artillery officer, then joined the tour in 1970. He earned $355 that first year but jumped to $55,786 in 1971, when he won the Greater Greensboro, holing a putt from the fringe on the first hole of a sudden-death playoff. He added the Florida Citrus Open in 1973, and the Doral Eastern Open and the Byron Nelson Classic in 1974. He is capable of very hot streaks with the putter, such as when he holed five times, from 10 to 40 feet, all for birdies in the opening round of the Greater Milwaukee in 1973. In the Professional Match Play Tournament that year, he defeated Masters champion Tommy Aaron in the first round, then lost to John Schroeder, the eventual winner, in the second. His winning margin of 8 strokes in the Florida Citrus was the biggest on the tour for the year. In 1974 Allin cleared almost $138,000, bringing his short career total to about $380,000.

ANDERSON, WILLIE B. May 1880, North Berwick, Scotland, D. 1910. This dour, flat-swinging Scot set a record in 1905 that has been equalled twice but never surpassed. That was the year he won the USGA Open for the fourth time—the last three in a row, a feat not yet matched. A business-like chap who wasted no words, he first won the Open in 1901 when he defeated Alex Smith, of the famous Smith brothers, in a playoff, scoring 85 to Smith's 86. He missed out the next year but in 1903, 04, 05 he won, with scores of 307, 303, and 314 respectively. He was 25 years old then, and five years later he died of arteriosclerosis. Only two players since Anderson have won the Open four times: Bob Jones and Ben Hogan. No one has won it twice in a row since Hogan in 1950, 51. Anderson's first victory was accomplished with the gutta-percha ball, his last three with the Haskell rubber-core. The ball made a great difference, for Willie's winning score in 1901 was 331. In 1904 he set a record for the Open by shooting a 73, and the next year scored a 72. For his first victory he represented the Pittsfield (Mass.) Country Club and during his last three, the Apawamis Club in Rye, N.Y. In 1897 Anderson finished second in the Open to Joe Lloyd when the tournament was played at 36 holes. Between 1902 and 1909 Willie won the Western Open four times. He was a charter member of the PGA Hall of Fame, established in 1940, and was voted into the World Hall of Fame in 1975.

ANDREWS, EUGENE S. B. 8/1/13, Kirkwood, Mo. Gene Andrews has several distinctions. He has won two USGA championships: the Public Links in 1954 and the Seniors in 1970. In the former he defeated Jack

Zimmerman and in the latter Jim Ferrie, each by 1 up, in the finals. Defending his Public Links title in 1955, he went to the semifinal, but was beaten then by the winner, Sam Kocsis. Gene also has the distinction of twice carrying Jack Nicklaus to the 36th hole, once in the semifinal of the USGA Amateur and the second time in the final of the North and South. The first earned him a place on the Walker Cup team of 1961. He played only in the foursomes, in which he and Bob Cochran defeated Mike Bonallack and Ronnie Shade, 5 and 4. Andrews set something of a record in the British Amateur that year by playing the "loop" holes at St. Andrews (7 through 11) in 3-2-3-3-2, five consecutive birdies. In 1962 he won the Gardena Valley Open, a secondary tour tournament. A thinker as well as a player, Andrews is noted for his analysis of putting. One of his findings was that the best professionals hole 6-foot putts 50 percent of the time.

ANTHONY, BESSIE B. 1880, Chicago, Ill. D. 11/22/12, Chicago, Ill. Miss Anthony won the USGA Women's Amateur in 1903, in her third try. In 1901 she met the redoubtable Margaret Curtis, who was later to dominate the tournament, and lost in the second round. The next year she ran into Genevieve Hecker, the eventual winner, and was beaten again, in the second round. But in 1903 Miss Anthony went all the way, defeating Miss J. A. Carpenter in the final, 7 and 6. Perhaps feeling that she had proved her point, she did not play in the tournament again. Among her other victories were three in the Western Women's in 1901, 02, 03.

ARCHER, GEORGE B. 10/1/39, San Francisco, Cal. 6'6", 200. The tallest regular ever on the tour, Archer reached his peak when he won the Masters in 1969 with 281, nipping Weiskopf, Casper, and Knudson by a stroke. He has been a money winner on the tour since 1964, with his best year in 1968 when he won $150,972. The strongest part of his game has been his putting. At his peak he was deadly on the greens, especially in the clutch. He has been known as the "Gilroy Cowboy" but claims he only worked around the barns of a Gilroy (Cal.) friend. Among his other victories was the 1968 PGA Team Championship with Bobby Nichols.

ARMOUR, THOMAS D. (Tommy) B. 9/24/1895, Edinburgh, Scotland. D. 9/11/68, Larchmont, N.Y. One of the great figures of international golf, Armour had many distinctions. He was wounded and decorated in World War I. He played on a British team against the Americans in a match which preceded the Walker Cup. After he had come to the U.S. and turned pro in 1924, he played with an American team against the British in a match before the Ryder Cup was established. In 1927 he holed a 10-foot putt to tie Harry Cooper for the USGA Open and defeated Cooper in the playoff. He won the PGA Championship in 1930, beating Gene Sarazen in the final, 1 up. And in 1931 he won the British Open at Carnoustie. Among the many other tournaments Armour won were the Canadian Open (three times), the Western, and the Miami. Tommy was a striking figure, sharp featured and with prema-

12

turely gray hair, which gave him the nickname of "Silver Scot." He was also a fluid conversationalist and raconteur and the author of several books. His advice to any player trying to qualify still holds good: "Take no sixes, no double bogeys, and remember there are lots of ways to make four." On the course Armour was famous for his long-iron play but also was an excellent wooden-club player. Deliberation was one of his hallmarks; he would waggle as many as 25 times before starting his swing. In 1940 Armour was named a charter member of the PGA Hall of Fame.

ASTROLOGES, MARIA B. 8/10/51, Valparaiso, Ind. As an amateur Miss Astrologes won only one title, the Los Angeles County Women's, but when she joined the tour her game picked up remarkably. In her second year as a pro, she won more than $21,000, was 21st on the money list, and 20th in scoring average. She was very long off the tee, and it was remarked that her consistency someday would make her a winner. It did. In May of 1975 she won the Birmingham, and she did it the hard way. On the last round she shot a 70 and tied veterans Judy Rankin and JoAnne Carner. Then she defeated them in the playoff by holing an 8-foot birdie putt on the first extra hole. Miss Astrologes attended San Fernando Valley State College and the University of New Mexico.

AUCHTERLONIE, LAURIE B. 1868, St. Andrews, Scotland. D. 1/20/48, St. Andrews, Scotland. Winner of the eighth USGA Open in 1902 at the Garden City (N.Y.) Golf Club. This tournament marked a milestone in golf, because it was the first Open played with the Haskell rubber-core ball. And Auchterlonie's claim to fame, besides the victory, was that he was the first player in the Open to break 80 on all four rounds. He had 78-78-74-77—307. His brother, Willie, won the British Open in 1893, one of only two cases on record of brothers dividing the two premier titles on either side of the Atlantic. Auchterlonie lost a playoff for the first Western Open in 1899 and won it in 1901.

AUSTIN, DEBORAH E. B. 2/1/48, Oneida, N.Y. 5'4", 140. Without a victory in seven years on the tour, Miss Austin scored her first in a tournament that had trouble. When the sponsors failed to get up the money for the $100,000 Gulf Coast Tournament in Houston in mid-March of 1975, the Women's Golf Charities, Inc., and pro Jack Montgomery put together a $35,000 purse and the girls played anyway. Debbie and Sue Roberts tied for first place, both shooting 69s on the last round. Prior to that Miss Austin had been a consistent money winner ($89,883 career) with several high finishes. As an amateur she was a finalist in the New York State Amateur and was low amateur in five straight LPGA events before she turned pro in May 1968.

13

BAIRD, FRED (Butch) B. 7/20/36, Chicago, Ill. 5'8", 155. Baird came out of Lamar Tech in 1959 and went on the tour the next year. In 1961 he won the Waco Turner Open, and in 1965 he teamed with Gay Brewer to win the first PGA National Four-Ball Championship. Butch also has won twice on the Caribbean tour: the Los Lagartos and Maracaibo Opens.

BALDING, AL B. 4/24/24, Toronto, Canada. 6'2", 185. Balding turned pro in 1949 and came on the U.S. tour in 1952, where he won four times. He lost three others on playoffs. He won the Canadian PGA four times. He numbers the Mayfair Inn, West Palm Beach, and Miami Beach Opens among his victories in the United States.

BALL, JOHN B. 12/24/1861, Hoylake, England. D. 12/2/40, Holywell, Wales. Greatest of the British amateurs before World War I. Ball's father owned a hotel hard by the Royal Liverpool course in Hoylake, and John practically grew up on it. When he was only 15, he finished sixth in the British Open. In 1887, the third year of the British Amateur, Ball reached the final. The next year he won it, the first of no less than eight times. His other victories came in 1890, 92, 94, 99, 1907, 10, 12. He was a runner-up only twice; when Ball reached the final, he usually won it. As late as 1921, when he was 60 years old, he reached the sixth round. To his Amateur championships Ball added the British Open in 1890, and was the first amateur to win it. In 1892, when Hilton won, Ball tied for second. He was said to have the smoothest, most beautiful swing ever developed in England. In 1927 Ball tried to win his 100th match in the Amateur but was beaten in the second round.

BARBARO, LOUIS B. 7/3/16, Harrison, N.Y. Coming out of Westchester County, the hotbed of so many fine players, Barbaro emerged with one of the best swings of them all—simple and natural, with no excess motion anywhere. Had it not been for his uncertain putting there's no telling where Lou might have gone. On one occasion when his putter behaved, Barbaro won the Providence Open on the PGA tour in 1941. He shot 273 and almost lapped the field. Toney Penna was second, 6 shots behind; followed by Sam Snead, 7 back; and Horton Smith, Gene Sarazen, and Craig Wood, 8 behind. Ben Hogan shot 288. In 1976 Barbaro started his 30th year at the Hollywood Golf Club, one of New Jersey's most prestigious. Despite his balky putter,

Lou won the New Jersey Open twice and the PGA, as well as the PGA Senior.

BARBER, JERRY B. 4/25/16, Woodson, Ill. 5'5", 137. Turned pro in 1940 but did not go on tour until 1948. He has won eight tournaments, with the big one being the PGA Championship in 1961, when he was voted Player of the Year. In the last round of the PGA, Barber trailed Don January by 4 shots with only three holes to go. But Jerry sank putts of 20 feet for a birdie, 40 feet for a par, and 60 feet for another birdie to catch January. In the playoff he caught January twice after falling behind and finally won by a single stroke with a 67. He made the Ryder Cup team in 1955, was playing captain of it in 1961, and was chairman of the PGA Tournament Committee in 1954, 55. He was perhaps the first of the top pros to emphasize an early wrist-break on the backswing.

BARBER, MILLER B. 3/31/31, Shreveport, La. 5'11", 200. Long known on the tour, until his marriage in 1970, as Mister X because of his large dark glasses and propensity for disappearing after a tournament round. Barber won the single biggest purse in American golf, $100,000, when he captured the World Open at Pinehurst in 1973. Total prize money was $500,000, and the tournament was played over 144 holes instead of the usual 72, and over a period of two weeks. Barber had a 69 on his last round, overtaking young Tom Watson. His total score was 570, an average of 71.25. This was the crowning achievement of a career which began at the University of Arkansas, where he earned a bachelor's degree in business. He turned pro in 1958, joined the tour the next year, and has won nine tournaments since then. His career earnings surpass $900,000. He has a peculiar, personalized swing which nobody can imitate.

BARNES, JAMES (Jim) B. 1887, Lelant, Cornwall. D. 5/24/66, East Orange, N.J. Because of his spare build and his height, 6 feet 3 inches, he acquired the nickname of "Long Jim." Although born abroad he developed his game in America and was generally classed as an American player. In Barnes's second appearance in the USGA Open, he tied for fourth place. This occurred in that historic finish at Brookline, Mass., in 1913, when Francis Ouimet beat Harry Vardon and Ted Ray in a playoff for the title. In 1916 the PGA Championship was started at the Siwanoy C.C., in Bronxville, N.Y., and Barnes won it, beating Jock Hutchison, 1 up, in the final. He won it again in 1919 when it was resumed after World War I, beating J. Douglas Edgar, again by 1 up. In 1921 Barnes won the USGA Open by nine shots, the greatest margin in Open history, with a score of 289. Twice more Barnes reached the final in the PGA, in 1921, 24, losing each time to Walter Hagen. There was no winter tour in those days, but there were tournaments in the other seasons and Barnes won his share of them. In 1919 alone, he took the North and South, the Western, the Shawnee, and the Southern. He won the Western in 1914, 17. Then in 1925 Jim climaxed his career by winning the British Open. He had tied for second in 1922. Truly one of the giants of

American golf, Barnes always will be associated with the lock of unruly hair over his forehead and the sprig of clover or grass which he continually sucked during play. Barnes has the distinction of being the only winner of the Open to have the trophy presented to him by a President of the United States, Warren G. Harding. Jim also was one of the charter members of the PGA Hall of Fame, an honor voted him in 1940.

BARNETT, PAMELA B. 3/2/44, Charlotte, N.C. 5'5", 122. She dominated Carolina golf for several years as an amateur, winning two Junior Girls' titles in 1958, 59 and the North Carolina Women's Championship in 1961. Pam became a pro in 1966 and joined the tour. Her forte has been consistency. After several high finishes she broke through for her first victory in the Southgate Open in 1971. With $18,800, she was eighth on the money list that year and seventh in scoring rank with a 74.11 average. In 1972 she tied for second in the USGA Women's Open. Miss Barnett is a graduate of Winthrop College in South Carolina.

BARRON, HERMAN B. 12/23/09, Port Chester, N.Y. For 20 years Barron was a contender to be reckoned with in the New York metropolitan district, and wherever else he chose to play. He won the Pinehurst Four-Ball title twice, 1931, 33, both times with Tom Creavy. He added the Philadelphia Open in 1934 and took the Metropolitan PGA in 1939, 40. In 1942 he won the Western Open, was second to Byron Nelson in the Canadian Open of 1945, and won the All-America and the Philadelphia Inquirer in 1946. As late as 1948, Barron won the Goodall Round-Robin from a fast field. Although he finished fifth in the USGA Open of 1941, Barron's chief bid for the national title came in 1946, when he closed with a 69 at Canterbury, 1 stroke behind Lloyd Mangrum, Byron Nelson, and Vic Ghezzi, who played off for the crown. He was on the Ryder Cup team of 1947. And in 1963 Barron won the PGA Senior Championship with a record score of 272.

BARTLETT, CHARLES B. 4/27/05, Chicago, Ill. D. 11/6/67. Bartlett was one of the best-known golf writers in the country during the 39 years he covered the game and other sports for the *Chicago Tribune*. When he died, he was golf editor of the *Tribune* and secretary of the Golf Writers' Association of America, a job he had held since it was organized in 1946. In 1929 he went to the *Tribune's* sports department, and his first major golf assignment was the 1931 USGA Open, the longest (144 holes) in its history. In 1933 he originated the *Tribune's* free golf school. During his 43 years with the paper (he was hired in 1924), Bartlett covered all sports except polo and soccer. He won many awards for his writing. His best-known project, however, is *Bartlett's World Golf Encyclopedia*, an exhaustive work covering all phases of the game. It is now edited by his son, Michael. In his memory the *Tribune* established a perpetual scholarship for a caddie interested in journalism. There is a Brunswick-MacGregor Award for the best golf writing, and a Charlie Bartlett Press Lounge at the Augusta National. At the 13th tee of the Dunes Golf & Beach Club in Myrtle Beach, S.C., there is a plaque honoring

Bartlett: "who once scored a 22 on this hole and was happy because he finished."

BARTON, PAMELA B. 3/4/17, London, England. D. 11/14/43, England. After twice being runner-up for the British Women's Championship, in 1934, 35, Miss Barton then won it twice, in 1936, 39. In 1936 she came to America and won the USGA Women's Championship, defeating Mrs. J. D. Crews (Maureen Orcutt), in the final round, 4 and 3. She was the first English girl to hold both the British and American titles in the same year since Dorothy Campbell in 1909. With the advent of World War II, Miss Barton enlisted in the Women's Auxiliary Air Force. She was killed in a plane crash while on duty.

BAUGH, LAURA B. 5/31/55, Gainesville, Fla. 5'5", 115. They don't get started in tournament golf any younger than Miss Baugh. By the time she was 10 years old she had won the so-called National Pee-Wee Title five times. In 1970 she won the Junior World and for the second year reached the quarterfinal of the USGA Amateur. Miss Baugh won the Amateur in 1971, defeating Beth Barry, 1 up, in the final. She was on the Curtis Cup and World Cup teams of 1972. She joined the LPGA tour in 1973, as soon as she reached the age requirement, and tied for second in her first tournament after leading the first two rounds. When Laura won the Amateur in 1971, she was 16 years, 2 months, and 20 days old, and thereby became the youngest winner of this championship, 13 days younger than Beatrix Hoyt when she had won it in 1896. Miss Baugh also was named by a golf magazine the most beautiful girl on the pro tour in 1972.

BAXTER, REX, JR. B. 2/28/36, Amarillo, Tex. Baxter had a splendid record as an amateur, reaching his peak in 1956-57. He was a quarterfinalist in the USGA Amateur in 1956 and a semifinalist the next year, losing to Hillman Robbins. That year he also won the Trans-Mississippi and the National Collegiate Athletic Association, the latter as a member of one of the many winning Houston University teams. And he crowned it in 1957 by making the Walker Cup team. In the victory over the British, Baxter won his singles match and teamed with Billy Joe Patton to win their foursome. In 1953 he won both the USGA Junior and the Hearst Junior, and in 1955 the Mexican Amateur. In 1958 he was on the Americas Cup team, and then turned pro. In 1963 he took the Cajun, and in 1966 the Brazilian Open. Baxter also won the National Club Professional title.

BAYER, GEORGE B. 9/17/25, Bremerton, Wash. 6'5", 250. Attended the University of Washington. He went on tour in 1955 and won the Canadian Open in 1957. He's one of the longest drivers in the history of the game, but is inclined to be erratic. In 1958 he won twice, the Havana Invitation and the Mayfair Inn, and took the St. Petersburg Open in 1960. A lineman on the football team in college, he had tremendous power. Bayer's drives averaged 280-295 yards.

BEARD, FRANK B. 5/1/39, Dallas, Tex. 6'0", 190. This quiet, business-like performer played on the University of Florida golf team and is more closely identified with his home in Louisville, Ky., than with Dallas. From $270 and 217th place in the money standings in 1962, his first year on the tour, he went to first place in 1969 with $175,224. His most notable victory was the Westchester Classic in 1969, although he twice won the Tournament of Champions, in 1967, 70. He has had phenomenal putting streaks: 12 putts on each nine of the second round in his second T. of C. victory. He made the Ryder Cup team in 1969, 71, and tied for first in the $300,000 World Open in 1974 with Johnny Miller and Jack Nicklaus, but lost in the playoff.

BECK, WILLIAM B. 4/25/19, Ashland, Ky. Beck began his newspaper career with the *Centralia (Ill.) Sentinel* in 1946, after 42 months as a combat crewman on heavy bombers in the Pacific Theatre during World War II. In 1948 he went to the *St. Petersburg (Fla.) Times.* His biggest accomplishment there was his series of stories which broke the Jim Crow grip on Florida baseball in 1953. At the *St. Louis Post-Dispatch* in 1968, he was nominated for a Pulitzer Award for his stories on the Masters golf tournament. A series on Jack Nicklaus and a story on Hale Irwin won him top awards from the Golf Writers' Association. Beck has been vice president and president and is now a permanent director of the GWAA. He is also a director of the Football Writers' Association. He is still with the *Post-Dispatch.*

BELL, MARGARET ANNE KIRK (Peggy) B. 10/28/21, Findlay, O. Mrs. Bell has had a long career in golf, as both amateur and professional, and as teacher and resort owner. After being the best athlete in her high school, she went on to the Sargent Physical Education School in Boston and then graduated from Rollins College in Florida with a degree in physical education. As an amateur she won the North and South, the Eastern Women's, and the Titleholders in Augusta, where she was the first to break 300 for that tournament. In 1947 she teamed with the late Babe Zaharias to win the International Four-Ball and in 1948 played on the Curtis Cup team. Mrs. Bell turned pro in 1950 and became a charter member of the Ladies' PGA. She went on the tour briefly but soon turned to teaching, an area in which she has become outstanding. In 1961 she was voted Teacher of the Year by the LPGA, and in 1966 she published a book, *A Woman's Way to Better Golf.* In 1953 she married Warren E. (Bullet) Bell, a former pro basketball player and, the same year, the couple, with Julius Boros and the Cosgrove family, bought a run-down course in Southern Pines, N.C. In 1955 the Bells bought out their partners and began building Pine Needles Lodge and Country Club, which they now operate. Mrs. Bell still continues her teaching and writes periodically for golf magazines.

BEMAN, DEANE R. B. 4/22/38, Washington, D.C. 5'7½", 150. The highly competitive Beman went from a top amateur with an insurance business to the pro ranks and then to commissioner of the Tournament Players' Division of the PGA. He won the USGA Amateur Championship in 1960, 63, follow-

19

ing his victory in the British Amateur in 1959, and thus became the ninth player to win both British and American Amateur titles. His victories in the American were over Bob Gardner, 6 and 4, and Dick Sikes, 2 and 1. In the British final he defeated William Hyndman, 3 and 2. Beman was on the Walker Cup team four straight times from 1959-65, on the World Cup team four times from 1960-66, and on the Americas Cup team in 1960, 61, 63. Noteworthy is that in all cup play he lost only two singles matches. He turned pro in 1967 and won on the PGA tour for the first time in 1969, the Texas Open. He was also runner-up that year in the USGA Open. A comparatively short hitter, Beman was extremely accurate and an outstanding putter. When Joe Dey stepped down as commissioner of the TPD early in 1974, Beman gave up the tour and succeeded to the post. His outstanding moves in 1975 were to drastically alter the format for the 1976 Tournament of Champions and to divide the campaign into seasonal segments.

BENEDICT, CLARENCE W. (Gus) B. 1/12/03, Katonah, N.Y. President of the United States Golf Association, 1964-65, after serving as vice-president the previous four years and as secretary in 1959. A graduate of Rensselaer Polytechnic Institute in 1924, Benedict kept close watch on the development of clubs and balls when he was chairman of the Implements and Balls Committee, from 1958-61. As chairman of the Championship Committee in 1962-63, he introduced several improvements in the technique of running tournaments. One was the use of the walkie-talkie for better long-distance communication; another, the use of lines painted on the turf instead of stakes to mark hazards; and a third, the employment of outside officials at each hole for speedy rule decisions. Benedict is a former president of both the Metropolitan G.A. and the Westchester County G.A. He has been a member of the USGA Executive Committee since 1956 and has a lifetime honorary membership in the Winged Foot G.C. Only three others have been so honored: Bobby Jones, Ben Hogan, and General Eisenhower. Benedict also is a member of the Royal and Ancient Golf Club of St. Andrews.

BERG, PATRICIA JANE (Patty) B. 2/13/18, Minneapolis, Minn. One of the great players of modern women's golf, Miss Berg has had a long and brilliant career. As an amateur she won the USGA Women's Amateur in 1938 and played on the Curtis Cup teams of 1936, 38. In her lifetime she has won 83 tournaments, 41 since the LPGA was formed in 1948. She helped form it and was its first president. She won the U.S. Women's Open Championship in 1946 and the World Championship in 1953, 54, 55, 57. Patty, three times, was the leading money winner on the tour, 1954, 55, 57; twice won six times in a single year, 1953, 55; and took the Vare Trophy for low average score in 1955. She plays the tour rarely now but is busy as an ambassador of women's golf, with clinics, speeches, and promotion work. She also teaches in the Fort Myers area of Florida.

BERNING, SUSIE MAXWELL B. 7/22/41, Pasadena, Cal. 5'2", 115. Starting golf at 15, Susie developed quickly enough to be the first girl to attend

Oklahoma City University on a golf scholarship, and she played on the men's team. She turned pro in 1964 and was Rookie of the Year. In 1965 she won twice, the first of her 10 victories on the tour. Mrs. Berning is one of three to win the USGA Women's Open three times, the others being Mickey Wright and Betsy Rawls. Susie's first came in 1968, shortly after her marriage. The others were in 1972, 73. Her best money year was also in 1973, when she collected $31,613. Mrs. Berning made a great finish to win the Open in 1972. She trailed Pam Barnett by a stroke coming to the 17th hole of the last round. She put her tee shot 20 feet from the hole on this 200-yarder, and dropped the putt for a 2. Miss Barnett was short, chipped weakly, and took a 4. In 1973 no such heroics were necessary, Mrs. Berning won by 5 shots. She likes all sports, especially horseback riding and tennis.

BESSELINK, AL B. 6/10/22, Merchantville, N.J. 6'3", 220. A graduate of Miami University in Florida. He turned pro and went on the tour the year he got his degree in 1949. In all he won seven tour tournaments, major and minor. His biggest victory came in the Tournament of Champions in 1953, the first year it was held. He also won the Kansas in 1957 and the Azalea in 1964, as well as the Caracas twice. He's always ready to play for a side stake in practice rounds.

BIES, DONALD B. 12/10/37, Cottonwood, Ida. 6'1", 170. Bies won his first tournament on the PGA tour in 1975, when he took the Hartford Open, after almost nine years of battling. But in that period he showed what could be done in the financial department with only one victory. He has won more than a quarter of a million dollars. Bies turned pro in 1957 but didn't go on the tour until 10 years later. Don has had his moments, along with his consistently high finishes. He set a course record of 64 at Firestone in the American Golf Classic and another, again a 64, on the NCR course during the 1969 PGA Championship.

BILLOWS, RAYMOND E. B. 6/12/14, Fond-du-Lac, Wisc. To reach the final of the USGA Amateur Championship three times, and yet fail to win it, has to be a disheartening experience. That was the lot of Ray Billows. But he could take solace in the knowledge that it is given to few men to gain the final three times. Billows fought his way to the last round in 1937, after reaching the last 16 the previous year. Johnny Goodman defeated him in the final, 2 up. In 1939 Billows made it again, this time bowing to Marvin (Bud) Ward, 7 and 5. After gaining the semifinal in 1940 and the quarterfinal in 1941, Billows did not play again until after World War II. In 1948 he was back in the final for the third time, and then it was Willie Turnesa who beat him, 2 and 1. Always a good match player, Billows went to the third round in 1949 and to the fourth in 1952, 55. In 1948 Ray won the Metropolitan Amateur. Twice he was on the Walker Cup team, in 1938, 49, and would have been on two other occasions but for the war. Billows also won the Great Lakes Amateur, the Sweetser Cup, the New York State Amateur (seven times), and the New York State Senior.

BISHER, FURMAN B. 11/4/18, Denton, N.C. Bisher is the sports editor of the *Atlanta Journal*. He started with the *Charlotte (N.C.) News* in 1946, went to the *Atlanta Constitution* in 1950, and to the *Atlanta Journal* in 1957. He has covered golf in one form or another since that time, as well as football, although in recent years as a columnist rather than as a news reporter. He plays golf, left-handed, and has a handicap of 12. He says: "The pleasure of playing golf courses all over the world has been one of the joys of my life." He also remarks that although he grew up within 35 miles of Pinehurst, he has yet to play a course there. Bisher has won the Georgia Associated Press Sports Writing Award for 14 years, has been the Georgia Sports Writer of the Year eight times, was president of the Football Writers' Association of America in 1959-60, and was president of the National Sportswriters and Sportscasters' Association in 1975.

BISHOP, GEORGIANNA M. B. 10/15/1878, Bridgeport, Conn. D. 9/1/71, Fairfield, Conn. Miss Bishop won the USGA Women's Championship in 1904, defeating Mrs. E. F. Sanford, 5 and 3, in the final. The following year she tied Margaret Curtis for the medal with 87, a new low for the Championship, but was beaten in the semifinal in defense of her title. She was one of a small group who went to England that year for the first time, to play informal matches and to play in the British Championship. Miss Bishop had a strong record in the Metropolitan Women's Championship, winning it in 1907, 08 and being the runner-up five times, in 1909, 13, 14, 16, 20. She also won the Connecticut Women's title three times, 1921, 22, 27. In 1914 she was again the medalist in the USGA Women's, her 85 tying what then was the record.

BISHOP, STANLEY E. (Ted) B. 1/10/13, Natick, Mass. Ted Bishop won the USGA Amateur Championship in 1946, the first year it was renewed after World War II. He defeated Smiley Quick on the 37th hole of the final at Baltusrol. Both missed holeable putts on the 36th hole but Bishop dropped a 4-footer on the first extra hole for the victory. This was only the fourth time in the history of the Amateur Championship, dating back to 1895, that the final had gone into sudden death. At the time of his victory Bishop also held the New England and Massachusetts Amateur titles. He was a member of the Walker Cup teams in 1947, 49.

BLACK, JOSEPH EDWARD B. 8/8/33, Snyder, Texas. Long identified with the PGA tour as an official, Joe Black is now chairman of the PGA Rules Committee. He was the assistant tour director from 1958-60, and tour director from 1961-64. At various times he has held membership on the Rules, Education, Manufacturer Relations, Championship, Ryder Cup, and Club Pro Championship Committees. He was president of the Northern Texas PGA in 1971, 72, and now is at the Brookhaven Country Club in Dallas, Texas.

BLALOCK, JANE B. 9/19/45, Portsmouth, N.H. 5'6", 125. This Rollins College graduate soon became the sensation of the LPGA tour after joining it in 1969. She didn't win that year but she did in 1970, and again in 1971. In 1972 she shot up with five victories and more than $57,000—$20,000 in the Colgate-Dinah Shore. She won once in 1973 (her second Angelo's Four-Ball with Sandra Palmer), then hit her biggest money year in 1974. Three victories and many high finishes brought her $78,417 in official money. With unofficial money she totaled $88,277, second only to JoAnne Carner. She was also second in the Vare Trophy for low scoring average with 73.11 strokes per round. At the end of 1975, Miss Blalock had won 14 times in six years. As an amateur, Jane won the New Hampshire State Amateur four times, 1965-68, the New England Amateur in 1968, and the Florida Intercollegiate in 1965. Biggest of her two victories in 1975 was the Colgate Triple Crown, worth $15,000. This brought her to 10th place on the all-time money list with $276,936.

BLANCAS, HOMERO B. 3/7/38, Houston, Tex. 5'10", 195. Of Mexican parentage, Blancas has a style all his own. His backswing, shorter than normal, is so fast he seems to be hitting the ball before his backswing is finished. He says he can't play like anybody else but has made his own style. While attending the University of Houston he once shot a 55 on a par-70 course in Longview, Tex. He turned pro in 1965 and promptly won the Mexican Open. He has won several tournaments, the most notable being the Colonial Invitation in 1970, a year in which he collected over $100,000. In 1973 he was a member of the Ryder Cup team. Blancas's career earnings top $500,000.

BLOCKER, CHRIS B. 11/10/39, Midland, Tex. 6'1", 190. A graduate of Texas Tech with a degree in education, Blocker turned pro in 1964, a year before he got out of college. He went on the tour in 1965 and in 1970 won the Magnolia, his only victory on the tour thus far. He has lost twice in playoffs. Chris was a third cousin of the late Dan Blocker, the actor who played Hoss in the "Bonanza" TV series. He is now co-owner of a golf course in Jacksonville, Florida.

BLOSSOM, GEORGE W., JR. B. 7/10/1890, Chicago, Ill. D. 12/12/60, Chicago, Ill. A graduate of Yale, 1914, he became an insurance executive in Chicago. In 1918 and 1919 he was a captain in the Chemical Warfare Service of the Army. Blossom was president of the United States Golf Association in the World War II years of 1942, 43. It was during this period that the Association's museum, containing ancient clubs, balls, tools of the clubmaker's craft, and other memorabilia of the game came into being. All USGA national tournaments were suspended during World War II, although in Blossom's first year as president, 1942, the USGA joined with the PGA and the Chicago Golf Association in running what was called the Hale America National Open Tournament, for the benefit of the Navy Relief Society and the USO. It was won, incidentally, by Ben Hogan.

BLUM, ARNOLD S. B. 4/21/22, Macon, Ga. 5'9", 160. Blum compiled an enviable record in Southeastern amateur golf from 1939-56. He won the Southern Amateur twice, 1951, 56; the Southeastern Amateur three times, 1939, 41, 47; and the Georgia State Amateur five times, 1946, 50, 51, 52, 56. On his sweep of these titles in 1956 and on the general excellence of his play, he was chosen for the Walker Cup team of 1957 and was on the winning American side in Minneapolis.

BOATWRIGHT, PURVIS J., JR. B. 11/8/27, Augusta, Ga. Boatwright is the executive director of the United States Golf Association, a post to which he rose in 1969, succeeding Joseph C. Dey. Educated at Georgia Tech and Wofford College, he became executive secretary of the Carolina Golf Association in 1955 and assistant executive director of the USGA in 1959. He has been secretary of the World Amateur Golf Council since 1969. Boatwright has an impressive record as a player as well as an administrator. He was the Carolina Open Champion in 1957, 59, the Carolina Amateur Champion in 1951, and played 72 holes in the USGA Open of 1950. His handicap now is 3, but he once played to a plus 1.

BODDIE, BARBARA WHITE B. 4/14/40, Shreveport, La. Mrs. Boddie did not win the USGA Women's Amateur, but she was twice a member of both the Curtis Cup and World Cup teams, with a remarkable record in each. Playing both singles and foursomes in the Curtis Cup in 1964, 66, first as Barbara Fay White and then as Mrs. Boddie, she won seven of the eight matches and halved the other. In World Cup play she was the low scorer on the United States team in 1966 with a four-round total of 292 and was second in 1964. She was a quarterfinalist in the USGA Women's in 1965, a semifinalist in 1966, and in 1969 won the qualifying medal but lost in the second round to Shelley Hamlin, a finalist. Mrs. Boddie also won the Western Women's in 1964, 65, the Broadmoor in 1964, the Southern in 1967, and the Louisiana State three times.

BOLSTAD, LESTER B. 5/19/08, New Prague, Minn. Nobody younger than Bolstad ever has won the USGA Public Links Championship. He won it in 1926, defeating Carl Kauffmann in the final, 3 and 2. The following year Kauffmann won the first of his three straight Public Links titles. For 36 years Bolstad was the youngest champion, having been 18 years, 2 months, and 19 days old when his match with Kauffmann ended. But in 1963 Bob Lunn took the title and, incredible though it is, Lunn was also 18 years, 2 months, and 19 days old at the time. Bolstad was a student at the University of Minnesota when he won, and he twice took the individual Big Ten Conference title, in 1927, 29. He went on to win every Minnesota championship except the Senior—the State Amateur, the Open (four times), the PGA, the Public Links, and the Junior. Les also was the first Minnesota golfer to win a national crown. He was a quarterfinalist in the 1931 USGA Amateur, and in 1934 he turned pro. He has been the golf coach at the University of Minnesota since 1947. In 1945 Bolstad and Joe Coria shot a record 59 in a best-ball tournament while defeating Chick Harbert and Joe Turnesa.

BOLT, THOMAS B. 3/31/18, Haworth, Okla. 5'11", 180. Won USGA Open in 1958, 12 years after turning pro and joining the tour. He has won 13 tour tournaments, and was on the Ryder Cup team in 1955, 57. He was one of the tour's most colorful players, with a reputation for having an explosive temper. Later he wrote a book on temper control. His uncomplicated, efficient swing enabled Bolt to finish third in the PGA Championship in 1971, at the age of 53, and to win the PGA Senior in 1969. His most notable victories, aside from the U.S. Open, were the Los Angeles Open and the Colonial National. Bolt won the National Seniors' Association title five times.

BONALLACK, MICHAEL B. 12/31/34, Chigwell, Essex, England. 6'1½", 192. Brilliant is the word for the record Bonallack established in British amateur golf. He won the British Amateur no less than five times, in 1961, 65, 68, 69, 70. Only the legendary John Ball, with eight victories, surpassed him; the best Harold Hilton could do was four. And no one in the history of the British Amateur, which goes back to 1885, has ever won it three years in a row. Bonallack played on the Walker Cup team in every match from 1959-73—eight in all—and captained the teams in 1969, 71, to a British victory in the latter year. He was likewise a member of every British World Amateur team from 1960-72—six times. He was captain of that team in 1968, 70, 72. In addition Bonallack was low amateur in the British Open of 1971, as well as English Stroke-Play Champion, and he has played for England in the Home Internationals many times.

BOOTH, JANE BASTANCHURY B. 3/31/48, Los Angeles, Cal. 5'2½", 115. Mrs. Booth is the living proof that you don't have to be very big to play very good golf. She was winning tournaments before she graduated from Arizona State in 1970 with a degree in education. In 1968 she was on the World Cup team, as she was again in 1970 when she was the low scorer, and also in 1972. She made the Curtis Cup team in 1970, 72, 74; won the Women's Western in 1969, 70; and won the Trans-Mississippi three times, 1967, 69, 71. Mrs. Booth was twice low amateur in the USGA Women's Open, tying for third in 1971 and for sixth in 1972. She was a quarterfinalist in the USGA Women's Amateur in 1968 and a semifinalist in 1970. Mrs. Booth was the North and South Women's Champion in 1972, and five times she has taken the International Four-Ball, in 1968, 69, 70 with Martha Wilkinson and in 1973, 74 with Cindy Hill. She was the Doherty Challenge Cup winner in 1972, 73. Of course she did not let the Women's National Intercollegiate go by, winning that in 1969. Invitation victories are numerous for this substitute teacher in the Whittier high school district. And she says she just plays golf for fun and has no intention of turning pro.

BOROS, JULIUS NICHOLAS B. 3/3/20, Fairfield, Conn. 6'0", 215. During 25 years on the tour, beginning in 1950, Boros won more than $900,000— $400,000 of that after he was 40 years old. He is one of a not overcrowded company which has won two USGA Opens, in 1952, 63. He's sometimes referred to as "Old Man River" because of his easy swing, calm temperament, and long success. When Boros won the PGA in 1968 he became its oldest winner, at 48. And when he defeated Arnold Palmer and Jacky Cupit in a playoff in 1963, he became next to the oldest winner of the U.S. Open. Ted Ray of England was 26 days older when he won it in 1920. In compiling his 18 victories, Boros almost made a habit of winning events twice, as in the Carling, Colonial, and Buick Opens. He was on the Ryder Cup team in 1959, 63, 65, 67. Boros's swing is strictly original, effortless, with a lazy look. The late Tony Lema said it was "all hands and wrists, like a man dusting the furniture." Boros twice won what was billed as the World Championship, 1952, 55. In 1971 he took the PGA Senior title and in 1974 was voted into the PGA Hall of Fame.

BOSWELL, CHARLES A. B. 12/22/16, Birmingham, Ala. One of the most remarkable persons in this book, Boswell is a 13-time champion of the United States Blind Golfers' Association. A three-year football player at the University of Alabama, he joined the Army early in 1941. His service with the 84th Infantry ended in November 1944, when he was wounded in Germany. The wound resulted in total blindness. While recuperating at Valley Forge General Hospital he learned to play golf. He retired from the Army in 1946 with the rank of major. Boswell won the first tournament of the USBGA in 1950, and through 1961 he was beaten only once. In 1958 he was honored with the Ben Hogan Award by the Golf Writers' Association of America, and in 1965 he received the Distinguished American Award by the Football Foundation and Hall of Fame. Many other awards followed, including the President's Distinguished Service Award from the Committee on Employment of the Handicapped. In 1971 Boswell was appointed revenue commissioner for the state of Alabama and the following year was elected to the Alabama Sports Hall of Fame. The last of his 13 victories came in 1970. He lost to Joe Lazaro (a seven-time winner) in a playoff in 1973. Boswell never had played a round of golf before he lost his vision.

BOURASSA, JOCELYN B. 5/30/47, Shawinigan South, Quebec, Canada. This girl is an all-around athlete. She was on the University of Montreal basketball, volleyball, skiing, and track teams. She won the Canadian Open twice, in 1965, 71, and the New Zealand Amateur in 1971. In 1972 she was French-Canadian Athlete of the Year, first time for a woman, and that year she turned pro. In her first year she almost won the Southgate but lost in a playoff to Kathy Whitworth. She was still voted Rookie of the Year, and her $16,000 was the most ever for a first-year player. In 1973 she won La Canadienne Open, a rich tour event, and received Canada's highest honor, a medal presented by the Queen.

BOWER, MRS. ALBERT BUNKER B. 10/4/22, Owensboro, Ky. Mrs. Bower capped a long career in golf by winning the USGA Women's Senior Championship in 1975. As Alberta Freeman Little she won her first tournament when she was 13, by breaking 100 for the first time. Three years later, in 1939, she won the Kentucky state title, the first of her four state championships. The others were the Maryland in 1945, the Massachusetts in 1957, and the New York in 1964. Mrs. Bower then won the Metropolitan Championship in 1966, 74. So far as is known, she is the only woman to have won state titles in four states, This does not count her four victories in the District of Columbia. Not a long hitter, Mrs. Bower depends on accuracy, chipping, putting, and intense concentration. All these paid off in her USGA Senior victory. She trailed by 3 shots after the first and second rounds, then shot a 73 on the last round to win by 6 strokes over Mrs. Philip Cudone, a former champion, with a score of 234. Mrs. Bower loves to sew almost as much as she loves to play golf.

BRADLEY, PATRICIA (Patty) B. 3/24/51, Arlington, Mass. Miss Bradley won her first important tournament as a professional late in 1975, after turning pro the previous year. This was the Colgate-Far East in Melbourne, Australia, the final tournament on the LPGA tour. She made it a good year financially, too, first prize being $12,500. This was more than she had earned in the entire 1974 tour, although she played consistently well then. She came from behind to win at Melbourne with a strong finish of three birdies on the last four holes, including a birdie putt of 40 feet on the final green. Miss Bradley started playing when she was 11 and won the New Hampshire Women's title in 1967, 69. She won the Massachusetts and New England Amateur Crowns in 1972, and the New England again the following year. On a golf scholarship at Florida International University, Miss Bradley was selected to the first All-America Women's Collegiate team in 1970. As a first-year player on the LPGA tour in 1974 her best finish was a fifth at Portland. In Japan she tied for first in the Sunstar Cup with Chako Higuchi but lost the playoff.

BRADY, MICHAEL J. B. 4/15/1887, Brighton, Mass. D. 12/2/72, Dunedin, Fla. Brady was "the man who came close." He had two chances to win the USGA Open and missed both times. In 1911 he tied Johnny McDermott and G. O. Simpson and lost the playoff as McDermott became the first native-born to win our National Open. In 1919, when the Championship was resumed after World War I, Mike seemed to have the Open won until Walter Hagen put on a late burst which caught him. Hagen then won the playoff by one shot, 77 to 78. Brady was seventh in the 1925 Open. But he did win a lot of tournaments, 11 in 1917, including the North and South. In 1922 he won the Western Open and in 1924 the Metropolitan. He, like many others, was capable of hot streaks. In 1917 he broke 100 for 27 holes—nine under even 4s. And in one round he had two holes-in-one. Brady was voted into the PGA Hall of Fame in 1960.

BRAID, JAMES (Big Jim) B. 1870, Fifeshire, Scotland. D. 11/27/50, London, England. One of the "Great Triumvirate," with Harry Vardon and J.H. Taylor, that dominated British golf from 1894 to World War I. In total they won 16 British Opens. Braid was the first to win five, in 1901, 05, 06, 08, 10. Vardon passed him with his sixth in 1914. Braid was a powerful man and a powerful hitter. Coming to a bad lie in a divot hole one time, he sent his caddy to the shop to get him another brassie, whereupon he smashed the ball out of the hole and broke the shaft of the brassie he used, as he expected to. In 1908 Braid set the record score for the British Open, 291, a figure which stood until Jones broke it in 1927. He was runner-up twice and won the British Match Play Championship four times. He was the pro at Walton Heath from the year it opened, 1903, through the rest of his life. He had 18 holes-in-one.

BREER, MURLE MACKENZIE B. 1/20/39, St. Petersburg, Fla. 5'5½", 119. As Murle Lindstrom she became a pro by accident when as an amateur in a pro-am tournament she was announced on the first tee as the pro. This happened on her 18th birthday, and she tried her luck on the tour in 1958 and won a thousand dollars. Three years later she won her first tournament—the USGA Open at Myrtle Beach, S.C. She took that by two shots, over Jo Ann Prentice and Ruth Jessen, and went on later in the year to win the San Antonio Civitan. Then came marriage and a family, and she didn't play much the next three years. In 1967 Murle got back full-time on the tour and won the Carlsbad JC. In 1969 she took the O'Sullivan Ladies' and had her biggest year on the tour, winning over $19,600.

BREWER, GAY B. 3/12/32, Middletown, O. 6'0", 185. Brewer's long and illustrious career goes back to his victory in the USGA Junior Championship in 1949, when he defeated Mason Rudolph, 6 and 4, in the final. After two years at the University of Kentucky, he joined the tour in 1956. Greatest of his 11 tour victories was the Masters in 1967, when he led Bobby Nichols by 1 stroke. The previous year he had bogeyed the last hole to tie with Tommy Jacobs and Jack Nicklaus and then lost the playoff. In 1965 he had won the PGA National Four-Ball with Butch Baird, and in 1972 he added the Canadian Open to his string. The latter came after recovery from a bleeding ulcer suffered the night before the Masters that year. Brewer has done exceptionally well abroad. He won the Alcan Golfer of the Year Tournament in 1967, 68, worth $55,000 each time, and in 1972 he took the Taiheiyo Club Masters in Japan, which brought him $65,000. He was a member of the Ryder Cup teams of 1967, 73. His swing is unconventional with a loop at the top, but who argues with success? The man has won about $700,000, officially, in his long career.

BROSCH, ALFRED (Red) B. 11/8/11, Farmingdale, N.Y. D. 12/10/75, Mineola, N.Y. Brosch was the first player to shoot a 60 on the PGA tour, the lowest ever recorded on the circuit. The 60 came on Brosch's third round of the 1951 Texas Open, on the Brackenridge Park course in San Antonio. Unfortunately he didn't win the tournament, that honor going to Dutch Harrison. The 60 has been equalled by several others but never surpassed.

Brosch won the Long Island Open no less than 10 times, the Metropolitan PGA, and many other tournaments.

BROWN, PETE B. 2/2/35, Port Gibson, Miss. 6'1", 190. Joined the tour in 1963 after winning the Negro National Open the two previous years. Brown became the first black to win an official PGA tournament when he took the Waco Turner Open in 1964. His biggest victory, despite that significant breakthrough, came in 1970 when he won the Williams-San Diego Open. There Brown shot a 65 in the last round to tie Tony Jacklin of England for first money, and then won the first hole of the playoff. His career earnings are close to $190,000. Playing on the United Golf Association tour, Brown won the UGA title twice, in 1961-62.

BROWNE, MARY K. B. 6/3/1891, Ventura, Cal. D. 8/19/71, Laguna Beach, Cal. Miss Browne never was a golf champion, and in her time there was no Curtis Cup team to which she could have been invited. The remarkable thing about Miss Browne was that after being many times a tennis champion, she turned to golf and reached the final round of the USGA Women's Amateur. Mary Browne won the United States National Singles title in 1912, 13, 14; the National Doubles in 1913, 14; and the National Mixed Doubles in 1912, 13, 14, 21. It was after this that she turned to golf seriously. In her first stab at it in 1924, she went to the final, beating Glenna Collett at the 19th hole in the semifinal. In the final she met the redoubtable Dorothy Campbell Hurd and was beaten, 7 and 6. In 1925 she got to the quarterfinal and lost to Alexa Stirling Fraser. She gave it a last try in 1934, only to go down in the second round to, ironically, Mrs. Hurd once more. Mary K. Browne is the only person to have played in the championship rounds of both tennis and golf.

BRYANT, BONNIE B. 10/5/43, Tulare, Cal. Miss Bryant has the rare distinction of being a left-handed golfer. She is, in fact, the only left-hander on the LPGA tour. She is also the athletic type, being better known in the Fresno area for her feats as a softball player than as a golfer in her high school years. She attended the College of the Sequoias and did not turn professional until she was almost 28. She suffered the usual setbacks in her first two years but improved in her third year and made the breakthrough as a winner in 1974. This came in the Fort Myers and raised her total money for the year to $22,348.

BUDKE, MARY ANNE B. 11/16/53, Salem, Ore. Playing her first formal tournament when she was only 12 years old, Miss Budke rose steadily to the top. Her crowning effort came in 1972 when, not yet 19, she won the USGA Women's Championship. She defeated Cynthia Hill in the final, 5 and 4. In defense of her title in 1973, she won her first three matches but lost in the quarterfinal to Carol Semple, the eventual winner. A member of the Curtis Cup team of 1974, she won her singles match and divided two foursome matches. In 1974 Miss Budke played on the winning United States team in the World Espirito Santo Trophy competition. She has won the Oregon Women's four times, the Western and Pacific Northwest Juniors' twice each, in 1970, 71, and she took the National Intercollegiate in 1974.

BULLA, JOHN B. 6/2/14, Newell, W. Va. Bulla created something of a sensation by playing with a 35-cent golf ball in the Los Angeles Open of 1941, when the best balls cost 75 cents or more. He was paid to do this by Charles Walgreen, who was marketing the ball in his chain of drug stores. Sacrilege though it was, Bulla won the Los Angeles Open that year. John also may have been the first flying pro, for he was flown to the tournament by Walgreen. But Bulla was more than a stunt man. He was runner-up in the British Open in 1939 and tied for second in 1946 with Bobby Locke, behind Sam Snead. In 1949 he tied for second with Lloyd Mangrum, again behind Snead, in the Masters. Bulla was runner-up in the Los Angeles Open in 1944.

BURFEINDT, BETTY B. 7/20/45, New York, N.Y. 5'4", 115. Despite her tiny size Miss Burfeindt is one of the longest drivers on the tour. After a slow start when she became a professional and joined the tour in 1969, she hit her stride in 1972 winning the Birmingham and Sealy Opens and ranking third in scoring average with 72.99. In 1973 she won the Child and Family, was in the top 10 in half her 32 starts, and was second no less than five times. In two of these she lost playoffs. For the second year in a row she was an All-American selection. Miss Burfeindt had major surgery before the 1972 season. She won a mink coat for being closest to pin in the Sears and had to sell it to continue on the tour. Finances are no problem now, as she has won well over $130,000. In late May 1976, Miss Burfeindt added the LPGA to her string of victories.

BURKE, JACK, SR. B. 2/4/1888, Philadelphia, Pa. D. 2/10/43. The father of Masters champion Jack Burke Jr. was the leader in the clubhouse in the late stages of the USGA Open of 1920 at the Inverness C. C. in Toledo, O. That was the year Harry Vardon, then 50 years old, led the field by 5 shots with seven holes to go but was caught in a vicious windstorm which his advanced age could not handle. His compatriot, Ted Ray, seven years younger, withstood it well enough to nip Burke by 1 stroke. Burke, Vardon, Jock Hutchison, and Leo Diegel all tied for second. Ray, at 43, was, and still is, the oldest winner of the Open. After that disappointment Burke had to wait 21 years for a national title. But in 1941 he got it, winning the PGA Senior Championship with a score of 142.

BURKE, JACK, JR. B. 1/29/23, Fort Worth, Tex. 5'9", 165. Here was a man who came naturally by his golf. Three years before he was born, his father finished in a four-way tie for second in the USGA Open with Harry Vardon, Leo Diegel, and Jock Hutchison behind the winner, Ted Ray. Young Jack turned pro when he was 17, and in 1950 he began to win tournaments. He tied for first in the Crosby and added the Rio Grande Valley, St. Petersburg, and Sioux City Opens. In 1952 he took the Texas, the Houston, the Baton

Rouge, and the St. Petersburg all in a row as he hit a hot streak. He added the Inverness Invitation in 1953 and in 1956 hit the highlight of his career. That came when he made up 8 strokes on the last round to win the Masters' by 1 shot from Ken Venturi. Burke's winning score of 289 was the highest in Masters' history but weather conditions were abominable. Jack went on to win the Insurance City in 1958, the Houston in 1959, and the Lucky International and the St. Paul in 1963. He and Jimmy Demaret now own a course in Texas. He was on the Ryder Cup team in 1951, 53, 55, 57 and won seven of his eight matches. In 1958 he won the Japanese Open in a playoff with, oddly enough, Venturi.

BURKE, WILLIAM (Billy) B. 12/14/02, Naugatuck, Conn. D. 4/19/72, Clearwater, Fla. 5'11½", 172. Burke burst into sudden fame when he tied George Von Elm for the USGA Open Championship in 1931 and then defeated him in a marathon playoff which went another 72 holes. Actually it was Von Elm who tied Burke on the 72nd hole of regulation play, with a birdie 3, for a total of 292. The playoff was scheduled for 36 holes and Von Elm again birdied the last hole to tie at 149. Burke won the second playoff, 148 to 149. He was on the Ryder Cup teams of 1931, 33 and won the three matches in which he took part. He won a few other tournaments: the Glens Falls (twice), the Florida West Coast, and the Cascades. Burke had been an iron worker and had lost a finger in the process, but it never seemed to bother him. He was an inveterate cigar smoker, on the course and off. For a while he was the personal pro for Henry Topping, the industrialist. Burke was a partner in two four-ball victories, the Hagen Anniversary in 1939 with Ed Dudley and the Miami in 1940 with Craig Wood. Burke was the first winner of the USGA Open to play with steel-shafted clubs. Billy was voted into the PGA Hall of Fame in 1966.

BURKEMO, WALTER B. 10/9/18, Detroit, Mich. An excellent match player, Burkemo fought his way to the final round of the PGA Championship three times in four years. In 1951 he ran afoul of Sam Snead and was beaten. In 1953 he won, beating Felice Torza, and in 1954, defending his title, he lost to the long-hitting Chick Harbert. In the entire history of the PGA, though match play was the format up to 1957, only five players have reached the final more often than Burkemo: Barnes, Hagen, Sarazen, Nelson, and Snead. Burkemo made the Ryder Cup team in 1953. In 1957 he won the Mayfair Inn Open. Popular among his fellow pros, he was known as "Sarge." Burkemo was a sergeant in the Army in World War II and was wounded twice.

BURNS, GEORGE, III B. 7/29/49, Brooklyn, N.Y. Burns piled up an impressive amateur record before turning pro in the summer of 1975. He won the Metropolitan Amateur in 1972, the Canadian Amateur in 1973, and five prestige tournaments, including the North and South, in 1974. He was also a member of the United States World Cup team which won in the Dominican Republic in 1974, and played on the Walker Cup team which won at St.

Andrews in 1975. Later in the year, after becoming a professional, Burns won the Scandinavian Open and the Kerry Gold, an invitation tournament in Ireland, both in playoffs. For the latter he could take no money, however, because of British PGA rules. Burns went to the University of Maryland on a football scholarship but cracked up a knee and then turned to golf seriously.

BYERS, EBEN MACBURNEY B. 4/12/1880, Pittsburgh, Pa. D. 3/31/32, New York, N.Y. Eben Byers was a prominent figure in both golf and business for many years. He was runner-up for the USGA Amateur Championship in 1902, 03, and finally won the title in 1906, defeating George S. Lyon, the Canadian champion, in the final. His family had founded the A. M. Byers Company, a nationally known manufacturer of iron pipe, and he was chairman of the board at his death. Byers died in a New York hospital after an illness which was the result of drinking what was supposed to be a medicinal water but which contained radium salts. He was a sportsman of many interests: trap shooting, horse racing, and baseball, as well as golf. He was a Yale graduate.

BYRD, SAMUEL D. B. 10/15/07, Bremen, Ga. Sam Byrd is the only professional baseball player who made a successful transition to professional golf. Signed by Birmingham at 19, he eventually went to the New York Yankees in 1929 as the No. 4 outfielder behind Meusel, Combs, and Ruth. He played one year under Miller Huggins, hitting .312; one under Bob Shawkey; and then several under Joe McCarthy, until he was traded to the Cincinnati Reds in 1934. He had been Ruth's understudy while with the Yankees, relieving the Babe in late innings and starting when the aging Ruth was given days off. Byrd played with the Reds in the first night game in major league history but was injured that night in 1935 and quit the game after the next season. As a golfer, Byrd won many tournaments, his biggest being the Chicago Victory Open in 1943, with a score of 277. He had won at Greensboro in 1942, took the New Orleans and Philadelphia Inquirer Opens in 1944, and the San Antonio and Mobile in 1945. Sam lost to Jug McSpaden in a challenge match in 1943 but beat Craig Wood, Byron Nelson, and McSpaden in another in 1944. Byrd reached the final of the PGA Championship in 1945 before losing to Sam Snead, 4 and 3. He then settled for a club job.

BYROD, FREDERICK J. B. 1/5/11, Sunbury, Pa. Byrod is the senior golf writer in the Philadelphia area, having covered the game for the *Philadelphia Inquirer* since the late 1930s. He has been with the *Inquirer* since his graduation from Temple University in 1933, except for four years in the Army during World War II. He has covered most of the major championships. From 1946-52, when the *Inquirer* was actively engaged in big-time golf promotion, one of Byrod's primary duties was promoting and helping run those tournaments. The paper ran a regular PGA tournament through 1949, a U.S. Women's Open, and other events. He also has written numerous magazine articles for golf and other publications.

CAMPBELL, JOE E. B. 11/5/35, Anderson, Ind. 5'8½", 175. Campbell started serious tournament golf at Purdue University and has now returned there. As a student at Purdue he won the National Collegiate Athletic Association Championship in 1955 and the Big Ten title in 1956, 57. He was a quarterfinalist in the USGA Amateur in 1955 and a semifinalist in 1956, beaten then by Harvie Ward, the ultimate winner. He made the Americas Cup team in 1956 and the Walker Cup team in 1957. Campbell turned pro after the last round of the Masters in 1958 and joined the tour the following year. His tour victories included the Beaumont in 1961, the Baton Rouge in 1962, and the Tucson in 1966. In July 1974 the stocky, cigar-smoking Campbell went back to Purdue as the professional and golf coach.

CAMPBELL, WILLIAM C. B. 5/5/23, Huntington, W. Va. 6'4", 185. Campbell has been winning golf tournaments since 1941, when he won the Eastern Interscholastic, which he followed with the Eastern Intercollegiate in 1943, 46. He has been one of America's outstanding amateurs for more than two decades, having made the Walker Cup team six times, 1951, 53, 57, 65, 67, 71. He was on the Americas Cup team five times, 1952, 54, 56, 65, 67 and on the World Cup team in 1964. He was its non-playing captain in 1968. In 1964 Campbell won the USGA Amateur, defeating Ed Tutwiler in the final, 1 up. He was a semifinalist in 1949, 73. In 1954 Campbell reached the final of the British Amateur. He won the Mexican Amateur in 1956 and three times was runner-up in the Canadian Amateur. Among his victories Campbell was a four-time winner of the North and South Amateur, a three-time winner of the West Virginia Open, and has taken the West Virginia Amateur no less than 14 times, as late as 1974. In 1956 he received from the USGA the Bob Jones Award for sportsmanship and was a member of the USGA Executive Committee from 1961-64. Between shots Campbell has found time for politics. He was a member of the West Virginia legislature from 1949-51, and since 1971 he has been chairman of the West Virginia Citizens' Legislative

33

Compensation Commission. Attesting to the soundness of his golf is his record of qualifying for the USGA Amateur a total of 32 times.

CARLSMITH, MERRILL L. B. 11/2/05, Hilo, Ha. Carlsmith was the first to successfully defend his USGA Senior Championship and is still one of only two to do it, the other being Curtis Person. He first won it in 1962, 63. During this stretch and through the first round in 1963, Carlsmith won 12 straight Championship matches. He was also a member of the United States team in the Senior World Amateur in 1969, which the U.S. won. In 1970 he took the World Senior and was runner-up the next year. Carlsmith also was runner-up in the North and South Senior in 1963, and in 1958 he won the Hawaiian State Amateur, at stroke play. He has qualified for the USGA Senior 10 times, and, in addition to his winning efforts, he reached the semifinal round in 1966, 69.

CARNER, JOANNE GUNDERSON B. 3/4/39, Kirkland, Wash. A graduate of Arizona State, JoAnne Gunderson brought an outstanding record into professional golf. She won the USGA Amateur, in 1957, 60, 62, 66, 68, as well as the Women's Western, the Doherty Challenge Cup, the Intercollegiate, the Trans-Mississippi, the Pacific Northwest, the Southwest, the Northwest, and the Eastern. And she took the LPGA Burdine in 1969, as an amateur. Four times she was on the Curtis Cup team. She went on the tour in 1970 and immediately won the Wendell West. In 1971 she took the USGA Women's Open and also the Bluegrass Invitation. Then, after some high finishes during the next two years, she exploded with six victories in 1974 and official money of more than $86,000. These were the Bluegrass, Hoosier, Desert Inn ($20,000), St. Paul, Dallas Civitan, and Portland. With three victories in 1975, her career money rose to $226,681. Equally good at match and stroke play, she is one of the longest drivers ever among the women. Mrs. Carner picked up two more victories in early 1976. She won the Orange Blossom, on the fourth extra hole of the playoff with Sandra Palmer, and the Lady Tara.

CARR, JOSEPH B. B. 2/18/22, Dublin, Ireland. Joe Carr, Ireland's best and most colorful amateur, won the British Amateur three times, in 1953, 58, 60. He was runner-up in 1968. The first of these three victories came over Harvie Ward, when Ward was defending the title that he had won the previous year. His third triumph also was over an American, Bob Cochran. Carr won the Irish Amateur four times, 1946, 50, 54, 56, and reached the semifinal of the USGA Amateur in 1961. He was on every British Walker Cup team from 1947-65, when he was playing captain. He was also on the British World Cup team in 1958, 60, 62 and was non-playing captain in 1964. In 1961 Carr received the Bob Jones Award for sportsmanship given by the USGA and in 1967 was awarded the Hagen Trophy for his efforts in promoting Anglo-American good will. Carr had the distinction of seeing one of his five sons play on the British Walker Cup team in 1971. Tall and slim, Carr hit an unusually long ball.

CASPER, WILLIAM EARL, JR. B. 6/24/31, San Diego, Cal. 5'11", 195. One of the giants of American golf, Casper turned pro in 1954, after briefly attending Notre Dame University, and went on the PGA tour in 1955. He won his first tournament the following year, then rose to the top like a rocket. He won the USGA Open in 1959, 66, the Masters in 1970, the Canadian in 1967, and 52 tour tournaments all told, the second highest in the modern, or post-Hogan, era. He also won the Alcan Golfer of the Year title in 1967. Casper won the Vardon Trophy for low stroke average in 1960, 63, 65, 66, 68 and was voted PGA Player of the Year in 1966, 68, 70. He has been on every Ryder Cup team from 1961-75—eight times. In the process he has won more than $1,600,000 and ranks third in the all-time money list. He has won more than $100,000 seven times, six of them in a row. When Billy won the Open at Winged Foot in 1959, he used only 112 putts for the 72 holes. His victory in the Masters came in a playoff with Gene Littler, 69 to 74. Most spectacular, though, was Casper's feat in the final round of the 1966 Open when, 7 strokes behind Arnold Palmer with nine holes to play, he caught Palmer and defeated him in the playoff the next day, 69 to 73, after being 2 shots behind after nine holes. Billy is a fast player with one peculiarity in his swing: he drags his right foot on every full shot. His marvelous putting has been done with a wristy tap. Plagued by allergies during his career, Billy went on a diet at one time of such exotic foods as elephant and whale meat. He is still bothered by the insecticides that are sprayed on the courses. Casper has cut his tour schedule markedly, and now does a great deal of work for the Mormon Church.

CERRUDO, RONALD B. 2/4/45, Palo Alto, Cal. 5'11½", 180. While a student at San Jose State College in 1965, Cerrudo tied for eighth in the USGA Amateur Championship. He graduated in 1966 with a B.S. degree. That same year, he played on the World Cup team and in 1967 on the Walker Cup team. Later in 1967 he qualified for his ATP Card and started on the tour in 1968. As a freshman he won the Cajun Classic and added the San Antonio Open in 1970. Shortly before turning pro, Cerrudo went to the final round of the British Amateur, where he was beaten by Bob Dickson, 2 and 1.

CESTONE, MICHAEL B. 10/12/04, Montclair, N.J. Cestone hit two peaks in a long career on both public links and private courses. As far back as the 1930s and 1940s, he was a persistent challenger for the New Jersey State Championship, being a finalist four times. In 1941 he won the prestigious Metropolitan Amateur. Mike's second peak came in 1960, when he made a "grand slam" of winning the USGA Senior Championship, the Metropolitan Senior, and the New Jersey Senior. His high competitive spirit showed in the USGA tournament when he went 21 holes to win in the quarterfinal and 20 holes in the final there to beat David T. Rose. A post office employee for many years, Mike was known as "the Montclair mailman."

CHAPMAN, RICHARD D. B. 3/23/11, Greenwich, Conn. 5'10", 168. Dick Chapman had a long and distinguished career in amateur golf, from 1930 when he won the Eastern Interscholastic Championship to 1967 when he won the International Senior. Blessed with a strong competitive spirit and an inquiring mind into the technicalities of the swing, Chapman not only played the game but wrote about it and worked at its many phases. He reached his first peak in 1940 when he won the USGA Amateur, overwhelming W. B. McCullough, 11 and 9. He was also the medalist with 140. Eleven years later he won the British Amateur, defeating Charley Coe, 5 and 4, in the final after having been runner-up in 1947, 50. At various times he won the amateur championships of France (1939, 52), Canada (1949), and Italy (1960). He also took the state titles of Connecticut, Massachusetts, New York, and the Carolinas, plus the United North and South. He was on the Walker Cup teams of 1947, 51, 53. Seven times he has had holes-in-one. In 1934 Chapman wrote articles for the old *American Golfer* and in 1940 a book, *Golf as I Play It*. In 1953 he invented the Chapman System of foursome play and later worked with the USGA in developing handicapping for this method. On the 50th anniversary of the Walker Cup matches in 1971, he and Roger Wethered (then 78) had a foursome score of 69. In 1972 Chapman suffered a stroke which affected his peripheral vision and depth perception, but he still manages to play.

CHARLES, ROBERT B. 3/14/36, Cartenton, New Zealand. 6'0", 200. Charles is without question the best left-hander golf has known. He came on the U.S. tour in 1963, the year in which he won the British Open. He won four times on the tour and collected more than $450,000. He won the Piccadilly World Match Play Championship in 1969, defeating Gene Littler on the 37th hole of the final. In 1968, he reached the final, then lost to Gary Player. A quiet, reserved person, Charles is not a long hitter, but his fellow players regard him as a superlative putter. He putts stiff-wristed, with an arm and shoulder stroke. He won the Canadian Open in 1968.

CHENEY, LEONA PRESSLER B. 7/1/04, Stockton, Mo. Mrs. Cheney never quite gained the National Championship, but she had the remarkable record of reaching the quarterfinal of the USGA Women's Amateur no less than seven times from 1927-34, and went on to the final in 1929. She was beaten on that occasion by Glenna Collett, 4 and 3. It took good players to beat Mrs. Cheney. Besides Miss Collett, she was defeated by Miriam Burns Horn, Helen Hicks (twice), and Virginia Van Wie. In her final charge she took Mrs. Opal S. Hill to the 24th hole before bowing. Mrs. Cheney also was the first, and one of the select few, who was chosen for the Curtis Cup team three times. She played in the first three matches of that competition, 1932, 34, 36. She won two of three singles matches and, paired with Maureen Orcutt, all three foursome matches. In 1955 she was honored by the Helms Foundation as the greatest woman amateur golfer from the Los Angeles area.

CHERRY, DONALD R. B. 1/11/24, Wichita Falls, Tex. 5'10", 177. A singer by profession, Cherry turned pro in 1961 after a considerable career as an amateur. In 1952 he was a semifinalist in the USGA Amateur and was chosen for the Walker Cup team in 1953, 55, 61. He won all singles and foursomes matches in which he played. In the third and fourth rounds of the 1952 Amateur he defeated Frank Stranahan and Gene Littler. Littler was to win the championship the following year and become one of the greatest professionals. Cherry was on the Americas Cup teams of 1954, 60.

CHOATE, MRS. ALLISON B. 5/18/10, Buffalo, N.Y. In winning the USGA's second Women's Senior Championship in 1963, Mrs. Choate did it in about the hardest possible way. Four shots behind defending champion Miss Maureen Orcutt, with five holes to play, she drew even at the 54th hole. In an 18-hole playoff she was 3 strokes back with three holes to play, but again managed to tie. She finally won on the fourth extra hole of sudden death with a birdie 2. Mrs. Choate was the non-playing captain of the Curtis Cup and Women's World Amateur teams in 1975. She won the U.S. Women's Senior Golf Association title five times, 1964, 65, 66, 68, 69.

CLARK, CLARENCE B. 9/22/07, Burlington, Kans. A big, blond, likeable chap, Clark won the Lake Placid Open in 1936. He came to the Forest Hill Field Club in New Jersey as the pro in the early 1930s, succeeding Craig Wood. It was while at Forest Hill that Clark made his big bid for the USGA Open, in 1936. His 69 in the first round at Baltusrol tied for the lead with Paul Runyan and Ray Mangrum. A 70 in the third round kept Clark in contention and he finally finished third, behind Tony Manero and Harry Cooper. While in New Jersey he won both the State Open and the PGA. Later he moved back to his native Kansas.

CLARKE, WILLIAM B. 5/10/23, Baltimore, Md. Clarke was president of the PGA of America in 1973-74, during which time he helped in smoothing out affairs within the organization, which had become somewhat ruffled earlier with the formation of the Tournament Players' Division. It was during his term also that Mark Cox was hired as PGA executive director. Clarke's interest in the game began when he was stationed in Norfolk, Va., during World War II. After professional jobs in Maryland and Florida, he became head pro at the Hillendale Country Club in Phoenix, Md., in 1964 and has been there ever since. In 1974 he was made executive director of the club. Previous to his election as PGA president, Clarke had served as vice president, treasurer, and secretary.

COCHRAN, ROBERT E. B. 10/8/12, St. Louis, Mo. Cochran's tournament golf activity covers a long span. In 1931 he won the Western Junior Championship, and in 1971 he was the medalist in the USGA Senior. Between those victories he was runner-up in the British Amateur of 1960, losing to Joe Carr; a member of the Walker Cup team in 1961; runner-up in the Western Amateur in 1960; winner of the Tam O'Shanter World Amateur in 1945; and twice winner of the North and South Senior in 1967, 70. In 1945 Cochran also won the Chicago Victory Amateur, the Great Lakes Amateur, and the Decatur Open, a tour tournament at the time. He has been Missouri State Champion four times and Missouri Senior Champion three times, besides winning numerous St. Louis open, amateur, and senior titles.

COE, CHARLES ROBERT B. 10/26/23, Ardmore, Okla. 6'1", 135. One of America's outstanding amateurs, and one who never turned pro. Coe won the USGA Amateur Championship twice, in 1949, 58, and was runner-up to Jack Nicklaus in 1959. In 1951 he was a finalist in the British Amateur. Charley had a great record in the Masters, finishing as low amateur no less than six times, and in 1961 came within a stroke of tying for first. If Gary Player hadn't gotten down in 2 from a trap at the 72nd green, he would have. He was low amateur in the USGA Open of 1958, and he was on the Walker Cup team six times, 1949, 51, 53, 59, 61, 63, as well as the Americas Cup team, 1952, 54, 58, 60, 61, 63, and the World Cup team in 1958. Coe won the Western Amateur in 1950 and the Trans-Mississippi four times, in 1947, 49, 52, 56. He was a great player by any standards.

COLBERT, JAMES B. 3/9/41, Elizabeth, N.J. 5'9", 165. A graduate of Kansas State University in 1964, Colbert turned pro the following year and went on the PGA tour in 1966. His first tour victory was the Monsanto in 1969. He has won four individual titles in all on the tour, and in 1975 he teamed with Dean Refram to win the National Team Championship. He has had high finishes many times, tying for third in the USGA Open of 1971 and being third in the rich Westchester Classic in 1972. Colbert started early. He won the Kansas State Junior title when he was only 11, was second in the NCAA Championship in 1964, and took the Kansas State Amateur in 1965. Colbert was an All-State football selection in high school and went to Kansas State on a football scholarship, but gave up that game for golf after his freshman year. He is strong physically and a strong competitor.

COLLINS, WILLIAM (Bill) B. 9/23/28, Meyersdale, Pa. 6'4", 205. Collins went on the tour in 1955, four years after turning pro. His activity often has been interrupted by back trouble, yet he has won four tour tournaments and in 1961 made the Ryder Cup team. His best years came in the late 1950s and early 1960s. Collins won the New Orleans Open in 1959, the Houston Classic and Hot Springs Open in 1960, and the Buick Open in 1962.

COLM, WILLIAM F. B. 5/23/15, Bakersfield, Cal. Colm refused to become discouraged by earlier setbacks, and in 1975 he won the USGA Senior Championship. In 1970 he was beaten in the first round. In 1971 he went to the semifinal, where he lost to Tom Draper, the eventual winner. Two years later he again was put out in the first round, but then went all the way. In the final round he defeated Steve Stimac, 4 and 3, after overcoming Keith Compton in the semifinal. The latter was a retired Air Force general who had the unorthodox technique of looking at the hole instead of the ball as he putted.

COMPSTON, ARCHIE B. 1893, England. D. 8/8/62, London, England. A tall, rawboned man, Compston's greatest claim to fame was his shocking defeat of Walter Hagen in a match at Moor Park in England, just before the British Open of 1926. The score was 18 and 17 in what was supposed to be a 36-hole match. He never won the British Open, although he was only 1 stroke away in 1925 when Jim Barnes won. He was the "coach" of Edward VIII when Edward was Prince of Wales, King, and later Duke of Windsor. In 1936 when the King was taking a cruise in the Mediterranean, Compston boarded the royal yacht with three thousand golf balls for the King to hit into the sea while practicing. Compston was a member of the British Ryder Cup team in 1927, 29, 31.

CONGDON, CHARLES W. (Chuck) B. 11/12/09, Blaine, Wash. Congdon came along with a group of good pros who made their mark when golf was resumed on a full-time basis right after World War II. In 1947 he won the Portland Open, and he reached his peak in 1948 when he took the Canadian Open from a good field. He made many other strong efforts but never quite recaptured his form of those two years. Congdon won the Canadian Open by 3 shots over Vic Ghezzi, Ky Laffoon, and Dick Metz, his score being 280.

CONLEY, PEGGY SHANE B. 6/10/47, Seattle, Wash. Peggy Conley was the youngest girl ever to reach the final round of the USGA Women's Amateur Championship. She was 16 years, 2 months, and 14 days old when she played Mrs. Anne Quast Welts for the title in 1963; this was seven days younger than Laura Baugh when she won in 1971. She lost to Mrs. Welts, 2 and 1. In 1967 Miss Conley reached the semifinal, where she was beaten by the eventual winner, Mary Lou Dill. Twice she was selected for the Curtis Cup team, in 1964, 68, winning three of her four singles matches and halving the other. Peggy won the USGA Junior Girls' title in 1964, the Western Women's in 1966, the Pacific Northwest Women's in 1972, and the Pacific Northwest Junior Girls' in 1961, 62, 64. She was also runner-up in the Western Women's in 1975 and the Trans-National in 1966. In 1965 Miss Conley became the first woman to be given an athletic scholarship at the University of Washington—$250. As an indication of the change in women's athletics, 10 years later a girl was given a scholarship at the University of Oklahoma for $10,000. Peggy is now a free-lance photographer in Spokane, Washington.

CONRAD, JOSEPH W. B. 3/14/30, San Antonio, Tex. Coming out of North Texas State College, that hotbed of fine golfers, Joe Conrad became the 10th native-born American to win the British Amateur. This victory came in 1955, with a 3 and 2 win over A. Slater in the final round. Joe also was low amateur in the British Open that year and a member of the American Walker Cup team which won easily at St. Andrews. In 1954, 56 he played on the Americas Cup team. Returning to Britain in 1956 to defend his Amateur championship, he reached the quarterfinal round. Previously Conrad had won the Mexican Amateur in 1950, the Texas State in 1951, the Trans-Mississippi in 1953, and the Southern in 1953, 54. He also had been a member of the North Texas State team which won the National Intercollegiate title in 1951, 52, 53. Conrad turned pro late in 1956, tried the PGA tour one year, and then took a club job. His forte, as he says, was match play.

COODY, CHARLES B. 7/13/37, Stamford, Tex. 6'2", 185. Another of the college men with which the tour is sprinkled, Coody is a graduate of Texas Christian University. He won some 30 amateur tournaments in Texas, was a semifinalist in the USGA Amateur in 1962, and thus made his first appearance in the Masters. He was on the tour as an amateur in 1963 and turned pro in 1964. A careful, methodical player, Coody reached the heights in 1971 when he won the Masters. He had led by a stroke with three holes to go the previous year but then bogeyed in. In 1971 he birdied the 15th and 16th holes on his final nine, then parred in the rest of the way for a 70 and 279 total. Coody has not won on the tour since then, though he had two previous wins, but in England, in 1973, he took the Wills Open and in Scotland, the John Player Classic. He is a consistent money winner, having collected more than $600,000.

COOPER, HARRY E. B. 8/4/04, Leatherhead, England. 5'8½", 152. One of a trio of superlative players who somehow failed to win either the USGA or British Opens, the other two being Macdonald Smith and Leo Diegel. Cooper was the son of Syd Cooper, who at one time was the personal pro to a crony of Edward VII. The Coopers came to this country when Harry was a young child and settled in Texas. Harry grew up swinging clubs, and at 18 became a pro in Dallas. Four years later, in 1926, he won the first Los Angeles Open with a score of 279. And from there on he won 32 tournaments. As late as 1955 he won the Metropolitan PGA and PGA Senior. And at 70 he shot a pair of 69s. With his fast swing and quick movements he soon became known as "Light Horse Harry," and the name stuck. Cooper didn't lose the United States Open so much as he had it taken away from him. He appeared to have won at Oakmont in 1927, but Tommy Armour holed a 10-foot putt on the last green to tie and then beat him in the playoff. In 1936, at Baltusrol, Cooper broke the Open record by 2 strokes with 284, only to have Tony Manero break that record by 2 more later in the afternoon. He tied for the Canadian Open in 1938 but lost the playoff to Sam Snead. An excellent match player, Cooper once beat Walter Hagen, 10 and 9, in a 72-hole challenge match. In 1939 Cooper won the Goodall Round-Robin and in 1942 the Crosby Pro-Amateur with John Dawson. Because of his foreign birth he was not eligible for the Ryder Cup team, and he never played in the British Open. So consistent was he in his tournament days that his second-place finishes equalled the number of his victories. In 1959 Cooper was voted into the PGA Hall of Fame.

COOPER, PETE B. 12/31/14, Lakeland, Fla. After a promising career as an amateur, Cooper turned pro in 1938. He won the St. Petersburg Open in

1949, 57, the Virginia Beach in 1954, and the West Palm Beach in 1958. It was farther south, though, that Cooper worked up a reputation. He won the Panama in 1959, 61, the Puerto Rico in 1959, and the Maracaibo and Jamaica Opens in 1960. His success in this area led to his being referred to as "The King of the Caribbean." Pete also won the Metropolitan Open in 1953.

CORCORAN, FRED J. 4/4/05, Cambridge, Mass. The vice president and tournament director of the International Golf Association since 1954, Corcoran is a living success story. From a caddy at the Belmont Springs C.C. in 1916 he became secretary of the Belmont C.C. in 1920. From 1925-36 he was the official scorer for 34 USGA Championships. From 1937-48 Fred ran the PGA tour as its tournament manager. In 1937, 39, 53 he managed the U.S. Ryder Cup teams. Meanwhile during World War II he toured the country arranging golf matches with Bing Crosby and later Bob Hope for the War Bond drive. He also dreamed up and promoted matches which raised more than $300,000 for the Red Cross. In 1944 he put on sports programs for the Fifth Army in Italy. Promoter that he was, Corcoran had a great penchant for starting things. He founded the Golf Writers' Association of America and the Ladies' PGA. He served as tournament director for the LPGA and founded its Hall of Fame. From 1952-55 he was promotional director of the PGA. He promoted the Thunderbird Classic, the first $100,000 tournament in golf, and since 1967 has been tournament director of the Westchester Classic, a $250,000 tournament, which has raised $2.25 million for Westchester hospitals. With all these activities Fred found time to manage the business affairs of Sam Snead, Babe Didrikson Zaharias, Tony Lema, Ken Venturi, Tom Weiskopf, Stan Musial, and Ted Williams. He gave up management in 1970. Corcoran received the William D. Richardson Award from the GWAA in 1960, the Achievement Award from the Boston golf writers in 1962, and the Walter Hagen Award from the writers of America and Great Britain in 1968. He was voted into the World Golf Hall of Fame in 1975.

CORNELIUS, KATHERINE B. 10/27/32, Boston, Mass. 5'6", 124. Although born in Boston, Kathy graduated from high school in Lake Worth, Fla., in 1949. While attending Florida Southern College, she won the Southern Amateur in 1952, and was runner-up in the Intercollegiate in 1952, 53. Kathy went on the LPGA tour in 1957 and won her first tournament in 1959, the Cosmopolitan Open. She added a second, the Tippecanoe, in 1961, and was a co-winner in the Zaharias in 1962 with Betsy Rawls. Then came a long drought during which she played the tour intermittently and did not win again until 1972. That came with the Bluegrass Invitation and the era of the bigger money. In 1973 Kathy added her fifth, the Sealy-Faberge, along with $44,246 for the campaign. Her career earnings now surpass $174,000.

COTTON, THOMAS HENRY B. 1/26/07, Cheshire, England. Great Britain's greatest player since the days of Harry Vardon. After 10 straight American victories in the British Open, Cotton broke the string when he won in 1934. He won again in 1937 and for a third time in 1948. He also won three British PGA Championships, as well as many titles all over the European continent. He rarely came to America, but in 1948 he won the White Sulphur Springs Invitation. Because of differences with the British PGA, Cotton played on only three Ryder Cup teams, in 1929, 37, 47. He won his first two matches, against Al Watrous and Tony Manero, and lost the third to Sam Snead. In his later years Cotton turned to golf architecture and designed courses in several European countries.

COURTNEY, CHARLES (Chuck) B. 10/11/40, Minneapolis, Minn. 5'10", 160. Turned pro in 1963 after attending San Diego State College. He made his first year on tour a big one by winning the St. Paul Open. He won three tournaments altogether. His career earnings approximate $250,000.

COWAN, GARY B. 10/28/38, Kitchener, Canada. 6'0", 185. Cowan stamped his name among golf's celebrities by winning the USGA Amateur Championship in 1966. This was the first time the title had gone to a foreign entrant since 1932, when C. Ross Somerville, another Canadian, took it. Cowan's victory came in the second year the Amateur was played at stroke play rather than match. He finished the 72 holes tied with Deane Beman, at 285, then defeated Beman in the playoff by 1 shot. He won the Canadian Amateur in 1961 and was a finalist in 1968. He was low amateur in the Masters in 1965. A strong player and big hitter, Cowan was on the World Amateur Cup team from 1960-66.

COX, MARK H. B. 5/23/16, Wyoming, Ill. Cox became executive director of the Professional Golfers' Association on August 1, 1973, after a long career in the business world and as a writer. From 1945-58 he was director of advertising, public relations, and promotion for Wilson & Co. This included all subsidiaries, including the Wilson Sporting Goods Company. He was director of corporate advertising and public relations of the Brunswick Corporation from 1959-66. In the latter year he became president of Victor Golf, a position he held until August 1973. Cox also is a former president, and is still a trustee, of the Evans Scholars Foundation. He has co-authored many books with a variety of sports figures, including Sam Snead, Bart Starr, Jack Kramer, Lou Boudreau, Patty Berg, and others.

COX, WILFRED H. (Wiffy) B. 10/27/1897, Brooklyn, N.Y. D. 2/20/69, Washington, D.C. After serving as a fireman on the battleship USS *Nevada,* Cox got into golf seriously. By 1930 he was winning. That year he and Willie Macfarlane took the Pinehurst Pro-Pro, and Wiffy tied for first in the Florida Open (there was no playoff) with Joe Turnesa. Coming north that spring he won the North and South Open, a tournament with much prestige at that time. In 1931 he won the San Francisco Match-Play and in 1932 the Pinehurst Pro-Pro, again with Macfarlane. Two years later Cox took two good ones, the Agua Caliente and Texas Opens, and in 1936 the Sacramento

Open. Cox made two bids for the USGA Open, finishing fourth in 1931 and fifth in 1932. Wiffy made the Ryder Cup team in 1931.

CRAMPTON, BRUCE B. 9/28/35, Sydney, Australia. 5'11", 180. One of the game's great players, Crampton has won 15 titles on the U.S. tour since he went on it in 1957. He has made his compact, no-nonsense swing pay off for him to the tune of more than a million dollars. He joined the "Million Dollar Club" in 1973 when he won four tournaments, finished second in five, and took in $274,266. He also won the Vardon Trophy that year (for low score average) with 70.576 and was the first foreign-born pro to win it since Harry Cooper in 1937. He also is known as the "Iron Man" because of the number of tournaments he enters. During one stretch from 1962-63, he played in 38 consecutive events. He is one of only six players who have won over a million dollars, joining Nicklaus, Palmer, Casper, Trevino, and Player.

CRAWFORD, JEAN ASHLEY B. 1/10/39, Chanute, Kans. 5'9", 130. At 16 Mrs. Crawford, as Jean Ashley, won the Kansas Women's Amateur and then repeated her win in 1961. In 1960 she reached the final of the USGA Women's Championship, where she lost to JoAnne Gunderson. But in 1965 she won the USGA title, beating Mrs. Ann Quast Welts in the final, 5 and 4. Two years later she reached the final for the third time, losing then to Mary Lou Dill. Mrs. Crawford was a playing member of the Curtis Cup teams of 1962, 66, 68 and was the non-playing captain of the 1972 team.

CREAVY, THOMAS B. 2/3/11, Tuckahoe, N.Y. Creavy won the national PGA Championship the first year he played in it, in 1931, when he was a mere 20 years old. He had failed to qualify the two previous years, knocking himself out by taking 11 on the last hole of the qualifier in 1929 and missing by 2 shots. But in 1931 Creavy swept through, beating Cyril Walker in the quarterfinal, Gene Sarazen in the semifinal, and Denny Shute in the final, 2 and 1. In 1932 Tom reached the semifinal of the PGA but lost to Frank Walsh on the 38th hole. He made a great comeback in this match, squaring it after being 8 down after 16 holes. He reached the quarterfinal of the 1933 Championship and that year won the San Francisco Match Play Open. Shortly afterward, Creavy's tournament career was ended by a near-fatal illness. Since then he has devoted most of his time to teaching and promoting the game. Creavy is next to the youngest winner of the PGA, losing that honor to Sarazen by a few weeks.

CREED, CLIFFORD ANN B. 9/23/38, Alexandria, La. 5'4", 105. A graduate of Lamar Tech in 1960, with a degree in physical education, Miss Creed had an impressive record as an amateur. She won the Louisiana State Championship six times; the Western Junior in 1956; the Southern Amateur in 1957, 62; and the North and South, the South Atlantic, and a place on the Curtis Cup team in 1962. She turned pro later that year. She played in only one tour tournament but tied for third. In 1964, 65, 66, Miss Creed won three times each year. Four times she has earned more than $20,000 and has been as low as second in scoring average. Clifford was named for her father. She is one of the smallest players on the tour.

CRENSHAW, BEN B. 1/11/52, Austin, Tex. 5'9", 163. If ever anyone came into the pro ranks with stardom marked all over him, it was Crenshaw. Three times, while a student at the University of Texas, he won the NCAA Championship, although he shared it one year with a Texas teammate, Tom Kite. He won the Western Amateur and in 1972 was a member of the U.S. World Amateur Cup team. Ben turned pro in 1973, leading the qualifiers for his Approved Tournament Players' Card by 12 strokes. He promptly won his first start, the San Antonio-Texas Open. It was the first time this had happened since Marty Fleckman won his first pro start in 1967. Crenshaw then came out of the pack and finished second in the World Open at Pinehurst later in the year. His earnings in less than two years on the tour were over $147,000. Early in 1976 Crenshaw won the Crosby and Hawaiian Opens.

CROCKER, FAY B. 8/2/14, Montevideo, Uruguay. Miss Crocker came to the United States and turned pro in 1953, after winning the Uruguayan Women's Amateur no less than 20 times. In an earlier appearance here in 1950, she had gone to the quarterfinal of the USGA Women's Amateur before losing to Mae Murray. In 1955 she won the USGA Women's Open, beating Louise Suggs and Mary Lena Faulk by 4 shots. She led after every round in winds that at times reached 40 miles an hour. Miss Crocker also added two victories on the Ladies' PGA tour that year. In all, from 1955-60, she won 11 tournaments, including the Serbin Open three times and the LPGA Titleholders once, in 1960. In 1958 she finished third in the USGA Women's Open.

CROCKER, MARY LOU DANIEL B. 9/17/44, Louisville, Ky. 5'2½", 115. Crocker won the USGA Junior Girls' title in 1962, as well as the Western Junior. Just before she turned pro in 1965 she won the Kentucky state title. She joined the LPGA tour in 1966. A tie for fourth that year was the best she did on the tour until she broke through in 1973, winning the Marc Equity. That was her best year financially too, with more than $11,100. Her development has been hampered by a knee injury.

CROSBY, HARRY LILLIS (Bing) B. 5/2/04, Tacoma, Wash. One of the best-known entertainers on the American screen, radio, and television, Crosby started singing with dance bands in 1925, after attending Gonzaga University. He got into broadcasting in 1931 and has been a screen actor since that time. An enthusiastic golfer, he got into the tournament picture in 1937, sponsoring an 18-hole tournament on the West Coast. Sam Snead was the winner, as he was the next year when it was increased to 36 holes. After

World War II, Crosby raised it to 54 holes and in 1958 to 72. It has a pro-amateur format, with celebrities playing the first three days. It is one of the most popular tournaments on the circuit, and is played at Pebble Beach. Crosby was the first of the big-name entertainers to get into the golf picture. He was also the first of the "crooners," singing with the Paul Whiteman band. He was a good enough golfer to once qualify sectionally for the USGA Amateur. Crosby got his nickname from his fondness for a comic strip called "Bingsville Bugle."

CRUICKSHANK, BOBBY B. 11/16/1894, Grantown-on-Spey, Scotland. D. 8/27/75, Delray Beach, Fla. 5'5", 165. One of golf's remarkable figures, especially for continued excellence into old age. He came to America in 1921 and turned pro the same year. Playing in the comparatively meager number of tournaments in that era, he won 13 of them, including the North and South (three times) and the Los Angeles Open. He never won a national championship, coming closest when he tied Bob Jones in the USGA Open of 1923 but lost the playoff. He was close again in 1924, 32, 34, 37. Known affectionately as "The Wee Scot" or "Wee Bobby," Cruickshank's sound swing stayed with him as age crept up. In the PGA Senior and Stroke Play events, over a three-year span, 1971, 72, 73, Cruickshank shot rounds which matched or bettered his age in 12 competitive starts. At the age of 79 he had two 75s and a 79. The PGA calls it "the most remarkable competitive scoring record in PGA annals." Cruickshank was voted into the PGA Hall of Fame in 1967.

CRUMP, GEORGE ARTHUR B. 9/24/1871, Philadelphia, Pa. D. 1/24/18, Merchantville, N.J. Crump's place in golf history rests on his role as builder and chief designer of the Pine Valley course in Clementon, N.J. It is generally regarded as one of the most difficult layouts in the world. Crump was a Philadelphia hotelman who decided to build a golf course different from any he'd ever seen. He got out of the hotel business and built a bungalow in the New Jersey pine barrens where he lived almost as a recluse while the course was under construction. This was in 1913. By 1918 14 holes had been completed, hacked out of the pine forests over acres of sand. Then Crump died of a gunshot wound. Hugh Wilson, a Philadelphia amateur, helped the heirs complete the course. Pine Valley had never been the design of Crump alone. He hired H. S. Colt, an English architect, to help him from the beginning. After his death several others had a hand in it. The course might best be described as one vast tree-studded sand bunker, with strips of fairway running through it. It is a monumental work.

CUDONE, CAROLYN B. 9/7/18, Oxford, Ala. Mrs. Cudone dominated the USGA Women's Senior Championship for five straight years, winning it from 1968-72. But this was not unusual, for she won the Women's Senior North and South six times, from 1969-75, missing only 1971. In 1953 she was a semifinalist in the USGA Women's Amateur and in 1956 a member of the

Curtis Cup team, of which she was the non-playing captain in 1970. Three times Mrs. Cudone won the National Mixed Foursomes title, partnered by William Hyndman III. In 1960 she took the Women's Eastern at stroke play and in 1958 the Women's North and South at match play. She won the tradition-packed Women's Metropolitan title five times, 1955, 61, 63, 64, 65, and the New Jersey Crown six times from 1955-65. She won the Women's New Jersey G.A. stroke play title no less than 11 times in 16 years and the Carolinas G.A. and the Women's South Carolina Championships five times each. In 1962 Mrs. Cudone and her partner won the International Four-Ball.

CULLEN, MARY ELIZABETH (Betsy) B. 8/14/38, Tulsa, Okla. 5'4", 125. A graduate of the University of Oklahoma with a degree in physical education, Miss Cullen moved into competitive golf by an unusual route. She was the State Junior winner in 1953, 54 and was a semifinalist in the USGA Junior Girls' in 1955. She became a professional in 1962, but unlike many of the girls she became a teaching pro for three years instead of jumping immediately to the tour. In 1965 Miss Cullen hit the tour full time. She had several high finishes each year but didn't break into the winner's circle until 1972. That's when she won the Sears Classic. She followed in 1973 with her second win, in the Alamo Open and in 1975 with her third, the Hoosier, bringing her career earnings to about $150,000.

CULLENWARD, NELSON B. 7/28/13, Vancouver, B.C., Canada. One of the country's leading and veteran golf writers, Cullenward has the distinction of playing the game as well as he writes it. He has been working for the *San Francisco Examiner* for 40 years, 39 of them covering golf. The fact that he is left-handed has not bothered him, for he has won the California Lefty Championship a total of 14 times. In 1965 he teamed with George Archer to win the Crosby Pro-Amateur. He won the Golf Writers' Association title, played annually at Myrtle Beach, in 1964, 70. He now has a handicap of 8. For 39 years Cullenward has run the San Francisco City Junior Championship and also various charity events. He is a former Golf Writers' Association of America president.

CUMMINGS, EDITH (Mrs. Curtis Munson) B. 3/26/1899, Chicago, Ill. Described by one writer as "a cool, blonde," Miss Cummings was one of the most beautiful girls ever to win a title in golf or any other sport in America. One reporter claimed she far outshone Julia Sanderson and Marilyn Miller, the reigning stage beauties of the period. And she also could play golf. In 1920 she was beaten by Alexa Stirling, the eventual winner, in the USGA Women's Amateur. In 1922 she went to the semifinal before falling to Glenna Collett, who won her first title the next day. And in 1923 she went all the way to the championship. After three easy matches in which her smallest margin of victory was 5 and 4, she disposed of Mrs. C. H. Vanderbeck, who had won the title in 1915, on the 20th hole, and then defeated Alexa Stirling in the final, 3 and 2. Defending her title in 1924, Miss Cummings was upset in the second round by Miriam Burns. In 1925 she went to the semifinal, where she was beaten by Glenna Collett. She reached the quarterfinal in 1926 but then dropped out of tournament golf. In 1924 Miss Cummings won the Western Women's. All the talent in the Cummings family was not confined to Edith. Her brother Dexter won the National Intercollegiate in both 1923, 24, while at Yale.

CUPIT, JACKY B. 2/1/38, Longview, Tex. 5′ 10″, 180. Cupit turned pro in 1960 and three years later tied for first place in the USGA Open at Brookline with Julius Boros and Arnold Palmer. In the playoff Cupit shot a 73, 3 shots behind Boros and 3 ahead of Palmer. In his second year on the tour, 1961, Cupit won the Canadian Open. He took the Western Open in 1962. His other victories came in the Tucson and the Cajun, both in 1964. He had a pronounced loop at the top of his swing. He has been inactive recently.

CURL, ROD B. 1/9/43, Redding, Cal. 5′5″, 155. After being on the tour since 1969, Curl finally broke through with his first victory in 1974, taking the Colonial National. It had been a hard, uphill struggle for Curl, who says he barely made ends meet for the first four years. In 1973, however, he finished in the first 10 in five tournaments and earned over $55,000. Curl is three-quarters Wintu Indian and did not start to play golf until he was 19. He did not have an impressive amateur record but finished tied for 11th in the USGA Amateur in 1968. He then decided to turn pro.

CURTIS, HARRIOT S. B. 6/30/1881, Manchester-by-the-Sea, Mass. D. 10/25/74, Manchester-by-the-Sea, Mass. Miss Curtis won the USGA Women's Championship in 1906, defeating Mary B. Adams in the final, 2 and 1. The following year she went to the final again but was beaten by her younger sister, Margaret. In 1913 she reached the semifinal but lost to Marion Hollins. In 1906 Miss Curtis, her sister, and several other top players went to the British Isles to play an informal team match and take part in the British Championship. In May of 1932 Harriot and Margaret presented the Curtis Cup for competition between British and American women's teams. It has been played for ever since, except for the years of World War II. Miss Curtis was a civil rights activist, had been dean of women in Hampton Institute in 1927, and for many years was secretary of the New England United Negro College Fund campaign. She died, incidentally, in the same room in which she had been born 93 years before.

CURTIS, MARGARET B. 10/8/1883, Manchester-by-the-Sea, Mass. D. 12/24/65, Boston, Mass. Winner of the USGA Women's Amateur in 1907, 11, 12. She had three times tied for the medal in the qualifying rounds and had reached the final in 1905, before finally breaking through. When she did win in 1905, she defeated her sister Harriot, the defending champion, in the final. Miss Curtis was a large, driving, competitive woman, with a complete disregard for fashion. In World War I she threw herself into Red Cross work and established food clinics for children in the devastated countries of Europe. She also was an avid tennis player and, in 1908, she and Evelyn Sears won the National Women's Doubles title. In 1958 she received the Bobby Jones Award for sportsmanship from the USGA.

CUSHING, JUSTINE B. B. 8/3/18, Beverly Farms, Mass. Mrs. Cushing provided the upset of the year in 1974 by winning the USGA Women's Senior Championship. Mrs. Mark Porter, the former Dorothy Germain, was a heavy favorite for the title, closely followed by defending champion Mrs. David L. Hibbs and five-time winner Mrs. Philip Cudone. But Mrs. Cushing took the lead on the fourth hole of the last round with a birdie 2, and held it to the finish with Mrs. Cudone second. Mrs. Cushing was playing in the Senior for only the second time, although she had previously won the Women's Metropolitan Senior in 1973 and the Women's Long Island Championship in 1968.

DANIEL, ELIZABETH ANN (Beth) B. 10/14/56, Charleston, S.C. Miss Daniel is one of the few women in the modern era to have won the USGA Amateur in her first attempt. Not yet 19 years old she swept through the field to defeat Donna Horton, 3 and 2, in 1975. She was then about to enter her sophomore year at Furman University. Miss Daniel, growing up in a golfing family, began to play when she was 7 and entered her first tournament when she was 8. She was a quarterfinalist in the USGA Junior Girls' Championship in 1973, and she won the Twin State Junior Girls' (North and South Carolina) in 1973, 74, 75. On her way to the final in the National, Miss Daniel defeated Nancy Lopez in the second round and Carol Semple, the winner in 1973, in the third.

DANIELS, DEXTER B. 5/1/04, Haverhill, Mass. Accuracy has been the hallmark of this New England native but long-time resident of Florida. Keeping the ball always in play, plus a good competitive temperament, has brought the cigar-smoking Daniels two USGA Senior Championships. He first won in 1961, when he defeated Col. William K. Lanman in the final, 2 and 1. In 1966 he won again, this time beating George C. Beechler, 1 up, in the final. It was the second time Beechler had been a finalist. Daniels has taken the Florida Senior title no less than eight times.

DANTE, JOSEPH J. B. 12/11/20, Denville, N.J. Dante is the teaching pro par excellence and one of the deep thinkers about the swing for the average club member. He has authored two books, in one of which he pioneered the square-face system 20 years before it drew national attention. In his second book, *The Four Magic Moves,* he exploded the myths and fallacies which have grown up around the swing, and it became recommended reading in the PGA golf school. His firm belief is that the position at the top of the swing is the key to a good swing. "If you get it up there right, you'll hit it right, ninety percent of the time," he says. Dante has three times been president of the New Jersey PGA, has twice been selected as Professional Golfer of the Year in New Jersey, and was the innovator, and is still the guiding light, of the Dodge Open, the richest tournament ($25,000) for local state pros in the country. He also has the remarkable record of 14 holes-in-one. He is a son of the late James J. Dante who authored, with Leo Diegel, *The Nine Bad Shots of Golf.*

DARWIN, BERNARD B. 9/7/1876, England. D. 10/18/61, London, England. An editorial in the *New York Times* once commented that "no one writes about golf with such intimate knowledge or more genial charm" as does Bernard Darwin. Educated at Eton and Cambridge, he had a style all his own which was a delight to read. And behind it was the authority of a player of no mean ability. He led a team against the Americans in a forerunner of the Walker Cup matches and played in the first formal match. He won his singles, too. Darwin represented England several times in the matches against Scotland, and twice was a semifinalist in the British Amateur. He once called golf "this damnable and seductive art." He was the golf correspondent for the *London Times* for a great many years. He was the grandson of Charles Darwin, the English naturalist.

DAVIS, WILLIAM H. B. 3/6/22, Chicago, Ill. Davis was the original founder of *Golf Digest* magazine. He and a friend put out two local (Chicago) issues in 1950—from his bedroom, as he puts it. In 1951 Howard Gill and Jack Barnett joined him; all three had gone to New Trier High School together and then on to Northwestern University. Four local issues were published in 1951, and the magazine went national in 1952 with six issues. The format was enlarged to the conventional size in 1962. Davis became an avid weekend golfer on Chicago's public courses after his release from the Navy following World War II. He got the idea to start his own magazine because he was dissatisfied with golf publications then in existence. He wanted a magazine with easy-to-understand instruction and service articles. Davis is still president and editor-in-chief, although the magazine was sold to the *New York Times* in 1969.

DAVIES, RICHARD D. B. 10/29/30, Pasadena, Cal. 6'2", 210. A graduate of the University of Southern California, Davies hit the peak of his golf career when he won the British Amateur in 1962. It was not a Walker Cup year but 30 Americans still entered the tournament. Davies defeated John Povall, 1 up, in the final at Hoylake. The next year he was selected for the Walker Cup team as well as for the Americas Cup team. Also in 1963 he won the Southern California Amateur. In 1962 Davies reached the fourth round of the USGA Amateur. By his victory at Hoylake he became the 12th American to win the British Amateur.

DAWSON, JOHN W. B. 12/20/02, Chicago, Ill. A fine amateur player whose career spanned World War II but which was interrupted by a long interlude away from USGA competition. Dawson was a quarterfinalist in the 1928 Amateur, losing to Phil Perkins who eventually lost the final to Bobby Jones. But Dawson worked for A. G. Spalding, the biggest maker of golf equipment at the time. In 1932 the USGA ruled he could not play in national competition as an amateur. He left Spalding in 1945 and again became eligible. In his first crack at the USGA Amateur in 1947, he reached the final, losing then to Skee Riegel. He was promptly selected for the Walker Cup team of 1949 and won in both singles and foursomes play. He was also a semifinalist in the

British Amateur and a runner-up in the French Amateur twice. To previous victories in the Trans-Mississippi, California Open and Amateur, Iowa Open, and Southern California Amateur, Dawson added the Championship of the United States Seniors' Golf Association three times running, 1958, 59, 60.

DEMARET, JAMES NEWTON B. 5/10/10, Houston, Tex. 5'10½", 190. A smiling extrovert, who loved galleries and racy clothes (especially caps), Demaret left his stamp on the golf scene without winning a national title. What he did do, however, was win the Masters three times, the first to do so. And he won most others, about 40 in all, over a span of roughly 20 years. Jimmy won the Masters for the first time in 1940, closing with a 30 on the last nine holes. In 1947 he took it for the second time, grabbing the lead in the second round and holding it to the end. His third victory came in 1950, when he overtook Jim Ferrier on the last nine in the process of making a 69. Demaret's best bid for the Open came in 1957 when he finished 1 shot behind Cary Middlecoff and Dick Mayer. His triumphs stretched all the way from Argentina to the Crosby and included the Western, the Los Angeles, the New Orleans (twice), and the Thunderbird (three times). Jimmy made the Ryder Cup team in 1947, 49, 51 and won all his matches. He won the Vardon Trophy in 1947. He and Jack Burke now own the Houston Champions G.C. Demaret was voted into the PGA Hall of Fame in 1960.

DENENBERG, GAIL B. 1/17/47, New York, N.Y. Miss Denenberg started slowly when she came on the LPGA tour in 1969 after winning county and Hudson River titles as an amateur. But by 1970 she was getting in the top 10 finishers, and in the next three years increased her earnings steadily. Early in 1974 Gail broke through with her first victory. This came in the Sears, with its unconventional format of a match-play elimination qualifying a limited number for one round of stroke play. Gail survived the matches and shot a 71 to win. It was a rich one, too, with a $15,000 first prize. She has a B.A. degree from the University of Miami.

DENT, JAMES B. 5/11/42, Augusta, Ga. 6'2", 222. Big and strong, as his statistics indicate, Dent is acknowledged to be the longest driver now on the tour. Tee shots of more than 300 yards are not uncommon for him. He came on the tour in 1971 through the qualifying school. He hasn't won yet, but he made $48,500 in 1974, his best money year so far. His best finishes have been ties for 11th in the Doral-Eastern and the San Antonio-Texas in 1973. In 1974 Dent won a PGA driving contest with a smash of 324 yards. He won the United Golf Association Championship in 1969.

de VICENZO, ROBERTO B. 4/14/23, Argentina. 6'1", 190. Despite all his other accomplishments, de Vicenzo always will be remembered for the tournament he didn't get a chance to win, the 1968 Masters. Here on the final round he shot a 65 for total of 277. But his playing partner, who kept his score, inadvertently marked down a 4 on the 17th hole instead of the 3

Roberto got. De Vicenzo signed the card without a careful check, and his round became a 66 and his tc⁺al 278. Bob Goalby came in with a blazing 66 for 277. After an hour's delay the Masters committee ruled that de Vicenzo's score had to stand and there would be no playoff with Goalby. Roberto turned pro in 1938, when he was only 15 years old. He went on the U.S. tour in 1947 and has won nine tour tournaments and more than 130 times in tournaments all over the world. His most notable victory came in the British Open of 1967, also with a score of 278, which was enough to beat Jack Nicklaus by 2 shots. The Argentine always has been one of the most popular men on the tour, where he is known as "the happy fella." But he wasn't that day in the Masters, which also happened to be his 45th birthday.

DEVLIN, BRUCE B. 10/10/37, Armidale, Australia. 6'1", 158. One of the outstanding and most engaging foreign players, witty and popular. Once a master plumber in Australia, Devlin turned pro in 1961 after attending St. Patrick's College and joined the tour in 1962. In 1964 he began to win and since then has rung up nine victories on the tour, including the St. Petersburg, the Colonial National, the Carling, the Byron Nelson, the Bob Hope Desert, the Cleveland, the Houston, the USI, and the Alcan Player of the Year. He also has won the French and New Zealand Opens and has earned over $600,000. He once underwent an operation for varicose veins in his legs. Recently, he has curtailed his tournament activity to devote more time to golf course design.

DEY, JOSEPH C., JR. B. 11/17/07, Norfolk, Va. Frequently referred to as "Mr. Golf," and with good reason, Joe Dey was a landmark figure in American golf for 40 years. He joined the administrative branch of the United States Golf Association in 1934 as executive secretary, a title later changed to executive director. There he remained as the top administrator, except for service in the Navy during World War II, until 1968. In 1969 Dey moved to the professional side as commissioner of the newly formed Tournament Players' Division of the PGA. After five years he resigned in the winter of 1974. During his long stay with the USGA he helped initiate five championships and four international team championships, and aided also in developing a uniform code of rules with the Royal and Ancient Golf Club, the ruling body in Great Britain. He was secretary of the World Amateur Golf Council from 1958-69. Dey has been the recipient of the William D. Richardson Trophy, presented by the Golf Writers' Association, the Distinguished Service Award by the Metropolitan G.A., and the Gold Tee Award of the Metropolitan GWA. In Dey's honor an oak tree was added to the "Hill of Fame" by the Oak Hill Country Club in Rochester, N.Y. In September 1975 Dey became captain of the Royal and Ancient Golf Club of St. Andrews, the only American, besides Francis Ouimet, to be so honored. He also was elected to the World Golf Hall of Fame. The Tournament Players' Championship trophy has been named for him. Dey attended the University of Pennsylvania and wrote sports in New Orleans and Philadelphia before joining the USGA.

DICKINSON, GARDNER B. 9/27/27, Dothan, Ala. 5'10", 144. A grim and determined competitor, Dickinson is a graduate of the University of Alabama, where he majored in clinical psychology. He turned pro in 1952 and immediately joined the tour. That first year he made only $100 but quickly jumped to four figures, then to five, where he has been since 1961. He has won eight tour tournaments and his earnings are well in excess of $500,000. Most notable of his eight tour victories is the Colonial National of 1969. As a member of the Ryder Cup teams of 1967 and 1971, Dickinson won nine of his 10 matches. Small but wiry, he swings hard at the ball. He seems to have modeled himself after Ben Hogan, even to always wearing a white, Hogan-type cap on the course. He will always be remembered for leaping on Sam Snead's back when partner Sam sank the winning putt to beat January and Boros in the CBS Classic in the snow in 1967. He was TPD player director in 1969.

DICKSON, ROBERT B. B. 1/25/44, McAlester, Okla. 6'3", 195. After receiving a bachelor of science degree in business from Oklahoma State University, Dickson came on the PGA tour in 1968 with faultless credentials. In 1967 he won the USGA Amateur by a stroke from Vinny Giles, when the tournament was at stroke play, and earlier that year he won the British Amateur, beating Ron Cerrudo in the final, 2 and 1. That same year he was a member of the Walker Cup team and won all his matches. Dickson promptly justified expectations as a pro by winning the Haig Open in 1968 but then fell off. He lost his swing and didn't do well in 1970-72 but found it again in 1973 and won the Williams-San Diego Open, as well as tying for second in the Shrine Robinson and finishing third in the Byron Nelson. He won $89,182, making 1973 his best year financially. Shortly before turning pro Dickson received the Bob Jones Award from the USGA for "Distinguished Sportsmanship in Golf."

DIEGEL, LEO B. 4/27/1899, Detroit, Mich. D. 5/8/51, No. Hollywood, Cal. 5'10", 164. A brilliant, high-strung player, Diegel won almost everything there was to win except the U.S. and British Opens. He took the PGA Championship in 1928, 29, breaking a string of four straight victories in this event by Walter Hagen. He won the Canadian Open four times, in 1924, 25, 28, 29. He had great chances to win the USGA Open in 1920 and 1925 but fell short, as he did in the British Opens of 1930 and 1933 when he barely failed. Records for his era are hazy but he won at least 10 important tournaments. He was on four Ryder Cup teams, 1927, 29, 31, 33. In many ways Diegel was a genius. He could break 75 regularly by playing his shots while standing on one leg. Once, on a bet that he could break 30 for nine holes, he shot 29. Often dissatisfied with his putting, Leo, at one time, set a style by bending far over at the waist and pointing both elbows straight out, right and left, as he took his stance. It became known as "Diegeling." Diegel was voted into the PGA Hall of Fame in 1955.

DIEHL, T. J. (Terry) B. 11/9/49, Rochester, N.Y. 6'0", 200. Terry attended the University of Georgia, won the New York State Amateur in 1969, and got on the tour by passing the 1973 qualifying school test. He had rough going almost to the end of the 1974 campaign, when he bobbed up with his first victory, in the San Antonio-Texas Open.

DILL, MARY LOU B. 2/18/48, Eastland, Tex. Miss Dill won the USGA Women's Amateur in 1967, defeating Peggy Conley, a former finalist, at the 19th hole in the semifinal and Jean Ashley, the champion in 1965, in the final, 5 and 4. On the Curtis Cup team in 1968, she played in one singles match and won it. She and Miss Conley halved one foursomes match and lost another, in a United States victory. In 1963 she won the Texas Junior Girls' title. Miss Dill was graduated from the University of Texas in 1971, majoring in biology and English, and turned pro. She did not, however, pursue the tournament trail. Instead she took to teaching and, becoming interested in television, has worked up a program of instruction with video tapes at the Baywood C.C. near Houston, Texas. She sees great possibilities for this teaching aid.

DOUGLAS, DAVID B. 1/1/18, Philadelphia, Pa. With a name like that, Douglas should have come from Scotland but he didn't. Nor is he any relation to the Dale Douglass who still plays the PGA tour intermittently. On the circuit in the boom years following World War II, he won twice. He took the Orlando Open in 1947 and the Texas Open in 1949. In the 1949 USGA Open, Douglas tied for sixth place with 290, 4 shots behind the winning Cary Middlecoff.

DOUGLAS, FINDLAY S. B. 1875, St. Andrews, Scotland. D. 3/29/59, New York, N.Y. This young Scot, who had captained the St. Andrews University golf team, came to this country in the Gay Nineties and proceeded to win the USGA Amateur Championship in 1898. He was a long hitter for those days and a consistent player. He was runner-up in the Amateur in 1899, 1900. In that 1900 final he was beaten by Walter J. Travis. He won the Metropolitan Amateur in 1901, 03, and the United States Seniors' Golf Association title as late as 1932. He was also the first president of that organization. Douglas prospered along the way and was elected president of the United States Golf Association for the 1929-30 term. He also served as president of the Metropolitan Golf Association from 1921-25.

DOUGLASS, DALE B. 3/5/36, Wewoka, Okla. 6'2", 160. This graduate of Colorado University in 1959 has been on the tour since 1963. He broke into the winner's circle in 1969 and, in all, has won three times: the Azalea, Kemper, and Phoenix Opens. His best year was 1969 when he took home $91,533. His overall earnings are in excess of $400,000. Douglass also made the Ryder Cup team in 1969 and was TPD player director in 1971, 72. He enjoys traveling and plays in a great many tournaments each year.

DRAPER, TOM B 8/4/14, St. Louis, Mo. Draper, who apparently improves with age, reached the peak in 1971 when he won the USGA Senior Championship. He defeated Ernest Pieper Jr., the one-time California star, in the final, 3 and 1. He won the tradition-packed North and South in 1965. Long before that he made a monopoly of the Missouri Valley Intercollegiate, taking it four times from 1933-36. In 1945 he won the San Diego County Open while in the Navy and in 1949 took the Michigan State Amateur. He also won the Michigan Closed Championship three times, 1956, 60, 74. Despite taking the latter when he was 60 years old, he is still trying to improve. Draper's deep feeling for the game is expressed in his philosophy: "The greatest thing is to play well and win; next best is to play well. The unthinkable is not to play at all."

DUDLEY, EDWARD BISHOP B. 2/10/02, Brunswick, Ga. D. 10/25/63, Colorado Springs, Col. This quiet, soft-spoken man was a prominent figure in the PGA and a player who won a lot of tournaments but never the national championships. He won his first, on what was then the tour, when he took the California Open in 1929. He followed with the Shawnee in 1930, the Los Angeles and the Western in 1931, the Pennsylvania and Philadelphia in 1932, the International Four-Ball with Armour in 1932, the Hershey in 1933, the Shawnee again in 1936, and the Sacramento in 1937. That latter year he was chosen for the Ryder Cup team and finished third in the Masters behind Byron Nelson and Ralph Guldahl. The esteem in which Dudley was held is evidenced by his service as the PGA president from 1942-48. In 1964 Dudley was named to the PGA Hall of Fame.

DUNLAP, GEORGE T., JR. B. 12/23/08, Arlington, N.J. The 1933 winner of the USGA Amateur Championship, Dunlap was noted for his ultra-fast swing, "like a hummingbird's wing," as one writer described it. George was one of 12 in a playoff for the last eight places in the field of 32. In the semifinal he defeated Lawson Little and in the final, Max Marston, who had won the title in 1923. The score against Marston was 6 and 5. Dunlap was on the Walker Cup teams of 1932, 34, winning both his singles matches and one foursome. He made a habit of winning the North and South Amateur.

DUNN, WILLIE B. 1870, Musselburgh, Scotland. D. 1952. One of the earliest of the Scottish professionals who came to this country, and the man who won the Open here before it became an official USGA Open. That was in 1894, in December of which the USGA was formed. Dunn, doubling as pro and golf course architect, laid out the first seaside course in America, Shinnecock Hills on New York's Long Island, in 1891. It was a 12-hole course, later enlarged to 18. Dunn won that unofficial Open in 1894 by beating two other Scots. In 1895, when the Open became official, Willie was second to Horace Rawlins. The tournament was played then at 36 holes and Rawlins had 173 to Dunn's 175. They played with the rock-like gutta-percha ball. Dunn had an inquiring turn of mind and, even in those early days, he experimented with steel shafts and with wooden pegs for use on the tees. He was far ahead of his time.

DUTRA, MORTIMER F. B. 10/3/1899, Monterey, Cal. 6'2¼", 189. Brother of Olin, the USGA Open winner in 1934, Mortie won the Northern California PGA in 1922 and was runner-up in the Pacific-Northwest Open in 1924, 25. He was a semifinalist in the PGA in 1925 and had high finishes in the Western Open, the Pasadena, the Caliente, and the Canadian. He was seventh in the USGA Open of 1931, 5 strokes off the pace set by Billy Burke and George Von Elm. In 1955 Mortie won the National PGA Senior Championship and the World Senior, the latter in Glasgow, Scotland. Although no records are kept, it is possible that Mortie has given more golf lessons than anyone in the profession. He has been teaching for 51 years and estimates he has given 150,000 lessons.

DUTRA, OLIN B. 1/17/01, Monterey, Cal. 6'1¾", 188. Dutra turned pro in 1924 and in the next decade, after knocking around the pro tour (such as it was then), won both the PGA Championship in 1932 and the USGA Open in 1934. In the PGA he defeated Frank Walsh in the final, 4 and 3. But his greatest feat came in the Open, when he made up a deficit of 8 strokes on the last day. Thirty-six holes were played on the last day at that time. This is still the greatest catch-up performance in the Open, matched only by Arnold Palmer in 1960. There were 17 men ahead of Dutra at the halfway mark, but he passed all of them with rounds of 71 and 72, to beat Gene Sarazen by 1 stroke. Dutra also won the Metropolitan Open and was fourth in the British Open of 1933. He was a member of the Ryder Cup teams of 1933, 35. To make matters even more remarkable, when Dutra won the USGA Open, he suffered from an intestinal disorder all through the tournament. Among Dutra's other victories were the Miami-Biltmore in 1934, the Sunset Fields and Santa Monica in 1935, and the True-Temper in 1936. In 1962 Dutra was voted into the PGA Hall of Fame.

DYE, PAUL, JR. (Pete) B. 12/29/25, Urbana, O. Dye is something of a maverick among modern golf course architects. He leans heavily toward the Scottish school of natural design and does not turn out the clean-cut, manicured course that has become conventional in America today. The result is a course that looks as though it just happened to grow there. Instead of one long and terrifying tee, he likes two or three smaller ones at a hole. He doesn't build outsized greens, claiming that a 95-foot putt is not a part of the game; a chip with finesse to a small green is more interesting, he says. He doesn't like elevated greens and water, either. Dye was a good amateur player and was in the insurance business before he turned to building golf courses. His first was a nine-hole job in 1959. Since then he has built three of what *Golf Digest* has rated the 100 best courses in America. Most recent of these is the Harbour Town Links in Hilton Head, S.C. Dye is a close friend of Jack Nicklaus, who works with him as an advisor.

EDGAR, J. DOUGLAS B. 9/30/1884, Newcastle-on-Tyne, England. D. 8/8/21, Atlanta, Ga. Edgar came to America in 1918, took a job at the Druid Hills Golf Club in Atlanta, Ga., and soon made his presence felt. He was capable of incredibly hot streaks when his hands "felt thin," as he put it. In 1919 he won the Canadian Open with a record score of 278, a mark which stood for 10 years. His hands must have felt very thin on the final day, for both rounds then were under 70, the final one a 66, and he won by no less than 16 shots. He is believed to have been the first to shoot two tournament rounds under 70 on the American continent. He won again in 1920. Incidentally, tied for second in 1919 was Bobby Jones, then 17. In 1921 Edgar was struck by an automobile in Atlanta and killed. For a while police theorized it was murder but later accepted it as an accident.

EGAN, H. CHANDLER B. 8/21/1884, Chicago, Ill. D. 4/5/36, Everett, Wash. Egan was a strong force in amateur golf for a long time. He won the Western Amateur four times, 1902, 04, 05, 06, the first two while he was an undergraduate at Harvard. In 1904, 05 he won the USGA Amateur and was runner-up in 1909. In 1904 the USGA introduced a 54-hole system of qualifying for the Amateur (32 places), and Egan won the medal. In 1929 Egan, then 44 years old, reached the semifinal of the Amateur again, and in 1933 he knocked off Johnny Goodman, then the Open champion, in the first round, 2 up. Long before that he had moved to Oregon, where he built golf courses and raised apples. While there he won the Pacific Northwest Amateur no less than five times. Egan was on the Walker Cup team of 1934. He was always a long hitter and in his younger days was very wild, thrilling galleries with his recovery shots.

EHRET, GLORIA JEAN B. 8/23/41, Allentown, Pa. 5'8", 138. As an amateur Miss Ehret won the Tri-State Championship in 1963, 64. She became a professional in 1965 and in her first year tied for fifth in the LPGA title tournament. In 1966 she won it and made $12,000 that year. From then until 1973 she had a succession of high finishes but did not win. Then in 1973 she chalked up her second victory, in the Birmingham. She ranked sixth in scoring average, and her prize money jumped to over $30,600. She has now topped the $120,000 mark in career earnings.

EICHELBERGER, DAVID B. 9/3/43, Waco, Tex. 6'1", 180. Eichelberger served in the Marine Corps, after graduating from Oklahoma State University in 1965, and he went on the tour in 1967. His big year was in 1971, when he won his only tour victory, the Milwaukee Open, and $108,312 for the campaign. As an amateur Eichelberger reached the semifinals of the USGA Amateur in 1964 and was a member of the U.S. Walker Cup and Americas Cup teams in 1965.

ELDER, LEE B. 7/14/34, Dallas, Tex. 5'8", 175. After banging on the door for six years without a victory, Elder broke through by winning the Monsanto Open in 1974. He thereby became the first black to automatically be invited to play in the Masters of 1975. Charley Sifford and Pete Brown, previous black winners on the tour, were not eligible for the Masters under the then existing rules. Elder played for 10 years on the United Golf Association tour, taking the UGA title four times and at one time winning 21 of 23 events. He joined the PGA tour in 1968 and immediately created a stir by tying for first with Jack Nicklaus and Frank Beard in the American Golf Classic. Beard dropped out early in the sudden-death playoff but Elder carried Nicklaus to the fifth extra hole before Jack's birdie finally won it. In 1973 he had a big money year, winning $84,730, and in two successive efforts he was 25 under par but not a winner. He was 3 shots behind Bruce Devlin in one and lost the other when Lee Trevino dropped an 18-foot birdie putt on the first hole of a playoff. In 1971 Elder was invited by Gary Player to play the South Africa tour. The trip drew world-wide attention because of South Africa's apartheid policy. While there Elder won the Nigerian Open. His career earnings on the PGA tour are now over $360,000. In 1975 he tied for second in the rich Japan Masters, behind Gene Littler. In early 1976, Lee won his second tour victory, the Houston Open.

ELLIS, WESLEY B. 1/27/32, Kansas City, Mo. 6'1", 170. Ellis graduated from the University of Texas in 1953, where he majored in zoology. He turned pro the next year and went on the tour in 1958. He made his freshman year a great one by winning the Canadian Open with a score of 267, the third lowest score in that championship's history. In 1959 he won the Texas Open, one of the older, more prestigious tournaments on the circuit. His other tour victory came in the San Diego Open of 1965. Off the tour for many years in one of the more esteemed club jobs, Ellis retained his liking for animals and has kept at various times such striking ones as ocelots.

ENGLEHORN, SHIRLEY B. 12/12/40, Caldwell, Ida. 5'7", 135. In spite of numerous injuries and bouts with surgeons and hospitals, Miss Englehorn has won 11 tour titles, capped by the LPGA Championship in 1970. After taking several regional competitions as an amateur, she turned to the professional side in 1959, entered one tournament, and won $57. But from 1962-70 she won at least once every year except two. During this streak she won the Carling Eastern, Eugene, Lady Carling, Waterloo, Babe Zaharias, Englehorn Invitation, Concord, Londoff, O'Sullivan, Lady Carling (Balt.), and LPGA. The last four all were won in 1970 and consecutively. Her career earnings now are well over $150,000.

ESPIE, J. CLARK B. 1/29/1899, Kattawa, Ky. Espie has left his mark on senior golf. He won the USGA Senior in 1958, after being runner-up in 1956 and winning the qualifying medal in 1958. His 71 then still stands as the record for 18-hole qualifying. His victory in the 1958 final was by 3 and 1 over J. Wolcott Brown. He has won the Western Senior twice, 1950, 53, been runner-up three times, and Indiana State Senior Champion six times. He was the Indianapolis District Champion in 1939. Espie also lays claim to the longest measured drive, 400 yards made in 1936, a shot witnessed and attested in Indianapolis, during a city tournament there.

ESPINOSA, AL B. 3/24/1894, Monterey, Cal. D. 1/4/57, San Francisco, Cal. This genial descendant of the Spanish who settled California came close to the big ones, but the top titles eluded him. After winning the Mid-America and the Florida West Coast Opens in 1927, Espinosa fought his way to the final of the PGA Championship in 1928. There he was beaten by Leo Diegel, 6 and 5. In 1929 he almost won the USGA Open. If Bobby Jones hadn't sunk a 12-foot putt on the last green, Espinosa would have won. But in the 36-hole playoff the next day he lost by 23 shots. In 1930 he lost what was called the National Match Play Title, again to Diegel. And he lost it again in 1932, to Craig Wood. However, he made the Ryder Cup team in 1929, 31. He and Denny Shute won the Miami Four-Ball in 1934, and he took the Indianapolis Open in 1935.

EVANS, CHARLES, JR. (Chick) B. 7/18/1890, Indianapolis, Ind. 5'10½", 158. An outspoken, free spirit and one of the giants of amateur golf in America. Up from the caddy ranks at the Edgewater Golf Club near Chicago to which city his family had moved when he was 3 years old, Evans quickly established himself. At 19 he reached the USGA Amateur semifinal. He did the same the next two years. He reached the final in 1912 and the semifinal again in 1913. At each stage he lost, although usually favored. In 1914 he almost tied Hagen in the Open. Finally, in 1916, Evans broke through, and with a vengeance. In the summer he won the USGA Open with 286, breaking the record by 4 shots. In the fall he won the USGA Amateur which had so long eluded him, beating Bob Gardner, the defending champion, 4 and 3, in the final. Chick thus became the first to win the Open and the Amateur the same year. He won the Amateur again in 1920, beating Francis Ouimet, 7 and 6, in the final. Local and sectional tournaments Evans won by the dozen. He took the Western Amateur, a prestigious event, no less than eight times, the last four in a row from 1920-23. They played the Western Open at match play in 1910 and Chick won that, too. Evans had a beautiful swing and was especially adept with his irons. Shaky putting alone kept him from reaching the top before he did. Harry Vardon once called Chick "the best amateur in America." He was a great gallery favorite, talking and joking on the course, and he loved galleries. Evans was on three Walker Cup teams, 1922, 24, 28, played in 50 consecutive amateur championships and won 86 matches in major championships. In later years he established the Evans Caddie Scholarships and was a leader in the movement. In 1940 Chick was voted into the PGA Hall of Fame, one of only four amateurs, as a charter member. He was named to the World Golf Hall of Fame in 1975. Incredible as it seems in these days of 14-club armament, Evans used only seven clubs when he won the Open and set the record in 1916. They were the brassie, spoon, midiron, jigger, lofter, niblick, and putter. In the modern numbering system they would be, approximately, No. 2 and No. 3 woods and Nos. 2, 4, 6, and 9 irons.

FARRELL, JOHN J. (Johnny) B. 4/1/01, White Plains, N.Y. 5'10½", 160. Coming out of that hotbed of golf, Westchester County, N.Y., Farrell always will be remembered as the man who beat Bobby Jones when Jones was almost unbeatable. That momentous victory came in a 36-hole playoff for the USGA Open Championship in 1928. They had tied at 294 in the regulation play at Olympia Fields C.C. in Illinois. On Sunday, June 24, Farrell scored 70-73—143 and Jones 73-71—144. Farrell decided the issue when he sank a 7-foot putt on the last green. Johnny had been knocking at the door for several years. He was 1 shot behind Jones and Macfarlane in the Open of 1925, 4 behind Jones in 1926, and 7 behind Armour and Cooper in 1927. He had been consistently brilliant in other tournaments. Through 1923-24 he had been in the money in every start. In 1927 he won seven tournaments in a row during the spring, and in the winter of 1928 he shot a 63 on the last round to win the rich LaGorce Open. Farrell had an easy, graceful swing, once he got himself settled to the ball, and he was one of the best putters of all time. Handsome and always a flashy dresser, Johnny perhaps set the tone for later sartorial standards. In 1929 Farrell was runner-up in the PGA to Leo Diegel and second in the British Open. He was fourth in the latter in 1931. Three times he was a member of the Ryder Cup team, 1927, 29, 31. Farrell was voted into the PGA Hall of Fame in 1961.

FAULK, MARY LENA B. 4/15/26, Chipley, Fla. As an amateur Miss Faulk reached the top in 1953, defeating Polly Riley, 3 and 2, in the final round of the USGA Women's Amateur. She reached the semifinal the following year, but lost to Mickey Wright, and then turned to the professional side. She won her first LPGA tour tournament in 1956, the Kansas City Open. This was the first of 10 she took through 1964. The year 1961 was her big one, with four victories, the Triangle Round-Robin, the Zaharias, the Eastern, and the Western. She won her last in 1964, the St. Petersburg, for the second time. In 1954 Miss Faulk played on the Curtis Cup team.

FAZIO, GEORGE B. 11/14/12, Norristown, Pa. Better known now for his work in designing and laying out golf courses, Fazio had his moments of glory as a player. In 1946 he won the Canadian Open, defeating Dick Metz by 1 stroke in a playoff. He tied for the Crosby with Ed Furgol in 1947. He was runner-up at various times in the Utah, Jacksonville, and Carling Opens, and twice in the Azalea. With his penchant for getting into playoffs, Fazio found himself tied for the top spot in the USGA Open of 1950 with

Ben Hogan and Lloyd Mangrum at Merion. Hogan shot 69 in the playoff to win his second Open title; Mangrum shot a 73 and Fazio a 75.

FERRARIS, JANIS JEAN (Jan) B. 6/2/47, San Francisco, Cal. 5'4", 120. Miss Ferraris had a strong amateur record, winning the USGA Junior in 1963, reaching the quarterfinal in the USGA Amateur in 1965, and winning the Western Junior in 1963, 64. She joined the tour in 1966 and by 1969 was second in the Tournament of Champions. In 1971 she started a string of victories for three campaigns. These came in the Orange Blossom, Atlanta, and Japan Opens. The latter was the last tournament of the year, and Jan was not even an official entry; she had been sent to Japan by her sponsor and didn't go with the LPGA invitees. Her victory gave her unofficial money for the year of slightly more than the $10,079 she made on the tour. She attended Odessa College.

FERRIER, JAMES B. 2/24/15, Sydney, Australia. 6'4", 192. Ferrier is one of the grand old foreign players who crowned his career with success in America. Ferrier won the Australian Amateur in 1935, 36, 38, 39, and as an amateur he won the Australian Open in 1938, 39, and 16 other regional titles. A football injury to a knee gave him a peculiarly uneven, dipping type of swing but didn't deter him. He turned pro in 1940 and went on the U.S. tour the following year and won his first tournament here in 1944, the Oakland Open. For 17 years he was a continual threat, due in part to his consistently excellent putting. In 1947 he won the PGA Championship, defeating Chick Harbert in the final, 2 and 1, and 13 years later was runner-up to Jay Hebert when the PGA was changed to stroke play. Meanwhile Ferrier won the Northern California, the Seminole, the St. Paul (twice), the Grand Rapids, the Kansas City, the Canadian Open (twice), the St. Petersburg, the Miami Beach, the Jacksonville, the Fort Wayne, the Empire State, and the Almaden. With Cary Middlecoff he won the Miami Four-Ball in 1948, 49, and with Sam Snead the Inverness Four-Ball in 1950, 52.

FETCHICK, MICHAEL B. 10/13/22, Yonkers, N.Y. 6'1", 200. Turned pro late in life, in 1950 at age 28, yet won four tournaments on the tour. His biggest victory came in the Western Open of 1956. This was his best year, too, with two other victories, the St. Petersburg and Mayfair Inn Opens. He took the Imperial Valley the year before. Mike won the Western the hard way, tying with three others, Jay Hebert, Doug Ford, and Don January, and then shooting a 66 in the 18-hole playoff to win by 5 shots.

FEZLER, FORREST B. 9/23/49, Hayward, Cal. 5'9", 175. After knocking at the door until it became chronic, Fezler finally broke in with his first PGA tour victory in the Southern Open of 1974. Obviously talented, he had been second in the Gleason, the Canadian, and the Southern Opens in 1973; tied for third in the IVB Philadelphia; tied for fifth in the American Golf Classic; and had had other low finishes in less than three years on the tour. He earned $106,390 in 1974 and stood 13th in the money list, playing in 38 events. He got on the tour after passing the qualifying tests in 1971 and graduating from San Jose City College in 1970, though he turned pro the year before. His long mustache and hair style prompted the nickname "Fuzzy." In high school he was a back-up quarterback to Jim Plunkett and is still an avid football follower. Fezler won $90,000 in 1974 and $52,000 in 1975, which brought his total to about $275,000.

FINSTERWALD, DOW B. 9/6/29, Athens, O. 5'11", 160. Turned pro while still in Ohio University, from which he was graduated in 1952, and set out on the tour immediately. By 1954 his earnings had dropped to a mere $180, yet two years later he was the second leading money winner on the tour. He was known for his conservatism, shooting for the "fat" part of the greens, minimizing his mistakes, and rarely gambling. Finsterwald made it pay off to the tune of 12 tour victories including the PGA Championship in 1958, the year the tournament was changed from match play to stroke play. Other triumphs came in the Fort Wayne, British Columbia, Carling (twice), Tucson, Utah, Greater Greensboro, Kansas City, Los Angeles, Greater New Orleans, and "500" Festival. In 1962 Finsterwald was engaged in the first triple tie in the Masters, with Arnold Palmer, the eventual winner, and Gary Player. His career earnings are well over $400,000. Dow made the Ryder Cup teams of 1957, 59, 61, 63, was Player of the Year in 1959, and winner of the Vardon Trophy in 1957. He also was a member of the PGA Tournament Committee in 1957-59. He is highly respected for both his playing and his judgment.

FISCHER, JOHN W. B. 3/10/12, Cincinnati, O. Fischer always will be remembered for turning back the British threat to the USGA Amateur Championship in 1936. At Garden City Golf Club, Fischer was one down with three to go against the Scot, Jock McLean. He saved a half on the 34th by laying McLean a stymie, squared the match on the 36th with a 12-foot birdie putt, and won on the 37th with another birdie, this time from 20 feet. Among Fischer's victims on his way to the final were the veteran Chick Evans, who first played in the Amateur in 1909, and Johnny Goodman, who won the Open in 1933. In 1937 he defeated the venerable Evans again but lost to Ray Billows in the semifinal. Goodman then beat Billows for the title. Fischer had a penchant for meeting the top players. In the third round in 1938 he lost to Willie Turnesa, the ultimate winner. In 1940 he beat Jess Sweetser, the 1922 champion essaying a comeback, but went out in the fourth round. In 1932, after he had won the NCAA Championship, while still a Michigan student, Fischer knocked off W. Lawson Little in the first round of the USGA Amateur but then lost to Francis Ouimet in the third round. Three times Fischer made the Walker Cup team, in 1934, 36, 38, and won all three of his singles matches. Twice he was medalist in the Amateur, his 141 in 1933 breaking the record. He won the Big Ten title three times and his record 281 in 1935 still stands. Three times Fischer won the Queen City Open, 1930, 31, 32, and he was runner-up to Johnny Revolta in 1935. And three times he was low amateur in the Western Open.

FITZGERALD, THOMAS J. B. 4/6/12, Boston, Mass. Tom Fitzgerald is one of the best known golf writers in the Boston area. This veteran has been covering the game for 35 years for the *Boston Globe*. All of his newspaper experience has been with the *Globe,* where he started as a copy boy in 1930. From local golf coverage he worked up to national and international tournaments, including some in Great Britain. He was one of the original board of directors of the Golf Writers' Association of America. Fitzgerald's other assignment with the *Globe* is covering the Boston Bruins in the National Hockey League. He was the first president of the Professional Hockey Writers' Association, serving two terms in 1967, 68.

FITZSIMONS, PATRICK B. 12/15/50, Salem, Ore. 5'10½", 160. This former student at the University of Oregon won the Oregon Open in 1968 and the Northwest Open in 1969 while still an amateur. In 1969 he was medalist in the Western Amateur. He came through the PGA qualifying school in 1972 and hit the tour the following year. His best finish then was a tie for 10th at Atlanta and winnings of about $16,600. In 1974 he had less success and won only about $10,000. But in February of 1975 Pat put it all together in the Glen Campbell-Los Angeles Open. His flaming red hair easy to spot anywhere on the course, Fitzsimons moved far out front with a course-record 64 in the third round and won easily. The victory was worth $30,000.

FLECK, JACK B. 11/8/22, Bettendorf, Ia. 6'1", 167. If any man ever had one brief hour of glory, it was Fleck when he first tied Ben Hogan in the USGA Open of 1955, and then defeated him in the playoff at the Olympic C.C. in San Francisco. Hogan appeared to have won his fifth National Open when he finished with 287. But Fleck, playing out of a municipal course in Davenport, Ia., and in his first full year on the tournament tour, finished with two birdies on the last four holes to tie. Then in the playoff he led Hogan by 3 shots after 10 holes and finally won by 3, with a 69. In the four rounds of the tournament Fleck shot 76-69-75-67. In the playoff Hogan was only 1 shot behind after 17, but he hooked his drive to heavy rough and wound up with a double bogey. Fleck, a likeable fellow, tried desperately but he never could recapture the form he showed that week. In 1960 he won at Phoenix and in 1961 at Bakersfield. In 1960 he tied for third in the Open behind Palmer and Nicklaus.

FLECKMAN, MARTIN A. B. 4/23/44, Port Arthur, Tex. 5'10", 170. A graduate of the University of Houston, which has turned out so many fine players, Fleckman won the NCAA Championship in 1965. He graduated from both Houston and the PGA qualifying school in 1967 and went on the tour. Marty then won the first tournament he entered, the Cajun Classic. In the summer of 1967 before turning pro, Fleckman created a sensation in the USGA Open at Baltusrol. He led the field by 2 strokes after the first round, with a 69, and by 1 stroke after the third round, in which he had another 69. It was the first time since 1933 that an amateur had led the Open after three rounds. An 80 on the last round left him tied for 18th and the leading amateur.

FLEISHER, BRUCE B. 10/16/48, Union City, Tenn. 6'3", 201. In 1968 Fleisher won the USGA Amateur with a score of 285, a stroke better than Vinny Giles, despite Giles's 65 on the last round. Bruce also won the NCAA Junior College title that year while attending Miami Dade. In 1969 he was a member of the Walker Cup and World Amateur Cup teams. He turned pro in 1970 and went on the tour in 1972. He has won more than $48,000 in official money. In Walker Cup play Fleisher made a remarkable comeback in his first singles match with Mike Bonallack, winning five holes in a row to square the match. He lost to Bonallack in the second encounter.

FLOYD, RAYMOND B. 9/4/42, Fort Bragg, N.C. 6'0", 185. This son of an Army officer almost became a professional baseball player, but a victory in the National Jaycees Tournament in 1960 turned him to golf. He went on the tour in 1963 and quickly proved he had made the right decision. In his first year he won the St. Petersburg Open, at the age of 20 years and 5 months, the second youngest winner in the tour's history. He added the St. Paul Open in 1965 and then had his big year in 1969 when he won the Jacksonville, the American Classic, and finally the PGA Championship. His score in the latter, 276, equalled the best (Dow Finsterwald's) since the tournament was changed to stroke play. In 1975 he added the Kemper Open to his victories and made the Ryder Cup team for the second time, the first having been in 1969. Floyd hit his second peak by winning the 1976 Masters. He lead all the way and won with a score of 271. Floyd's interest in baseball is still keen; he works out with his favorites, the Chicago Cubs, at every opportunity. He had his best money year in 1974 with a take of $119,000. His career total now is more than $600,000.

FLYNN, WILLIAM B. 12/25/1890, Milton, Mass. D. 1/24/44. A good schoolboy golfer in the days of Francis Ouimet, Flynn also was a good enough tennis player to be hired as an instructor at a summer resort in Lake Placid. He was only 20 years old when, somehow, he was asked to design a golf course in Vermont. This he liked better than tennis; it also paid more money. So before long Flynn was launched on golf architecture as a career. A convivial fellow with an outgoing personality, he found it easy to become friendly with leaders in business and industry. He designed a course for John D. Rockefeller Jr. in Pocantico Hills; one for Eugene Grace near Bethlehem, Pa.; Seaview, near Atlantic City for Clarence H. Geist, a Philadelphia utilities man; and two courses in Boca Raton, Fla. There are those who consider his revision of the ancient Shinnecock Hills course on Long Island his best effort, but he himself thought that Spring Mill, near Philadelphia, where Byron Nelson won the USGA Open in 1939, was his best. Among others Flynn laid out were Cherry Hills in Denver, where Arnold Palmer won his only Open, and Rolling Hills, near Philadelphia, where the

1976 USGA Women's Open was played. Flynn died of a heart ailment at 53.

FORD, DOUG B. 8/6/22, West Haven, Conn. 5'11", 180. Reared in the strong competitive atmosphere of Westchester County, N.Y., the oldest golf center in the country, Ford, the son of a golf pro, has proved tough to handle on the golf course. Going back to 1950, when he joined the tour, he has racked up no less than 19 victories. From 1952-63, there was only one year in which he failed to win at least once. Furthermore he has been in 12 playoffs of which he has won five—which means he tied for first in seven tournaments that he didn't win. Highlights of the Ford career include his victory in the Masters in 1957 and the PGA in 1955. He also won the Canadian Open (twice) in 1959, 63, and the Western in 1957. He defeated Cary Middlecoff, 4 and 3, in the PGA final. In the Masters he shot a final round 66, capped by a birdie 3 at the 18th, where he holed out from a bunker. Ford is one of the few fast players, wasting no time on any shot, and he attacks both the course and the ball. He likes to play for a side stake and says he can't concentrate unless he does. He was a member of four Ryder Cup teams, from 1955-61, Player of the Year in 1955, and twice a member of the PGA Tournament Committee. His career earnings go over $400,000. Ford's victory in the Masters with a score of 283 came two weeks after he had predicted he would win—by 283.

FOSHAY, WILLIAM WARD B. 9/14/10, Port Chester, N.Y. A graduate of Harvard and Oxford and a partner in the New York law firm of Sullivan & Cromwell. Foshay was president of the United States Golf Association in 1966, 67. He also is a past president of the United States Seniors' Golf Association. He served in the Navy from 1942-45 and was counsel to the U.S. Bureau of Ships. He was decorated with the Legion of Merit.

FOSTER, DAVID R. B. 5/24/20, London, England. Foster became president of the Colgate-Palmolive Co. in 1970 and chief executive officer in 1971. His stature in sports was established when, seeing the promotional possibilities for his products, he entered the field of women's golf and raised the prize money to a startling figure. This occurred in 1972 and led the way to a new financial era for the women. That year Colgate, in cooperation with Dinah Shore, put up $110,000 for a 54-hole tournament and followed the next year with $154,000 for 72 holes. In 1974 and 1975 the purse went to $200,000, far more than ever had been offered for a women's tournament. Those years, also, Colgate branched out to a European women's invitation and a Far East Women's Open, with the prize money hitting $77,315 and about $75,000 respectively. To top it all there was the Colgate Triple Crown, a 36-hole affair for the top nine players, and $50,000. In all, Foster's company sponsored 10 tournaments with the prize money totalling $1,024,315 through 1975. These purses had the effect of raising the ante for other sponsors and the women are playing now for more money than they ever dreamed of back in the 1960s. Although born in London, Foster's parents were American. He is a graduate of Cambridge University and, during his war service, he was decorated with the DSO and DSC by the British government.

FOULIS, JAMES B. 1868, St. Andrews, Scotland. D. 6/12/25, Chicago, Ill. This Scottish professional won the second USGA Open in 1896, with a score of 152. His second round in the 36-hole test was a 74, and it stood as the Open record for seven years. It must be admitted that the course measured only 4,423 yards, but it must also be remembered that they were playing with the old gutta-percha ball at that time. Probably because of the short course, Foulis's score was 21 shots under the winning total in the first Open in 1895. Horace Rawlins, the inaugural winner, finished 3 strokes behind Foulis.

FOWNES, WILLIAM C., JR. B. 10/2/1877, Pittsburgh, Pa. D. 7/4/50, Oakmont, Pa. Fownes always will be associated with the Oakmont Country Club, which his father helped found and which has been the scene of so many national championships. Fownes graduated from the Massachusetts Institute of Technology in 1898 with a degree in metallurgical engineering and set about building industrial plants. In 1910 he won the USGA Amateur and, as a resident of the Pittsburgh area, he won the Pennsylvania State Amateur eight times and was runner-up another five times. He served as president of the USGA in 1926, 27. In 1922 Fownes played in the first Walker Cup match with Great Britain and in 1924 was again a member of the U.S. team.

FRALEY, OSCAR B. 8/2/14, Philadelphia, Pa. As a contributing editor of *Golf Magazine,* with a monthly column, Fraley is one of the best-known golf writers in the country. He covered his first tournament in 1939, the USGA Open at Spring Mill, for what was then the United Press, now UPI. Since then he has covered 20 U.S. Opens and 24 PGA Championships, as well as tournaments in 14 foreign countries, from Japan to Argentina to Morocco. He has written several books, including instruction volumes with Sam Snead and Lee Trevino. Fraley has played 370 golf courses on every continent and virtually every one in the United States, with what he describes as a "flexible" handicap. Oscar has not confined all his activities to golf. He was the author of *The Untouchables,* from which the still popular TV series is taken, and his latest book is a biography of former Teamsters Union president, Jimmy Hoffa.

FRASER, ALEXA STIRLING (Mrs. W. G.) B. 9/5/1897, Atlanta, Ga. A childhood friend of Bobby Jones, Alexa took up golf as a child, encouraged by her Scottish-born parents. Like Jones, she was a student of Stewart Maiden, and was one of the top women amateurs of the first quarter of the 20th century. Alexa won the USGA Women's Amateur in 1916, 19, 20 and was runner-up in 1921, 23, 25. Other victories include the Southern Championship in 1915, 16, 19; the Metropolitan (N.Y.) in 1922; and the Canadian Women's Amateur in 1920, 34. She was runner-up in the Canadian in 1922, 25. She married Dr. Fraser of Ottawa in 1924. She has been seven times club champion of the Royal Ottawa G.C.

FRASER, LEO B. 6/2/10, Flushing, N.Y. A professional in Atlantic City, N.J., for many years, Fraser served as president of the PGA of America in 1969, 70. This was a critical time, for at one point the tournament players broke away from the PGA. Fraser was instrumental in getting them back under the PGA umbrella, although they have their Tournament Players' Division now. He was given the Richardson Award for outstanding contributions to the game by the Golf Writers' Association in 1970. While president, he also was the architect of the National Club Professional Championship and suggested a credit union for PGA members, now in successful operation. Fraser also was president of the Philadelphia section of the PGA and there originated the Philadelphia caddie scholarship program, started an insurance program, and originated the Philadelphia Golf Show.

FUNSETH, ROD B. 4/3/33, Spokane, Wash. 5'10", 170. Funseth worked at various clubs after turning pro in 1956 and finally joined the tour in 1962. His best year came in 1973, when he won the opening tournament of the tour, the Campbell-Los Angeles Open. That was also his biggest money year, as he raked in $89,145. He has won only one other tournament, the Phoenix in 1965, but his career earnings are over $400,000. He is capable of shooting super rounds, such as his 69 in gale winds in the last round of the Crosby in 1973, which gave him sixth place. He has one of the flattest swings on the tour.

FURGOL, EDWARD B. 3/27/19, New York Mills, N.Y. 6'1", 180. Furgol's greatest feat was his victory in the USGA Open at Baltusrol in 1954 with a score of 284. This was accomplished in spite of a left arm that was crooked, shortened, and stiff at the elbow—the result of an accident in his youth. His arm had a marked effect on his swing, forcing him to make it largely with his right arm. Yet Furgol scored consistently on rounds of 71-70-71-72, to win by a single stroke from Gene Littler. A feature of his play that day came on the long 18th, where he hooked his drive among some trees near a ditch. Blocked from playing down the fairway without losing too much distance, Furgol played his second shot through an opening to the 18th fairway of Baltusrol's upper course, and reached the green with his third for a par 5. Furgol also won the Phoenix, the Miller (with 265), the Caliente, and Rubber City Opens. He was a semifinalist in the PGA in 1956 and was voted Golfer of the Year in 1954. He was on the Ryder Cup team of 1957. In 1947 Ed tied with George Fazio for first in an early Bing Crosby Open.

FURGOL, MARTIN B. 1/5/18, New York Mills, N.Y. 6'0", 190. An outgoing, talkative chap, Marty won two good tournaments on the PGA tour in 1951, the Western and Houston Opens. In 1954 he won the National Celebrities, and the following year he made the Ryder Cup team. In 1959 he won the San Diego and El Paso Opens. Strangely enough, Marty was no relation to Ed Furgol, although they were born in the same town in upper New York State.

GARDNER, ROBERT A. B. 4/9/1890, Hinsdale, Ill. D. 6/21/56, Lake Forest, Ill. Gardner was not only a champion but a great competitor in various diverse pursuits. He won the USGA Amateur Championship in 1909, defeating Chandler Egan in the final, 4 and 3. At 19 years and 3 months, he was the youngest to win it. In 1912, as a senior at Yale, he won the NCAA pole vault with a leap of 13 feet 1 inch. He was the first to vault 13 feet. In 1915 Gardner won the Amateur again, this time beating John G. Anderson, 5 and 4. In 1920 he went to the final of the British Amateur, losing only when Cyril Tolley sank a long putt on the 37th green. And in 1926 he and Howard Linn won the National Squash Racquets Doubles Championship. Two more times Gardner reached the USGA Amateur final but didn't win, losing in 1916 to Chick Evans and in 1921 to Jesse Guilford. He was on four Walker Cup teams, 1922, 23, 24, 26, and captained the team the last year.

GARDNER, ROBERT W. B. 3/3/21, Hollywood, Cal. Gardner did about everything but win the USGA Amateur. He reached the final in 1960 but lost to Deane Beman. Gardner played on the 1961, 63 Walker Cup teams, the World Cup in 1960, and the Americas Cup team in 1961. He won both of his singles matches in the Walker Cup, one foursomes match, and halved the other. He was a finalist in the French Amateur, twice a quarterfinalist in the British Amateur, and a semifinalist in the North and South. Among his victories were the San Diego Open, the Southern California (twice), the California (twice; a finalist four times), and the Metropolitan (six times; five of them in a row from 1960 through 1964), the latter while Gardner was living in the East. He played in the Masters six times, and his even par 288 in 1960 was 8 shots behind Gary Player, the winner. A member of the Bel-Air Country Club in Los Angeles, where the USGA Amateur was played in 1976, Gardner still plays to a plus-1 handicap.

GARRETT, WILLIAM B. 9/6/40, Amarillo, Tex. 6'6", 220. Garrett was graduated from North Texas State in 1962, a school which has turned out many fine players, and he turned pro in 1964. In 1970, after taking a month off and almost quitting the tour, he came through with his first victory. This was the Coral Springs Open, the next to last tournament on the schedule. He was tied after 54 holes with Lee Trevino, got off to a shaky start in the fourth round but settled down with three straight birdies and was never headed after that. He says playing with Julius Boros had a good effect on him.

GEIBERGER, AL B. 9/1/37, Red Bluff, Cal. 6'2", 180. Geiberger is a graduate of the University of Southern California, with a degree in business. After piling up an impressive record in college golf (a 34-2 mark in matches), he came out in 1959 and promptly went on the tour the next year. He scored his first victories in 1962, in the Caracas and Ontario Opens, and followed in 1963 with the Almaden. Then Geiberger began to show a fondness for the Firestone Country Club course. He took the American Golf Classic there in 1965 and the PGA Championship in 1966. Two more good money years followed in which he won more than $60,000 but no titles. Then physical ailments kept him home for long periods. Not until 1974 did he come up with his sixth victory, that in the Sahara Invitation, although he had another $60,000-plus year in 1973. Al chalked up his seventh tour victory when he won the Tournament of Champions and his eighth in the TPD championship in 1975. He was a member of the Ryder Cup teams of 1967, 75. Geiberger and Dave Stockton won the CBS Classic in 1968, 69, the only team ever to repeat in this television tournament—which also was held at Firestone. His career earnings total about $700,000. His ninth win came in the Greater Greensboro early in 1976.

GHEZZI, VICTOR B. 10/19/12, Rumson, N.J. 6'4", 190. D. 5/30/76, Miami Beach, Fla. A big, strong player, Ghezzi won the Los Angeles Open in 1935, when he was only 23 years old, and went on, in 1941, to take the PGA Championship in a thrilling final match with Byron Nelson. Ghezzi won it on the 38th hole. Other outstanding victories in his career were the North and South, the Calvert, the Dapper Dan, the Inverness Four-Ball, the Hershey Four-Ball, and the Greater Greensboro. Ghezzi played on the Ryder Cup team in 1939. In the U.S. Open of 1936 Ghezzi got off to a fine start and was tied for the lead after 36 holes but faded in the third round. Ghezzi's best shot at the USGA Open came in 1946, when he tied Lloyd Mangrum and Nelson for first place. All tied at 72 after 18 holes of the playoff, and Mangrum won with another 72 in the afternoon to 73s for Ghezzi and Nelson. Vic was a close friend of the late Dan Topping, former owner of the New York Yankees, and played often with him. Ghezzi was voted into the PGA Hall of Fame in 1965.

GILBERT, C. L. (Gibby) B. 1/14/41, Chattanooga, Tenn. 5'9", 175. Gilbert sprang from being just another name on the tour in 1969, when he won only $2,800, to a winner in 1970, when he took the Houston International and pocketed $65,618 for the year. Gilbert, christened C. L., without a first name, made his high school and Chattanooga University golf teams, but married, dropped out of college in 1962, and became an assistant pro. Five years later he got his Approved Tournament Player's Card and in 1968 went on the tour. After two lean years he suddenly made his big jump. Scoring 282 at Houston he found himself in a tie with Bruce Crampton, but won on the first extra hole. After a slump in 1972 he talked about quitting the tour but decided to stay on and then shot a 62 in the first round of the $500,000 World Open at Pinehurst in 1973, breaking the course record by 3 strokes. He slipped during the second week of that tournament and finished 15th. His career winnings are now more than $300,000. Gilbert won for the second time in 1976, taking the Thomas Memphis Classic.

GILDER, ROBERT B. 12/31/50, Corvallis, Ore. 5'9½", 165. Gilder was an early and a surprise winner on the 1976 PGA tour, taking the Phoenix Open in mid-January. He is a 1973 graduate of Arizona State University, with a degree in business. He turned pro the same year and, although he did not qualify for the PGA tour until 1975, he won the New Zealand Open in 1974. In official money on the 1975 tour, Gilder earned only $905, but his victory in the Phoenix payed off to the tune of $40,000. As an amateur he won the Western Athletic Conference Championship.

GILES, MARVIN, III (Vinny) B. 1/4/43, Lynchburg, Va. 6'0", 170. Perseverance is the name for Giles. After finishing second in the USGA Amateur three straight years, 1967, 68, 69, he finally overcame the "bridesmaid" tag and won the championship in 1972. He did it convincingly, too, by 3 shots. This was the eighth and last year the tournament was contested at stroke play before reverting to match play. Finally over the championship hurdle, Giles went on to win the British Amateur in 1975. He played on the Walker Cup teams of 1969, 71, 73, 75 and on the World Cup teams of 1968, 70, 72. He was on the Americas Cup team of 1967. Giles was second low amateur in the Masters of 1972. In 1973 he was low amateur in the USGA Open and a semifinalist in the Amateur. That same year he won the Eastern Amateur and the Porter Cup. In 1974 he won the Virginia State Open and lost in the third round of the USGA Amateur.

GILL, HOWARD R., JR. B. 11/18/22, St. Louis, Mo. Gill is the publisher and one of the founders, along with William H. Davis, of the magazine *Golf Digest*. Gill is a graduate of Northwestern University, with a degree in electrical engineering. He also took journalism courses at the Northwestern night school. From 1949-51 he was assistant to the publisher of *Chicago Electrical News Magazine.* It was in 1951 that he joined Davis in a spare-time endeavor in publishing *Golf Digest.* This was done locally, with four issues, testing newsstand sales, etc. They went national in 1952, and the publishing business has become a full-time job. Gill has been the publisher of *Golf Digest* since 1952.

GIVAN, HARRY L. B. 8/26/11, Seattle, Wash. In the pre-World War II era of Lawson Little, Johnny Goodman, and Johnny Fischer, a man to be reckoned with on the national scene was Harry Givan. He reached the last 32 in the USGA Amateur of 1934, the last 16 in 1935, and the quarterfinal round in 1939. He was chosen for the Walker Cup team in 1936, the year the matches were played at the forbidding Pine Valley course and in which the British were shut out for the only time. Givan won the Pacific Northwest Amateur five times, the Open once, and the British Columbia Amateur once. He took the Northwest Senior twice. In the business world Givan has been selected as Seattle's Man of the Year.

GLUTTING, CHARLOTTE B. 1/29/10, Newark, N.J. Four times a member of the Curtis Cup team and three times a semifinalist in the USGA Women's Amateur—this is the record Miss Glutting accomplished in major competition. She was on the Curtis Cup team in 1934, 36, 38 and was chosen again for the 1940 team, but the match with the British never was played because of World War II. Charlotte won all three of her singles Cup matches, two of them against British champions Pam Barton and Wanda Morgan. She reached the semifinal of the USGA in 1932, 35, 39. Miss Glutting also won the Eastern once and the New Jersey State three times. She was runner-up in the Women's Metropolitan no less than four times.

GOALBY, ROBERT (Bob) B. 3/14/31, Belleville, Ill. 6'0", 195. One of the most determined players on the tour, Goalby crowned one of his ambitions when he won the Masters in 1968. To do it, he shot a sizzling 66 on the final round. This was characteristic of him too, for he has long been known for his ability to hit hot streaks. He holds the record, in fact, for the number of consecutive birdies on the tour, eight. These came in the fourth round of the St. Petersburg Open in 1961, one of his 11 tour triumphs. The other nine came in the Greensboro, Coral Gables, Los Angeles, Insurance City, Denver, San Diego, Robinson, Heritage, and Bahamas Opens. A four-sport athlete in high school, Goalby went to the University of Illinois to play football but dropped out after one year, won several amateur tournaments while an automobile salesman, then turned pro and went on the tour in 1957. He won his first tournament, the Greensboro, the following year. His best year financially was 1967, when he won $77,107 and was 10th on the money list. Career earnings are now well over $600,000.

GOLDEN, JOHN B. 4/2/1896, Austria-Hungary. D. 1/27/36, Stamford, Conn. Brought to this country from Central Europe as a child, Golden became one of America's premier golfers, twice a member of the Ryder Cup team. He started as a caddie in Tuxedo, N.Y., and in 1919 became the professional there. He later spent a period at the North Jersey C.C. in New Jersey and won the State Open while there three times in a row, 1927, 28, 29. He then went to the Wee Burn Club in Connecticut. Meanwhile Golden was a regular on the winter tour. He won the Texas Open in 1924, the La Jolla in

1928, the Agua Caliente in 1931 (where he was paid with a wheelbarrow full of silver dollars), and the North and South in 1932. Walter Hagen insisted on having Golden as a partner in the Ryder Cup foursomes of 1927, 29, counting on John's accuracy off the tee to counteract his own frequent wild spells. Thick-set and of medium height, Golden had a short backswing and was uncommonly straight. They won both their matches. John set what was then the record for the longest match in PGA championship play in 1932 at St. Paul, when he outlasted Hagen in the first round to win at the 43rd hole. He lost the next day. Playing at Jacksonville, Fla., on the tour in January of 1936, Golden was stricken with pneumonia. He was rushed to a hospital in Stamford, Conn., where he died. His longest-match record was later surpassed, by one hole, by Chick Harbert.

GOODMAN, JOHN G. (Johnny) B. 1910, Omaha, Neb. D. 8/8/70, Southgate, Cal. 5'9", 165. Goodman became the fifth amateur, following Travers, Ouimet, Evans, and Jones, to win both the USGA Open and Amateur Championships. He won the Open in 1933 and the Amateur in 1937, and he won them as the kid "from the wrong side of the tracks." Goodman was the fifth of 10 children. His family was poor and he grew up near the packing-house district of Omaha. When his mother died he had the task of supporting the younger children and had to quit school and go to work. He went to night school for a summer, finally got back into high school and graduated. Although he had won the Trans-Mississippi three times and other tournaments, Johnny shocked the golf world by beating Bobby Jones, 1 up, in the first round of the Amateur at Pebble Beach. He had gotten out there from Omaha on a free ride on a cattle car. In 1932 he reached the Amateur final but lost to Ross Somerville. Then he broke through in the Open. A 66 in the second round gave him the lead, and Walter Hagen and Ralph Guldahol couldn't quite catch him. Ignored by the Walker Cup selection committee in 1930, 32, Goodman kept banging away and won the Amateur in 1937. He beat the tough Bud Ward on the 19th hole in the semifinal and Ray Billows, 2 up, in the final. Goodman made the Walker Cup team in 1934, 36, 38 and won all but one of his six matches, singles and foursomes.

GRAFFIS, HERBERT BUTLER B. 5/31/1893, Logansport, Ind. The name of Graffis is as tightly linked to American golf as a non-player's name could be. Herb and his brother Joe have been identified with the game in one form or another since World War I. After doing some summer reporting for Chicago newspapers, Herb became golf columnist for the *Chicago Sun Times* when it was launched. The brothers are best known for founding the National Golf Foundation, *Golfdom Magazine* in 1919, and *Golfing Magazine* in 1933. The latter is now known as *Golf,* of which Herb is still a consulting editor. Both magazines were sold in 1965. Herb is a past president of National Golf Fund, which established National Golf Day, and also of the Golf Writers' Association of America. He is a member of three USGA committees and of two PGA committees. Herb collaborated in the writing of three instruction books by the late Tommy Armour and of a half dozen others, including *History of the PGA*. He also has been a monthly contributor to *Esquire* magazine.

GRAFFIS, JOSEPH MARKLEY B. 4/29/1895, Logansport, Ind. Because Joe and Herb Graffis worked together so closely, it is almost impossible to separate them. Joe got his start in golf by working for *Golfers' Magazine* in 1919, a publication edited by the secretary of the Western Golf Association. The possibilities of a magazine and the rapid gowth of the game prompted the brothers to start *The Chicago Golfer Magazine,* which they sold in 1926. Joe was the first president of the National Golf Foundation and is still a member of its executive board. He also founded the Golf Car Manufacturers' Association and the O. J. Noor Research Association, and was a founding member of the Midwest Turf Research Foundation. In 1962 the brothers were jointly honored with the Richardson Award by the Golf Writers' Association of America for outstanding service to the game. In 1972 they received the United States Golf Association's Green Section Award. Joe was associate publisher of *Golfdom,* a publication which dealt largely with the turf and maintenance of courses.

GRAHAM, DAVID B. 5/23/46, Windsor, Australia. 5'9", 152. Graham turned pro in 1962 and had a big year in the Far East in 1970, when he won the Tasmanian, Victorian, Thailand, and Tokyo Yomiuri Opens, as well as the French Open. He came on the American tour in 1972 and won the Cleveland Open. In 1971 he won the Caracas Open on the Caribbean tour. In 1973 he tied for second in the Campbell-Los Angeles Open.

GRAHAM, LOU B. 1/7/38, Nashville, Tenn. 6'0", 175. The steady, workmanlike, no-frills Graham hit the peak of his career by winning the USGA Open in 1975. It didn't come easily, for he had to beat one of the game's rising young stars, John Mahaffey, in an 18-hole playoff after they had finished regulation play with 287 each. Lou did it with a 71 to a 73. It was Graham's third victory in 13 years on the tour, but years which brought him in excess of $600,000. Starting golf when he was 10 years old, Graham played well enough to earn a scholarship at Memphis State University. That he quit after three years is not surprising, because he admits he never liked school. Then he enlisted in the Army and for a time was a member of President Kennedy's honor guard. Out of the Army in 1962, he turned pro and went on the tour in 1964. Graham won for the first time by taking the Minnesota Classic in 1967, but developed tendonitis in his left arm in 1968. This eventually needed surgery, but he came back strongly and in 1972 won the Liggett & Myers Open, beating Hale Irwin, Larry Ziegler, and Dave Graham in a playoff on the third extra hole with a 25-foot birdie putt. Lou was in the top 10 nine times in 1973 and made the Ryder Cup. He made it for the second time in 1975.

GRAINGER, ISAAC B. (Ike) B. 1/15/1895, Wilmington, N.C. Ike Grainger had one of the longest periods of service with the United States Golf Association of anyone connected with it. His presidency in 1954-55 was preceded by his being vice president from 1950-53 and secretary from 1946-49. He was chairman of the Rules Committee from 1948-53, the longest period of any chairman, and was a member of the Rules Committee from 1948-63. Grainger also was chairman of the Negotiating Committee, which worked out the first uniform code with the Royal and Ancient in 1951. It was then that the stymie was eliminated, to take effect in January 1952. He was captain of the 1964 World Amateur team, and in 1954 he presented Arnold Palmer with his first National Championship trophy, the USGA Amateur. Grainger was involved in and resolved three USGA Open problems, with Byron Nelson in 1946, Sam Snead in 1947, and Lloyd Mangrum in 1950, and with Roberto de Vicenzo in the Masters in 1968. He is vice chairman of the Masters' Rules Committee. He was president of the Metropolitan Golf Association in 1943, 44, 45 and of the United States Seniors' Golf Association in 1959, 60.

GRANT, JAMES A. B. 3/30/42, Hartford, Conn. 6'2", 185. A graduate of the University of Houston in 1954, Grant made the Walker Cup team in 1967, sharing in the easy American victory that year. He tied for eighth place in the USGA Amateur in 1965, 66, the first two years the tournament was contested at stroke play. He qualified for the PGA tour through the ATP school in the fall of 1967.

GRAY, A. DOWNING B. 8/1/38, Pensacola, Fla. Gray has made strong bids for the USGA Amateur Championship three times. In 1962 he was runner-up to Labron Harris, losing, 1 up. In 1966, when the format was stroke play, he tied for third, 1 stroke behind Gary Cowan and Deane Beman who tied for the top spot. In 1967 he was fourth. Gray played on three Walker Cup teams, in 1963, 65, 67, two Americas Cup teams, 1965, 67, and the World Cup team in 1966. In 1965, 67, he was low amateur in the Masters and was second in the Southern Amateur in 1965, 66.

GREEN, DUDLEY E. (Waxo) B. 8/1/12, Brownsville, Tenn. Green has been with the *Nashville Banner* for 42 years and has spent 29 of them as the paper's golf writer. During that time he has promoted the biggest hole-in-one tournament in the state, helped form the first state junior tournament for the Tennessee Golf Association and has run the state high school tournament. He was president of the Golf Writers' Association of America in 1967, 68, and is a member of the selection committees for the PGA Hall of Fame and the World Golf Hall of Fame. Of his own ability on the course, Waxo says he plays well "at times," which his handicap of 13 bears out.

GREEN, HUBERT (Hubie) B. 12/28/46, Birmingham, Ala. 6'1", 165. After winning seven amateur titles in the deep South, graduating from Florida State University in 1968, and turning down a nomination to the U.S. Walker

Cup team, Hubie turned pro and made the tour through the qualifying school in 1970. In five years on the circuit Green has won eleven tournaments, a rare accomplishment. He started winning in his second year, at Houston, slacked off in 1972, won the Tallahassee and B. C. Opens in 1973, and got up a head of steam for 1974. During that campaign Hubie proceeded to take the Hope Desert, Greater Jacksonville, Philadelphia, and finally the National Team Championship with Mac McLendon. These victories sent his earnings for the year soaring to $211,709 and for his career to upward of $440,000. Green bends over more and grips his putter lower than any of the top pros on the tour but finds it very effective. His eighth victory came in the Southern Open in 1975. Three more victories came in March 1976: the Doral, the Jacksonville, and the Sea Pines Heritage.

GREEN, RONALD B. 3/25/29, Greenville, S.C. Green, now sports editor of the *Charlotte News,* has been covering golf steadily since he came to the *News* in 1948. Among the tournaments he has reported are 21 consecutive Masters, beginning in 1955. He also has done several magazine pieces for *Golf Magazine, Golf Digest,* and other periodicals. In 1960 Green won the championship of the Golf Writers' Association of America, a tournament played annually in Myrtle Beach, and he has been runner-up several times. He is a co-founder of the Carolinas Golf Writers' Association.

GREENE, BERT B. 2/11/44, Gray, Ga. 6'0", 170. This former Tennessee State Amateur Champion has been beset by physical problems since he joined the tour in 1967. He has chronic back trouble and underwent surgery for a kidney condition. Added to those was a gunshot wound in his foot in the fall of 1972. Sandwiched around these various misfortunes Greene has had good years and bad ones. His best, financially, was 1969, when he took in over $76,000 without winning a tournament. He was second in the rich Westchester, third in the PGA, and tied for second at Tallahassee. Then in 1973, he won his first on the tour, the L. & M. Open, after a five-hole playoff with Miller Barber. That helped give him another good money year, nearly $57,000.

GRISCOM, FRANCES C. B. 1880, Philadelphia, Pa. D. 3/30/73. Miss Griscom won the USGA Women's Amateur Championship in 1900, after being a semifinalist in 1897, 98. With her victory she checked the first serious bid of Margaret Curtis, who was later to win the title three times. Miss Griscom won the final, 6 and 5. She was an active sportswoman. Besides trap shooting and fishing she liked nothing better than to drive a coach-and-four at full gallop. She also was reputed to be the first woman in Philadelphia to own and drive an automobile. During World War I she drove a Red Cross ambulance.

GROH, GARY B. 10/11/44, Chicago, Ill. 6'0", 165. Groh is the perfect example of what determination and sticking to it will do. After attending Michigan

State, he turned pro in 1968 and went on the tour in 1969. For seven years he failed to win on the big circuit, although he took two tournaments on the second tour. Then, in the third tournament of 1975, the rich Hawaiian Open, he came through. At one point in the last nine holes he trailed Al Geiberger and Arnold Palmer by a shot. But as they faltered Groh birdied the last hole and won by a stroke. His first money of $44,000 was more than twice as much as he won in all of 1973.

GROUT, JACK B. 3/24/10, Oklahoma City, Okla. Grout is one of the many professionals who teach, rather than play, and form the backbone of the game in all countries. He turned pro in 1928 in the Oklahoma section of the PGA but gravitated eastward and held head professional positions at clubs in Pennsylvania and Chicago before going to the Scioto C.C. in Columbus, Ohio. It was there that he met young and aspiring Jack Nicklaus. He taught Jack the game, and Nicklaus himself says Grout was the only teacher he ever had. He later went to the LaGorce C.C. in Miami Beach and now is the pro at Nicklaus's new club, Muirfield Village, in Dublin, Ohio. Grout's teaching thoughts center on basic fundamentals. As he puts them: "Proper grip and stance, full body turn, maintaining straight left arm with the head in a still position, which creates balance. And practice, practice, practice."

GUILFORD, JESSE P. B. 3/3/1895, Manchester, N.H. D. 12/1/62, Newton, Mass. A big fellow who hit tee shots incredible distances. When he played in the USGA Amateur in 1914, he was promptly labelled the "Siege Gun" and the name stuck. In 1916 Guilford reached the semifinal of the Amateur, and in 1921 he won it. Jesse's victims read like a "Who's Who" of amateur golf in this country, too. He beat George Von Elm in the first round, Jimmy Johnston in the third, Chick Evans in the semifinal, and Bob Gardner in the final, 7 and 6. All either had been or were to be national champions. Guilford was on the Walker Cup teams of 1922, 24, 26. He won the Massachusetts Amateur three times and the New Hampshire Amateur once. Jesse also was the first amateur to win the Massachusetts Open. A shy fellow, Guilford said when accepting the trophy in 1921: "If I'm expected to make a speech, I'm sorry I won."

GULDAHL, RALPH B. 11/22/12, Dallas, Tex. 6'2", 175. This big, rather tousled graduate of the public courses in Texas, and later an automobile salesman, became one of the mysteries of American golf. In 1933 he came within a 4-foot putt, on the last green, of tying Johnny Goodman for the USGA Open, then all but dropped out of sight for a couple of years. He came back and proceeded to win the USGA Open two years in a row, 1937, 38, something only three others had ever done up to that time. In 1937 he scored 281, breaking the tournament record set the year before by a stroke. Just before he stepped up to his last putt he stopped to comb his hair, then calmly knocked in the 4-footer. At that time Ralph was playing as an unattached pro from Chicago. The next year he all but ran away from the field, winning by 6 shots with 284. In 1939 Guldahl won the Masters and the Greensboro; he had won the Western Open three years running in 1936, 37, 38. It looked as though the man had come who would dominate the game as Jones had a decade earlier. But no. Ralph was never in the running for the Open in 1939, was 3 shots behind in 1940, and not in the first 20 in 1941. His game had deserted him, and no one could tell why. His swing was effective rather than classic; he fell back on his right foot after he hit the ball. Guldahl tried everything to regain his winning touch, but he never could. Ralph made the Ryder Cup team in 1937, the last one before World War II, but never had another chance. Among his victories were the Phoenix in 1932; the Miami-Biltmore in 1936; the Dapper Dan, the Greensboro, and Miami Four-Ball in 1939; and the Milwaukee and Inverness Four-Ball in 1940. Ralph was voted into the PGA Hall of Fame in 1963.

GUNN, WATTS B. 1/11/05, Macon, Ga. Gunn was a member of two Walker Cup teams, 1926, 28, and had several other distinctions. He was a finalist in the USGA Amateur in 1925, the year Bobby Jones won his second Amateur championship. It was the first, and so far the only, time that the Amateur finalists were members of the same club, East Lake in Atlanta, Ga. It was also the year the USGA tried a new format, qualifying only 16 players and playing all matches at 36 holes. The system was unpopular and was promptly dropped. Gunn won his first three matches by big margins (10 and 9 over Jess Sweetser) but was beaten by Jones, 8 and 7. Gunn won the Southern Amateur, the Georgia State, and the National Intercollegiate, the latter in 1927 while still a student at Georgia Tech. He also won all his matches in Walker Cup play.

HAAS, FRED B. 1/3/16, Portland, Ark. 6'1", 175. Haas graduated from Louisiana State in 1937 and won the National Collegiate Athletic Association Individual title as a senior there. He turned pro in 1945 and went on the tour that same year. He won four times on the tour and was a member of the 1953 Ryder Cup team. Haas also had the distinction of making the Walker Cup team in 1938, and thus joined a select group of players who were on both international teams. In 1966 Haas won the PGA Senior. He plays only an occasional tournament now.

HAGEN, WALTER CHARLES B. 12/21/1892, Rochester, N.Y. D. 10/5/69, Traverse City, Mich. 5'10½", 185. The first giant of American golf, prominent both on the course and in elevating the status of the professional. The man whose first idea was to become a baseball player wound up winning 11 national championships—four British Opens, two USGA Opens, and five PGA titles. And before he was through, he had so seized the public imagination that golf pros were walking in the front doors of clubhouses instead of the back doors. He made a million dollars in golf in a period when that was all but unthinkable—and he spent it. He was supremely confident and spectacular in his shotmaking. He was, in a word, colorful. In the first USGA Open that he played in, in 1913, he finished only a shot behind Ouimet, Vardon, and Ray at Brookline. The next year he won his first Open. In 1919 he won his second, beating Mike Brady in a playoff. Then came the riotous 20s, in which Hagen won his four British Opens, in 1922, 24, 28, 29, and his five PGAs, in 1921, 24, 25, 26, 27. In that stretch he defeated Jim Barnes (twice), Bill Mehlhorn, Joe Turnesa, and Leo Diegel in the finals. At one point he won 22 consecutive matches, until Diegel finally stopped him. His 290 in the USGA Open of 1914 was a record for the event. It is estimated that he played in 200 tournaments in his long career and that he won more than 60. He also played in about 1,500 exhibitions. He inflicted the worst defeat on Bobby Jones, winning 12 and 11 in 72 holes, for which he was paid

$6,800. He also took his worst defeat in one of these matches, from English-man Archie Compston, 18 and 17, for a purse of 500 pounds sterling. That was in 1926 and he followed it by promptly winning the British Open. He won three Metropolitan Opens, a big tournament in those days, and five Westerns, two North and Souths, along with a Canadian and a slew of others. He was on five Ryder Cup teams, 1927, 29, 31, 33, 35, and was non-playing captain in 1937. He lost only one match, to brilliant George Duncan. Hagen's swing was far from classic. He took a rather wide stance and swayed perceptibly. He would hit several bad shots in the course of a round, but he expected to and they didn't bother him. He was a master of recoveries from seemingly impossible situations, and he was a great putter, especially from middle distances. In 21 USGA Opens he finished in the first ten 15 times, and as high as third in 1935, when he was 41 years old. His long career as a contender spanned the era from Vardon to Nelson. Above all, Hagen was a great competitor, as well as a great showman. He was named to the PGA Hall of Fame as one of the charter members in 1940.

HAGGE, MARLENE BAUER B. 2/16/34, Eureka, S.D. 5'2", 120. Mrs. Hagge has had a sensational career. She started golf before she was 4 years old and has never stopped playing. At 15, as Marlene Bauer, she won the first USGA Junior Girls' Championship and the Western Junior Girls' Championship. That year she was voted Athlete of the Year by the Associated Press, and one of the Top Ten Women. She also won the Helms Award. The next year she turned pro, the youngest, at 16, ever to join the LPGA. In 1952 she won her first on the tour, the Sarasota Open, and has added no less than 24 victories since. Marlene had her greatest year in 1956, winning eight tournaments, topped by the LPGA Championship. This she took in a playoff with Patty Berg. She won five times in 1965 and is a three-time winner of the Babe Zaharias Open. Her prize money now is in excess of $300,000. In her early years, when she was part of a sister duo with Alice, Marlene had an extremely long, full swing. She has shortened it considerably.

HAHN, PAUL B. 6/12/18, Charleston, S.C. D. 3/3/76, Lake Worth, Fla. The best trick-shot artist in golf, Hahn had a patter, stage presence, and humor which enhanced his act. The things he did with a golf ball were incredible. Some of the clubs he used—one with a multi-jointed shaft, another with a rubber shaft—were equally as bizarre. Judged by spectator reaction, Paul might well have been called "The Wizard of Ahs." After four years in the Navy during World War II and a brief fling on the tour, Hahn started his trick-shot routine in 1949. Subsequently, he performed his show all over the world, in 48 of the 50 states and in 55 foreign countries. Paul appeared in the movies and on several TV talk shows. He flew his own plane and was given the Horton Smith Award by the PGA for his service to golf. Hahn's rugged constitution gave way when he underwent open heart surgery twice within seven months in 1974-75, but he was back on tour five months later. He retired late in 1975.

HAMILTON, ROBERT (Bob) B. 1/10/16, Evansville, Ind. Hamilton was a long-shot winner of the PGA Championship in 1944, and therein lies his major claim to fame. This was the year the PGA was resumed after a one-year lapse because of World War II. It was also one of the years in which Byron Nelson was sweeping tournament after tournament with his magic woods and irons. Hamilton had shown he could win by taking the venerable North and South Open in the spring of 1944. But even though he had fought his way to the final of the PGA, no one gave him much of a chance against Nelson. Yet he beat him, 1 up. One down going to the 36th hole, Nelson birdied it. But so did Hamilton. Hamilton won at Charlotte in 1945 and at New Orleans in 1948. He was on the Ryder Cup team of 1949.

HAMLIN, SHELLEY B. 5/28/49, Fresno, Cal. Miss Hamlin first drew attention when, at 17, she was low amateur and tied for 13th place in the 1966 USGA Women's Open. The same year she was the medalist in the USGA Women's Amateur with a qualifying record of 143. She shot 70 in that 36-hole qualifier, the lowest single round ever in this tournament. By 1968 she had played in two Women's World Amateur team competitions and that year she was also on the Curtis Cup team. In 1969 Miss Hamlin reached the final of the Women's Amateur, losing there to Catherine Lacoste, 3 and 2. In 1970 she made the Curtis Cup team again. While at Stanford University she won the National Collegiate Championship and is a four-time California State Champion. She graduated with a degree in political science and hopes someday to do some work in government. Miss Hamlin turned pro in 1972 and although she had several high finishes, did not win until 1975. That was a big one, though, the $100,000 Japan Classic, in which Shelley came out of a trap to a foot from the hole for her winning par 4.

HANNIGAN, FRANK B. 3/29/31, Staten Island, N.Y. Hannigan is the assistant director of the United States Golf Association, a position he has held since 1965. He was the golf writer for the *Staten Island Advance,* later became a magazine editor, and did some public relations work before joining the USGA in 1961 as its public information editor. In 1962 he was appointed tournament relations manager and was largely responsible for the administration of the USGA Open Championships from 1962-68. Since Hannigan was named assistant director he has been responsible for interpretations of the various USGA codes, such as the rules, handicapping, and amateurism, and he continues to assist in the conduct of tournaments. An engaging, humorous writer, his satirical piece "Golf Thru TV Eyes" and biographical feature on the late architect, A. W. Tillinghast, have gained national attention.

HANSON, BEVERLY (Mrs. Sfingi) B. 12/5/24, Fargo, N.D. Miss Hanson won the USGA Women's Amateur in 1950 and then went into the professional ranks where she carved an enviable record for the next 10 years. In the Amateur, she defeated Mae Murray, 6 and 4, in the final, after eliminating Philomena Garvey, the last foreign threat, in the quarterfinal. In 1953 Miss Hanson finished fourth in the USGA Women's Open, the first year the USGA ran the tournament. Then in 1955 she took the Ladies' PGA Championship. In this the two low scorers after 54 holes (Beverly was low with 220) played 18 holes at match play for the title. Miss Hanson defeated Louise Suggs, 4 and 3. In all, Beverly won 15 tournaments, from the Eastern in 1951 to the St. Petersburg in 1960. These included the Western in 1956 and the American Women's Open in 1959. She was a member of the Curtis Cup team of 1950, winning in both foursomes and singles.

HARBERT, MELVIN R. (Chick) B. 2/20/15, Dayton, O. 6'0", 175. Harbert, one of the long hitters of his era, was adept at match play as well as stroke play. He was a finalist three times in the PGA Championship, winning it in 1954 with a 4 and 3 victory over Walter Burkemo and losing in 1947, 52. Chick was on the Ryder Cup team twice, in 1949, 55, and captain the latter year. On the tour he won 10 tournaments, including the Beaumont, Texas, Jacksonville, Charlotte, and St. Paul Opens. As an amateur he won the Michigan Open in 1937 and the Trans-Mississippi and International in 1939. Harbert won over 50 driving contests, those at the national PGA, the Masters (twice), and the Western Open among others. Harbert won the longest match in PGA Championship history when he defeated Eddie Burke in the second round at Norwood Hills in 1951, at the eighth extra hole. This surpassed the Golden-Hagen match of 1932 by one hole. In 1968 Chick was voted into the PGA Hall of Fame.

HARLOW, ROBERT E. B. 10/21/1899, Newburyport, Mass. D. 11/15/54, Pinehurst, N.C. Bob Harlow, a familiar face on the golf scene for many years, was known for many things. Foremost of these, perhaps, is his founding of *Golf World,* a magazine widely read all over the country. Harlow started this in 1947 in Pinehurst, N.C. But he also was known as the manager of Walter Hagen, from 1921-29, and later of Joe Kirkwood. He handled Hagen during the Haig's conquests of the British Open, and he booked Hagen and Kirkwood on many of their exhibition tours. From 1930-35 he was the tournament manager of the PGA, setting up the tour. He was succeeded in 1936 by Fred Corcoran. Educated at the University of Pennsylvania, Harlow worked on the *Boston American* and the *New York Herald-Tribune,* among other papers. It was Harlow, while he was Hagen's manager, who arranged the match between Hagen and Bobby Jones in Sarasota, Florida, in 1926.

HARMON, CLAUDE B. 7/14/16, Savannah, Ga. Harmon was the only player not on the regular PGA tour to ever win the Masters. This occurred in 1948 and in the process Harmon tied the then low score for the Masters with a 279. He also won by getting in front and staying there. His margin of victory over Cary Middlecoff, in second place, was 5 shots, and this stood as a record until 1955 when Middlecoff himself won by 7. Eleven years later

Harmon made a strong bid for the USGA Open when it was held at his own club, Winged Foot, in Mamaroneck, N.Y. He tied for third, 2 shots behind Billy Casper. Aside from the Masters, Harmon is best known as a developer of young professional talent and as a teacher.

HARNEY, PAUL B. 7/11/29, Worcester, Mass. 5'11", 160. Coming out of Holy Cross in 1952 with degrees in both the arts and the sciences, Harney hit the tour two years later and won the first of his seven times in 1957 when he took the Carling. He followed with the Labatt, the Dorado, and the Pensacola, the latter in 1959. Uncertain health cut down his play for a while but he came back and took the Los Angeles Open two years in a row, 1964, 65. Harney skipped the winner's circle then until 1972, when he won the Williams-San Diego. For several years he has been holding down a club job and playing the tour infrequently. From the time he turned pro, Harney was noted as one of the longest hitters. His career earnings are over $360,000.

HARPER, CHANDLER B. 3/10/14, Portsmouth, Va. 6'0", 175. Harper turned pro in 1934 and won seven tournaments throughout his career. The highlight was his victory in the PGA Championship of 1950, when he defeated Henry Williams Jr., 4 and 3, in the final. In that match Harper won the first hole and never lost the lead through the 33 holes the match lasted. He reached the final the hard way, too, beating Jimmy Demaret, 2 and 1, in the semifinal, and Lloyd Mangrum, 1 up, in the quarterfinal—shooting two 68s at Mangrum. His other notable victories were in the Canadian Open in 1949, the Texas Open in 1954, and the Colonial Open in 1955. Harper holds one PGA record, the lowest score for 54 consecutive holes—189. He shot 63-63-63 in the last three rounds of the 1954 Texas Open. Two of those 63s tie the record for 36 holes. In 1947 Harper finished second in the Reed-Latham Pro-Amateur, partnered by the Duke of Windsor. In his later years Harper won the PGA Senior, the World Senior, and the U.S. National Senior. He also won the Virginia State Open 10 times. He was elected to the PGA Hall of Fame in 1969.

HARRIMAN, HERBERT M. B. 1876, New York, N.Y. D. 1/3/33, Aghadowey, Ireland. Harriman won the USGA Amateur Championship in 1899. His victory was a milestone in American golf because he was the first native-born to win the title. Previously it had gone to transplanted Englishmen and Scotsmen. Harriman's victory was a surprise. The favorites were Findlay S. Douglas and Charles Blair MacDonald. Yet Harriman beat the latter in the semifinal and Douglas in the final, 3 and 2. Harriman was a brother of Mrs. William K. Vanderbilt and a cousin of E. H. Harriman, the railroad magnate (Union Pacific) and Wall Street figure. He himself circulated through New York and Newport society and busied himself mostly with tennis and golf. In 1900 when Harry Vardon came to America for a tour, Vardon played better golf than Harriman and Douglas. Vardon beat them, 9 and 8.

HARRIS, LABRON, JR. B. 9/27/41, Stillwater, Okla. 6'4", 200. This graduate of Oklahoma State has a master's degree in mathematical statistics. He won the USGA Amateur Championship in 1962, defeating Downing Gray in the final. He turned pro and joined the tour two years later but did not win his first tour tournament until he broke through to take the Robinson Classic in 1971. Harris came close to having a playoff chance to win the richest 72-hole tournament in America, the Dow Jones, in 1970. He was leading until Bobby Nichols holed a 14-foot putt on the last green to win it. As a member of the 1963 Walker Cup team, Harris won three of his four matches. Harris also was a member of the World Cup team in 1962 and of the Americas Cup team in 1963.

HARRISON, ERNEST JOSEPH (Dutch) B. 3/29/10, Conway, Ark. Known as the "Arkansas Traveler," the engaging Harrison left his mark on the PGA tour. From 1937-58 he is credited with winning 21 times. His only national title came when he won the Canadian Open in 1949, but he took a raft of others, the Texas Open in 1939, 51, the Western in 1953, the Crosby in 1939, 54, and the All-America in 1956. Age seemed not to rust his game or dull his competitive urge. He made the Ryder Cup team once, in 1949. In his later years he became a commentator on televised golf, and watchers may still recall his Arkansas accent and form of address: "Mistah Bob." Strangely enough, Harrison started golf as a left-hander but quickly switched to his right. An indication of the soundness of Dutch's swing is that he tied for third in the USGA Open in 1960, when he was 50 years old. In 1962 Harrison was voted into the PGA Hall of Fame.

HARVEY, GLYNN (Bud) B. 7/30/12, Medford, Mass. Harvey is the editor of the *Professional Golfer,* the official publication of the Professional Golf Association of America, and of the *PGA Book of Golf,* an annual. The *Professional Golfer,* published monthly, keeps the pros up to date on what is going on in all sections of the country and carries feature material by and about the pros. Harvey came to the PGA in 1965 after a long career in newspaper work in sports and city rooms from Boston to Miami. He has been with the *Boston Globe,* the UPI in Boston and New York, the AP in New York, ABC News in New York and Wilmington, N.C., and the *Miami News.* He was also with Bob Harlow during the early days of the magazine *Golf World,* which Harlow founded. Harvey then went to the *Washington Times-Herald* and, after other jobs with industrial organizations, to the PGA.

HASKELL, COBURN B. 12/31/1868, Boston, Mass. D. 12/14/22, Cleveland, O. Coburn Haskell is the man who invented the rubber-wound golf ball, the first ball of its kind, and the one, basically, that we still play with today. Something of a dilettante, he was interested mainly in horses, books, shooting, and golf. But he was not a good golfer and longed for more distance. One day while sitting in the office of a friend in the Goodrich Rubber Co., in

Cleveland, Ohio, he got the idea of a ball made of rubber strands, wound tightly about each other. He made one, had it covered with gutta-percha and gave it to Joe Mitchell, the pro at his club, to hit. Mitchell promptly knocked it over a cross-bunker on the first hole, on the fly. This bunker was rarely reached by long hitters with a rolling ball, in dry weather. This was the ball, wound by hand by Haskell, and with the refinements which soon came, that replaced the old solid gutta-percha ball which had been in use since 1848. It was exactly 50 years later, in 1898, that Haskell came up with his invention. It should be remembered that this first Haskell ball had no core; the rubber strand was simply wound around itself. For the invention of the core, see the biography of Jack Jolly. It was with the Haskell ball that Sandy Herd won the British Open in 1902, with the rest of the field playing gutties, and with which Walter Travis won the British Amateur in 1904. The ball revolutionized the game.

HAVEMEYER, THEODORE A. B. 1834, New York, N.Y. D. 4/26/1897, New York, N.Y. Havemeyer was one of the founders and the first president of the United States Golf Association in December of 1894. That same year he donated a handsome silver trophy to be played for in the Amateur Championship. It was destroyed by fire in November 1925 and replaced in January 1926 with a trophy donated by Edward S. Moore, treasurer of the Association from 1922-25. Havemeyer was one of a family which founded the American Sugar Refining Co., now Amstar. The company got into trouble with state and federal legislators late in the 19th century as a monopolistic trust. Havemeyer then was known as the "Sugar King." He was instrumental in completing the country's first nine-hole course, at Brenton's Point, near Newport, R.I. He was elected president of the USGA for the third time in February of 1896.

HAWKINS, FRED B. 9/3/23, Antioch, Ill. 6'1½", 165. Hawkins attended the University of Illinois, then was moved to Texas Western while in Officers' Training School during World War II. He turned pro and went on the tour in 1947. He won the Cavalier Open in 1950, the Oklahoma City in 1956, and the Jackson in 1958. He was chosen for the Ryder Cup team in 1957.

HAYES, MARK S. B. 7/12/49, Stillwater, Okla. 5'11", 170. After two victories in the Oklahoma State Amateur, Hayes was the runner-up in the USGA Amateur in 1971, and tied for second in the 1972 Amateur Championship. Also in 1972 he was chosen for and played on the United States World Cup team. Hayes qualified for the PGA tour through the 1973 school. He failed to win in 1974, yet earned more than $40,000 in tour prize money, to which he added $49,297 in 1975. Hayes won for the first time on the tour in April 1976, when he took the Byron Nelson Classic.

HAYNIE, SANDRA B. 6/4/43. Fort Worth, Tex. 5'5", 120. With her six victories on the tour in 1974 and four in 1975, Sandra ran her professional triumphs to 39, next to the highest among active women pros. After cleaning up in Texas with the State Public Links twice and the Amateur twice, plus the Trans-Mississippi, Sandra hit the LPGA tour in 1961. Her best finish then was 10th. But in 1962 she started a remarkable string. From then through 1975 there was never a year in which she didn't win at least once. In 1964 she won four times, as she did again in 1971, 75; three times in 1969, 72, 73. In 1965 Miss Haynie won the LPGA Championship, and in 1974 she took both the LPGA and the USGA Women's Open. Her official money in 1974 was over $77,000 and in 1975 $61,600, raising her lifetime earnings to slightly more than $449,000. This placed her on the all-time money list second to Kathy Whitworth. In 1975 Miss Haynie also had the lowest per round scoring average, an even 72. She did not win the Vare Trophy, however, because her 60 rounds were 10 short of the required minimum. Sandra has accomplished all this despite corrective surgery on one wrist and injuries when struck by a car in South Africa.

HEAFNER, CLAYTON B. 7/20/14, Charlotte, N.C. D. 12/31/60, Charlotte, N.C. Heafner was a dangerous competitor through the 1940s and early 1950s. His first big bid was in 1942, when he finished second in the Tam O' Shanter. He tied Byron Nelson for the top spot but lost the playoff. In 1947 he won the Jacksonville Open, beating Lew Worsham in a playoff for the title. Heafner made the Ryder Cup team that year. In 1948 he won the Colonial, a Virginia tournament, with 272, holing a 90-foot putt on the last green. Heafner was a quarterfinalist in the PGA Championship of 1949 and again was selected for the Ryder Cup team. In Ryder Cup play he was always a winner, in both foursomes and singles play. Heafner made two strong challenges in the USGA Open. In 1949 he tied for second with Sam Snead, 1 stroke behind Cary Middlecoff, and in 1951 he was tied with Ben Hogan going into the last round and shot 69, only to lose to Hogan's 67.

HEARD, JERRY B. 5/1/47, Visalia, Cal. 6'0", 190. Touted as one of the most promising of the "young Turks," Heard has won four times since he went on the tour in 1969. He has been playing golf since he was 11 and equalling par since he was 12. This came from daily practice on a driving range at a municipal course run by his father. He turned pro in 1968 and went on the tour a year later, and it took him only three years to reach the high echelons. In 1971 he won the American Golf Classic and more than $112,000. In 1972 he took the Florida Citrus and Colonial National and went up to $137,000. He didn't win in 1973 and had to be satisfied with about $94,000. He added the Florida Citrus, for the second time, in 1974. Heard dropped out of Fresno State to take the qualifying test for the tour. Like many pros he likes to fish, but he also has the tour's most unusual hobby—raising quarter horses. Earnings in 1974, 75 pushed his career winnings to more than $620,000.

HEBERT, JAY B. 2/14/23, Lafayette, La. 6'0", 175. The older half of golf's most successful family, Jay has been associated with the tour for two decades, although he rarely plays now. After serving in the Marines during World War II, Jay scored his first tour victory in the Crosby Pro-Am in 1957. That was the year his younger brother, Lionel, won the PGA Championship. Three years later Jay won it, establishing the Heberts as the only brothers ever to win national championships. Jay did it with a score of 281 in the third year of the tournament's change to stroke play. He led after 36 holes, slipped back on the third day but came on strong with a 70 on the last round. Jay played on two Ryder Cup teams, in 1959, 61, and was the non-playing captain of the 1971 squad. He has won seven tour tournaments in all, the others being, besides the PGA and the Crosby, the Texas, Lafayette, and Orange County Opens and the American and Houston Classics. At his peak before the big money came into golf, Jay still collected career money of about $280,000.

HEBERT, LIONEL B. 1/20/28, Lafayette, La. 5'8½", 200. The younger half of the famous brother team. Lionel attended Southwestern University and Louisiana State and created a sensation the first year he joined the tour by winning the PGA Championship in 1957. He defeated Dow Finsterwald, 2 and 1, in the final, the last time the tournament was held at match play. He went on then to win four other tournaments in the 18 years he has been on and off the tour. He took the Tucson in 1958, the Cajun in 1960, the Memphis in 1962, and the Florida Citrus in 1966. He has been a steady money winner, though not a big one. One of his hobbies is music, and he is an accomplished jazz trumpet player, often sitting in with professional groups. He was on the Ryder Cup team in 1957, a member of the PGA Tournament Committee in 1961-62, chairman of that committee in 1962-63, and player-director of the TPD Policy Board in 1972-74. His career earnings approximate $400,000.

HECKER, GENEVIEVE (Mrs. C. T. Stout) B. 1884. D. 7/29/60, New York, N.Y. Miss Hecker was a strong player in the opening years of the century, winning the USGA Women's title two years in succession, 1901, 02. In both finals she won by comfortable margins, 5 and 3, and 4 and 3. She then dropped out of tournament golf for a while. When she returned in 1905, as Mrs. C. T. Stout, she found the scene all but monopolized by two giants of the period, Margaret Curtis and Dorothy Campbell, the latter just over from England. In 1905 Mrs. Stout lost in the third round to Miss Curtis and in 1909 to Miss Campbell. She won the Women's Metropolitan in 1900, 01, 05, 06.

HEFFELFINGER, TOTTEN P. B. 1/23/1899, Minneapolis, Minn. Heffelfinger was president of the United States Golf Association in 1952, 53. It was at his club, the Hazeltine National, many years later, that Tony Jacklin became the first Englishman to win the USGA Open in 50 years. Heffelfinger served in the Navy from 1942-45 and at one time was executive officer of the Naval Air Station in Honolulu. He is a graduate of Yale and a nephew of William W. (Pudge) Heffelfinger, all-time great Yale football lineman of the late 19th century.

HELD, EDMOND R. B. 11/12/02, St. Louis, Mo. Held was the winner of the first National Public Links Championship conducted by the USGA. This was in Toledo, Ohio, in 1922. Eddie defeated Richard J. Walsh in the final, 6 and 5, after putting out the medalist, George Aulbach, on the 20th hole of the semifinal. The tournament was a milestone in golf in more ways than one. During one of the matches a spectator shot and killed himself in the rear of the gallery. After his victory, Held joined a private club and did not defend. In 1929 Eddie became the first United States player to win the Canadian Amateur. He won the Trans-Mississippi in 1923, 26 and was runner-up in the Western Amateur in 1927. In the USGA Amateur, Held was a quarterfinalist in 1926, 27, 33 and reached the last 16 in 1935. He turned pro in 1940.

HENNING, HAROLD B. 10/3/34, Johannesburg, So. Africa. 6'0", 165. Playing around the world, Henning has won tournaments on four continents: Europe, Africa, North America, and Asia. He turned pro in 1953 and won the South Africa Open in 1957, 62. In 1965 he teamed with Gary Player to win what is now the World Cup for his native country. Henning came to America in 1960 but was on and off the tour for several years. In 1966 he won his first tournament here, the Texas Open, and in 1970 took the Tallahassee Open—the latter with a birdie-eagle-birdie finish. His brother Allan also won the South Africa Open.

HENRY, GEORGE W. (Bunky) B. 2/8/44, Valdosta, Ga. 5'11", 195. A graduate of Georgia Tech in 1967 with a B.S. degree in industrial management, he turned pro in 1967 and went on the tour the next year. In 1969 he won the National Airlines Open. Henry was a kicking specialist at Georgia Tech and in 1966 set a Tech season record for extra points, kicking 32 out of 32 attempts. He also holds the school record of 73 kick conversions during his three-year football career. He kicked 73 in 75 attempts. While still a student at Georgia Tech, Bunky won the Canadian Amateur, defeating William C. Campbell in the final. He is a nephew of Billy "Dynamite" Goodloe, a prominent amateur in the 1940s.

HERD, ALEXANDER (Sandy) B. 4/22/1868, St. Andrews, Scotland. D. 2/17/44, West Hertfordshire, England. Sandy Herd was one of the most popular of British professionals. He not only won the British Open in 1902 and finished second three other times, but he had the remarkable record of making 19 holes-in-one. When he won the title in 1902, the redoubtable Harry Vardon was second. He also won the British PGA twice, once when he was over 50. As late as 1920, when he was 52, Herd was second to George Duncan in the British Open. He was selected 10 times to play for Scotland against England. He also toured the United States with J. H. Taylor. Thirteen of his 19 holes-in-one came at Coombe Hill, where he was the pro for many years; three came at Huddersfield and one each at Ganton, Portrush, and Machrie. A characteristic of Herd's play was how quickly he hit the ball after he teed it up. This caused one spectator to remark: "Tak yer time,

Sandy, naebody's gaun to steal yer ba.'' Sandy's victory in 1902 was accomplished with the then new Haskell rubber-wound ball, a first for the British Open. Vardon and the others were still using the gutta-percha ball. Before the tournament Herd had said he wouldn't play the Haskell, but at the last minute he got one from John Ball, the great English amateur—and played that one ball all through the 72 holes.

HERD, FRED B. 11/26/1874, St. Andrews, Scotland. D. 3/14/54, Welwyn, England. 5'10½", 150. Herd was the fourth winner of the USGA Open, taking it in 1898 by a margin of 7 shots from Alex Smith, who was to win it himself many years later. The tournament was played at the Myopia Hunt Club, a nine-hole course in Massachusetts which required eight trips around it. This was the first year the Open was played at 72 holes. Herd came to this country in 1895 and returned to England when he became ill two years after his victory and did not return. He was the pro at Knebworth until his death. Fred was one of five brothers, all professionals. A nephew of Fred's, Bruce Herd, was the pro at Flossmoor, near Chicago, for 29 years and was named PGA Pro of the Year in 1963.

HERRON, S. DAVIDSON B. 10/16/1897, Pittsburgh, Pa. D. 1/27/56, Pinehurst, N.C. Davey Herron was the surprise winner of the USGA Amateur Championship in 1919, when he defeated Bobby Jones in the final, 5 and 4. A good club player and playing on his home course, the Oakmont Country Club, Herron nevertheless was the darkest of dark horses when the Championship began. Yet he tied for the qualifying medal, won most of his matches by big margins, and in the final was 4 under even 4s for the 32 holes the match lasted. Jones at the time was only 17 years old but even then was regarded as a future star. Davidson continued to play tournament golf but never again reached his pitch of 1919. He won the Pennsylvania state title in 1920, 29.

HIBBS, MRS. DAVID L. B. 8/16/18, Harrow-on-the-Hill, Middlesex, England. Gwen Hibbs startled the world of senior golf by dethroning Mrs. Philip J. Cudone in the USGA Women's Senior Championship in 1973. Although it was only her second attempt in the tournament, her total of 229 for 54 holes broke the record for this Championship by 2 shots. Not only that, but she won by 6 shots. She did it the hard way, too, after taking a 4-over-par 8 on the first hole of the tournament. She recovered from that for a 77 the first day and followed with a 74 and 78. Her victory ended a five-year string by Mrs. Cudone. Mrs. Hibbs has won her club championship, in Long Beach, Cal., for seven straight years but says she has not won anything else. But when you've won a USGA title, what else do you need? In 1974 she started a Southern California Senior Women's tournament.

HICKS, ELIZABETH (Betty) B. 11/16/20, Long Beach, Cal. Betty Hicks won the USGA Women's Amateur title in 1941, defeating Helen Sigel in the final, 5 and 3. She had made two runs at it, losing to Betty Jameson in the semifinal in 1939 and in the second round in 1940. She did not make the Curtis Cup team for two good reasons: World War II and the fact that when the matches were resumed in 1948, she was a professional. She turned pro in 1941 after winning the Amateur. Betty did hold the title a long time, though, like Craig Wood who won the Open in 1941, until competition was resumed after the war. In 1954 Miss Hicks finished second to Babe Didrikson Zaharias in the USGA Women's Open, and in 1957 she was third behind the winning Betsy Rawls. Betty now is coach of the women's golf team at San Jose State College.

HICKS, HELEN B. 2/11/11, Cedarhurst, N.Y. D. 12/16/74. Miss Hicks was the first woman golfer to turn pro, at least the first with a national reputation as a player to do so. She reached her peak at 20, when she won the USGA Women's Championship, defeating no less a personage than Glenna Collett Vare in the 1931 final, 2 and 1. She won the Women's Metropolitan the same year. In 1933 she went to the final in the National again, this time losing to Virginia Van Wie, 4 and 3. On her way to the final in 1931 Miss Hicks eliminated Marion Hollins, a former champion, and Enid Wilson, who won the British Women's title in 1931, 32, 33. In 1933 Miss Hicks won the Metropolitan for the second time. And in the spring of 1934 she turned pro, signing with the Wilson Sporting Goods Company. She was a member of the first Curtis Cup team in 1932.

HIGGINS, PAMELA SUE B. 12/5/45, Groveport, O. 5'5", 120. Miss Higgins went on the LPGA tour after winning the district championship in Ohio three years in a row, 1965, 66, 67, and being runner-up in 1963, 68. She did little the first two years, 1969, 70, but broke through in 1971 with a victory in the Lincoln-Mercury in Alamo, Cal. She had another good year in 1972, tying for fourth in the Alamo Ladies' Open. But although she did not win in 1973, she jumped her earnings from more than $12,000 to almost $21,000. Her best finish was a tie for second in the Waco. She had eight top 10 finishes.

HIGGINS, WILLIAM D. B. 2/6/05, San Fancisco, Cal. Higgins reached the peak of a long golf career when he won the USGA Senior Championship in 1964. He defeated Edward Murphy in the final, 2 and 1. In the semifinal he was one down with two to play against David Goldman, and he birdied the last two holes to win. This was retribution for Higgins, who had gone to the final in 1963 and lost to Merrill Carlsmith as the latter won his second Senior title in a row. When he was 35, Higgins won the San Francisco City Championship and five years later, in 1945, the Nevada State Amateur. After his victory in the USGA he added two more senior crowns: the California State and Northern California in 1970 and the latter again in 1971.

HIGUCHI, HISAKO MATSUI (Chako) B. 10/13/45, Tokyo, Japan. 5'4", 125. Chako is the No. 1 woman player in Japan, after starting golf only in 1963.

She has won three Japanese LPGA and Open titles. She plays the American tour infrequently and has not yet won, although she has been second twice since coming here in 1970. In 1973 she played in only eight events in the U.S., yet won more than $10,000. In 1974 she won $9,600 and the Japan Classic, with its first prize of $15,000. She is very popular with American galleries.

HILL, CYNTHIA (Cindy) B. 2/12/48, South Haven, Mich. The even years have been the big years in national and international competition for Cindy Hill. She won the USGA Women's Amateur in 1974, was a finalist in 1970, 72, and in 1970, 74 she was a member of both the Curtis and World Cup teams. In her march to the National Championship, Miss Hill never had to play the last hole in any match and was carried to the 17th only once. In the final she defeated Carol Semple, the defending champion, 5 and 4. Martha Wilkinson defeated her in the final in 1970, and Mary Budke in 1972. She also was the low amateur in the USGA Women's Open in 1970. In 1974 Miss Hill's 307 in the World Cup was the lowest score of any player for the 72 holes. Outside national competition Cindy had a good year in 1975, winning the North and South, the South Atlantic, and the Doherty Cup. In 1973 she won the Broadmoor.

HILL, DAVID B. 5/20/37, Jackson, Mich. 5'11", 145. This wiry, combative player has been on the tour since 1959, after attending Detroit University, and has been a consistent money winner. He has won 12 times. His favorite seems to have been the Memphis Open, changed to the Danny Thomas Memphis in 1973, when Dave won it for the fourth time. His other victories have come in the Home of the Sun, Denver, Hot Springs, Buick, Philadelphia, Monsanto, Houston, and Webb Sahara Opens. His best year was 1969, when he won three times and his $156,423 placed him second on the money list. In 1970 he was second in the USGA Open, although he did not like the course in Minnesota. Always a man to say what he thinks, Hill announced at that time that the best thing to do with that course was to turn it over to 40 acres of corn and some cows. He made the Ryder Cup teams of 1969, 73, 75 and won the Vardon Trophy in 1969 with an average score of 70.344 for 90 rounds. In the fall of 1973 he had cartilage removed from one knee, yet in May he won the Houston Open. His career earnings are more than three-quarters of a million dollars.

HILL, MICHAEL B. 1/27/39, Jackson, Mich. 5'9½", 168. The younger brother of Dave Hill, Michael has been on the tour since 1968, after attending Jackson Junior College and Arizona State. He has won twice: the Doral-Eastern in 1970 and the San Antonio-Texas in 1972. Mike dreamed of baseball as a career, but after high school he spent four years in the Air Force and there found himself playing more golf than baseball. So the career became golf. The Hill boys grew up on a dairy farm with a golf course right next to it, so it was natural for them to become caddies, as well as good golfers.

91

HILL, MRS. OPAL S. B. 6/2/1892, Newport, Neb. Mrs. Hill never won the USGA Women's Championship but she was so consistent that she reached the semifinal three times and the quarterfinal twice from 1929-36. For this and for her many victories in other tournaments, she was chosen three times for the Curtis Cup team, 1932, 34, 36. In the Championship itself, Mrs. Hill was perhaps unlucky in that her contemporaries were unusually strong— Glenna Collett, Virginia Van Wie, Maureen Orcutt, and Charlotte Glutting. Her record outside the USGA, however, was remarkable. She won the Western Women's five times, the Trans-Mississippi four times, the Western Open twice, the Missouri Valley twice, and the Missouri State three times, among others. In 1937 she shot a 66, a women's record which stood for 12 years. In 1930 she was the medalist in the USGA qualifying. More remarkable than her record, perhaps, is that Mrs. Hill ever played golf at all. When she was 22 the doctors gave her three years to live because of a kidney infection and anemia. Mild exercise was prescribed and, at age 31, she took up golf. Assiduous practice and lessons—and courage—turned her into one of the country's best. After her husband's death in 1942 she turned pro (the second woman to do so) and has been teaching ever since. Although born in Nebraska her family moved when she was a child and she is always associated with Kansas City, Missouri.

HILTON, HAROLD H. B. 1/12/1869, West Kirby, England. D. 3/5/42, Westcote, England. One of England's greatest amateurs of the pre-war period, he won four British Amateurs, in 1900, 01, 11, 13, and two British Opens, in 1892, 97. He also came to the United States in 1911 and won the USGA Amateur, defeating Fred Herreshoff, 1 up, on the 37th hole, in the final. Hilton was a great student of the game, was a careful, precise player, and wrote several books on the swing. He was the first of only three men to hold the British and American Amateur Championships at the same time, the others being Bobby Jones and Lawson Little.

HINES, JAMES (Jimmy) B. 12/29/05, Mineola, N.Y. A good competitor and big hitter during the days of the Great Depression, Hines won a lot of tournaments. In 1933 he won the first of three Glens Falls Opens and teamed with T. Suffern Tailer to take what was called the National Pro-Amateur Championship. In 1935 he won at St. Augustine, a regular tour stop in those days, and had a big year in 1963, winning the Los Angeles, Riverside, and Glens Falls Opens. Jimmy came out on top at Glens Falls for the third time in 1937. He also won the Metropolitan, which he repeated in 1938. He was a member of the Ryder Cup team of 1939.

HINSON, LARRY B. 8/5/44, Gastonia, N.C. 6'2", 155. A good college golfer at East Tennessee State, from which he graduated in 1968, Hinson joined the tour the same year. He has won once, when he defeated Frank Beard in a playoff for the Greater New Orleans Open in 1969. His biggest money year, though, was in 1970 when he took in over $120,000 and was eighth on the money list although he did not win. Hinson has gained his success in spite of a slightly withered left arm, the result of an attack of polio when he was a child. For this he was given the Ben Hogan Award by the Golf Writers of America in 1970. He was an excellent basketball player in high school, and he owns and flies his own plane on short hops when the tour is near his Georgia home. His career winnings exceed $300,000.

HISKEY, BRYANT (Babe) B. 11/21/38, Burley, Ida. 6'0", 175. Hiskey graduated from the University of Houston in 1961 and went on the tour in 1963, a trail which has been rough until recently. He won his first tournament in 1965, the Cajun Classic, but not until 1970 did he take one of the bigger money jousts. That was the Sahara Invitation, worth $20,000. Then in 1972 he won the National Team Championship, paired with Kermit Zarley. Hiskey is one of a group of touring pros that meets regularly for Bible study and readings. Hiskey says it helps his concentration.

HOGAN, WILLIAM BENJAMIN (Ben) B. 8/13/12, Dublin, Tex. 5'8½", 145. A colossus of modern golf. Wiry, grim, determined, and a tireless worker, Hogan reduced the hitting of a golf ball to almost machine-like precision. From caddy and local amateur in Texas, he turned pro in 1931, at the age of 19, and hit the tour briefly in 1932. From there it was a long, uphill struggle to the top. He qualified for the 1936 Open but missed the cut. In 1939 he finished second from last. His first pro victory came in the North and South in 1940, and from then his rise was rapid if we skip his years in the Navy in World War II. Hogan tied Byron Nelson in the Masters in 1941 but lost the playoff. Back from the service he promptly won the 1946 PGA, beating Porky Oliver in the final. He won it again in 1948, this time crushing Mike Turnesa. And in 1948 he won his first USGA Open. Then came Hogan's near-fatal automobile accident on a Texas highway in February of 1949. One of his greatest triumphs was his comeback, to win the Open in 1950, beating Lloyd Mangrum and George Fazio in a playoff although suffering from severe leg pains resulting from the accident. Ben won it again in 1951 and still again in 1953. This was his greatest year, for besides the Open he also took the Masters and the British Open—three of the four modern "Grand Slam" tournaments. He had won the Masters for the first time in 1951. He lost it in a playoff with Sam Snead in 1954. The record is phenomenal—four USGA Opens, two PGAs, two Masters, one British Open. He was the leading money winner in 1940, 41, 42, 46, 48 and the Vardon Trophy winner (for the lowest year's scoring average) in 1940, 41, 48. Hogan won 52 tournaments, and the figure might have been more. He lost a playoff for the Open in 1955 to Jack Fleck, and in 1946 he was second in both the Open and Masters by 3-putting the 72nd green in each. Two putts would have put him in a playoff with a chance for victory. His Open triumph in 1953 made Hogan the third man to win this championship four times, joining Willie Anderson and Bob Jones. All the more remarkable is that this record was achieved in spite of his years in the Navy and his devastating accident. Hogan truly is a monumental figure in the history of golf. Although he can be credited with four USGA Open victories, Hogan won the Hale America Open in 1942, sponsored by the USGA, the PGA, and the Chicago District G.A. for the benefit of the Navy Relief Society and United Service Organizations. In every respect except name, it was the United States Open. Hogan won it with 271, 3 strokes ahead of Jimmy Demaret and Jim Turnesa. In 1953 Hogan was named to the PGA Hall of Fame.

HOLLINS, MARION B. 1892, East Islip, N.Y. D. 8/27/44, Pacific Grove, Cal. Golfer, horse fancier, and promoter was Miss Hollins. Growing up in a golf-happy part of Long Island, Islip, she soon became adept at the game. In 1913 she went to the final in the USGA Women's Amateur, losing to Gladys Ravenscroft of England. In 1921 she won it, upsetting the great Alexa Stirling, who had won three years in a row, 5 and 4. She had a fluid swing, was known as "The Golden Girl," and to keep her rhythm she would hum "The Merry Widow Waltz," a great hit at the time. Today she might be called a feminist, for after deciding there should be a course for women only, she was instrumental in building the Women's National Course at Glen Head, L.I. She then went West and planned and promoted the great course at Cypress Point and another, Pasatiempo, at Santa Cruz. Miss Hollins made more than a million dollars in an oil deal but lost it all in California real estate and died broke. She won the Women's Metropolitan in 1913, 19, 24.

HOMANS, EUGENE V. B. 2/26/09, Englewood, N.J. D. 10/29/65, Englewood, N.J. Gene Homans always will be remembered as the player Bobby Jones defeated in the final round of the 1930 USGA Amateur Championship to complete his "Grand Slam." The score was 8 and 7, at the Merion Cricket Club. Homans, a strong player in Metropolitan circles, was still attending Princeton University, and he and Jones had tied for the qualifying medal the year before at Pebble Beach. Homans had reached the final by beating, among others, Lawson Little and Chuck Seaver, father of pitcher Tom Seaver. He had also met Jones in 1927 in Gene's first big tournament when he was 16 and had lost, 3 and 2.

HOPE, LESLIE TOWNES (Bob) B. Eltham, England, 5/29/03. Hope's parents brought him to America when he was 4 and settled in Cleveland. He discovered as a child that he had the knack of making people laugh, and he made it pay off in vaudeville, radio, movies and television. His fabulous memory for jokes, his faultless timing, and his delivery of "one-liners" have made him the country's most successful comedian. Hope's entertainment of the troops in World War II resulted in his being the only entertainer voted into the Living Hall of Fame by the Smithsonian Institution. After the war he took a troupe to entertain the troops overseas at Christmas time for many years. His last such trip was in 1973. In 1960 Hope, a good golfer himself, sponsored a PGA tournament, the Bob Hope Classic. It also had a pro-amateur format but differed from the usual tournament by running for five

94

rounds instead of four. Arnold Palmer won the first one and five altogether. In addition to the cash prizes, Hope put up a trophy named for the late President Eisenhower. Hope took the name Bob when he became a solo performer in vaudeville about 1929.

HOPKINS, J. MARK B. 11/13/42, Texas City, Tex. On the strength of reaching the semifinal round of the USGA Amateur in 1964, Hopkins was chosen for the Walker Cup and Americas Cup teams of 1965. In the semifinal of the Amateur he was beaten by William C. Campbell, the eventual winner. Previously Hopkins had been a member of the University of Houston team which had won the NCAA Championships in 1962, 64. He made the Collegiate All-America in 1963, won the Texas State Open as an amateur in 1962, the Texas Junior in 1960, and the National Hearst (Junior) the same year. In the Americas Cup Hopkins won all four of his singles matches as the United States finished second to Canada.

HORN, MIRIAM BURNS (Tyson) B. 2/3/04, Kansas City, Mo. D. 3/19/51, Kansas City, Mo. One of the most attractive women in golf, Mrs. Horn came along in an era marked by great players—Glenna Collett, Alexa Stirling Fraser, Virginia Van Wie, Maureen Orcutt, Edith Cummings, Mrs. Opal Hill, and the aging but still redoubtable Dorothy Campbell Hurd. In 1923, as Miriam Burns, she was beaten in the second round of the USGA Women's Amateur by Alexa Stirling. In 1924 she lost to Mrs. Hurd in the quarterfinal and the next year to Mary K. Browne, the former tennis champion. But in 1927 as Mrs. Horn, she went all the way. She defeated Mrs. Fraser in the semifinal, 1 up, and Miss Orcutt in the final, 5 and 4. It is worth noting that her early defeats all came at the hands of champions or finalists. In 1927, Mrs. Horn also won the Trans-Mississippi, and in 1930 she won the Women's Western for the third time.

HOWELL, WILLIAM R. B. 3/1/12, Richmond, Va. A high ranking amateur at the beginning of the Great Depression, Howell had his best years in 1931, 32. In the USGA Amateur of 1931 he knocked out Johnny Goodman in the first round and Lester Bolstad in the third. Then he ran into the veteran Francis Ouimet, staging his remarkable comeback, and was beaten in the semifinal, 2 and 1. Ouimet went on to win, 17 years after his first Amateur victory. Howell played on the Walker Cup team of 1932, pairing with Don Moe in a foursomes victory. Howell won the Virginia Amateur in 1928, 31, 32, 35, the Middle Atlantic in 1931, 32, the Old Dominion twice, and was a finalist in the Southern Amateur and the Intercollegiate. Making the Walker Cup team was his golf goal, Howell says, and he quit tournament golf after 1935.

HOYT, BEATRIX B. 7/5/1880, Westchester Co., N.Y. D. 8/14/63, Thomasville, Ga. Miss Hoyt started to dominate women's golf at an early age and then quit before maturity could overtake her. In 1896, the second year of the

USGA Women's Amateur, a qualifying round was held for the first time. Miss Hoyt won the medal and went on to win the title. At 16 she was and remained the youngest winner until Laura Baugh in 1971. Five years in a row Miss Hoyt won the qualifying medal, through 1900. Three years in a row she won the Championship. But after losing to Margaret Curtis in the semifinal and having reached the age of 20, Miss Hoyt retired from tournament golf. She was a granddaughter of Salmon P. Chase, Lincoln's secretary of the treasury. By her first victory Miss Hoyt won the Robert Cox Trophy, which is still in competition. Mr. Cox, a member of Parliament from Edinburgh, Scotland, gave it with the proviso that the tournament be played that year at the Morris County Golf Club, a course which he helped lay out.

HUNTER, HENRY MacGREGOR (Mac) B. 6/16/29, Santa Monica, Cal. Mac Hunter won the National Junior Championship in 1946 and the Western Junior the same year. In 1949 he took the California Amateur and the Mexican Amateur. In 1952 he turned pro. For many years Mac worked with his father, Willie Hunter, at the Riviera Country Club in California and did not play much tournament golf. He took over the job at Riviera when his father died in 1968. His godfather was Tommy Armour. The Hunter family has been associated with golf, one way or another, since the middle of the nineteenth century, in Scotland and America.

HUNTER, WILLIAM IRVINE (Willie) B. 1/29/1892, Forest Row, Sussex, England. D. 11/15/68. 5'8", 152. Although born in England, Willie Hunter was "as Scotch as the heather at Troon," as his son puts it. He won the British Amateur Championship in 1921 and was a semifinalist in 1922. He also was low amateur in the British Open of 1920. In 1921 he made a strong bid for the USGA Amateur, reaching the semifinal after beating Bobby Jones in an early round. He won the Royal St. George's Cup in 1922. In 1923 he turned pro after coming to America in 1922. Hunter won the California Open in 1926, 27, 28 and the Southern California title six times. He took the San Francisco match play in 1936 and the California PGA in 1940, 42.

HURD, DOROTHY CAMPBELL B. 5/6/1883, Edinburgh, Scotland, D. 3/20/45, Yemassee, S.C. As Dorothy Campbell she won the British Women's Amateur in 1909, 11. In 1909 she came to America and won the USGA Women's, repeated in 1910, and won for a third time in 1924, when she defeated Mary K. Browne, the tennis star, in the final. She was then Mrs. Hurd. To round out her sweep of international golf, Miss Campbell won the Canadian Women's three years in a row, 1910-12. She was truly the dominant figure in women's golf in the early years of the century. In 1938 she won a United States Women's Senior tournament with a 36-hole score of 159. She was then 55. She was killed by a train in 1945, while changing trains, in Yemassee, S.C.

HUSAR, JOHN B. 1/29/37, Chicago, Ill. This golf writer for the *Chicago Tribune* has had a varied career. He went to the University of Kansas on a football scholarship and studied journalism and theatre. Wilt Chamberlain was in his freshman class there, which he says encouraged him to give up any thoughts of playing basketball. After his first newspaper job with the *Clovis (N.M.) News-Journal* in 1960, he was drafted and spent a year and a half in Okinawa, where he edited an Army paper. After discharge he was city editor of the *Pasadena (Tex.) Daily Citizen,* followed by a year as police reporter and later business editor of the *Topeka (Kans.) Daily Capital* and two years as city hall reporter. Then he became regional news editor of the *Wichita (Kans.) Beacon.* He went to the *Chicago Tribune* in 1966 and began writing golf the next year. He has been a director of the Golf Writers' Association of America, and he conducted the *Tribune*'s golf school for three years. Husar claims he holds the record high score, 178, in the annual GWAA tournament in Myrtle Beach.

HUTCHISON, JOCK B. 6/6/1884, St. Andrews, Scotland. This little Scot, who came to America with so many Britons in the early years of the century, was one of the best. A dour, nervous, restless competitor, Hutchison was runner-up to Jim Barnes in the first PGA Championship. That was in 1916. The same year he also was runner-up to Chick Evans, when Evans became the third amateur to win the USGA Open. Evans set a record of 286 and Hutchison had 288, the first time anyone had broken 290. Between exhibitions for World War I charities, Jock won what was called the Patriotic Open, by 7 shots. In 1920 he won the PGA, beating J. Douglas Edgar, 1 up. The following year he won the British Open in a playoff with the amateur Roger Wethered. Jock had a hole-in-one in the first round and shot the last nine holes in 34 to tie Wethered. He won the playoff by 9 strokes. In 1920 he tied for second in the USGA Open and in 1925 tied for third. He won at least eight major tournaments, including the North and South and Western Opens. For several years he and Freddie McLeod were the lead-off pair in the first round of the Masters. Jock is credited with shooting a 66 when he was 66 years old. And it should not be forgotten that he won the PGA Senior in 1937, 47. Jock was voted into the PGA HAll of Fame in 1959.

HYNDMAN, WILLIAM, III B. 12/25/15, Glenside, Pa. 6'3½", 198. A man with a long and illustrious career in amateur golf. In 1955, when he was 40, he reached the final in the USGA Amateur, losing to Harvie Ward. Three times he reached the final in the British Amateur, 1959, 69, 70, losing first to Deane Beman and twice to Mike Bonallack. Five times he has been on the Walker Cup team, 1957, 59, 61, 69, 71, three times on the Americas Cup team, and twice, in 1958, 60, on the World Amateur team. In 1972 Hyndman was a semifinalist in the USGA Senior, and in 1973 he won it, defeating Harry Welch, 3 and 2. He has been equally successful in many other tournaments. In 1969, 70, at 55, he won the Philadelphia Open, in 1968 the Trans-Mississippi, in 1958, 67, the Sunnehanna Tournament of Champions, and in 1974 the Northeast Amateur. A durable golf game is Hyndman's, one that enabled him to make the Walker Cup team 14 years after making it the first time.

INMAN, JOE B. 11/29/47, Indianapolis, Ind. 5'11", 165. Inman was a graduate of Wake Forest University and a star amateur. He played on the Walker Cup team in 1969, won the North and South Amateur, and was on the college All-America team. In 1968 he won the Carolinas Open and in 1970 the North Carolina Amateur. He got his ATP Card in 1973 and played the full tour for the first time in 1974, winning $46,645 although he was without a victory.

IRWIN, HALE B. 6/3/45, Joplin, Mo. 6'0", 165. Irwin had had only two victories, but had won a lot of money in his six years on the tour, when he came through with a triumph in the biggest of them all, the USGA Open in 1974. That week, on the very tight and punishing Winged Foot course, Irwin was straighter than anyone, and he putted consistently well. From being 2 strokes behind after 54 holes, Irwin finished 2 in front. His 287 and Fezler's 289 were the only scores under 290. He was graduated from Colorado University in 1968 and had been an All-Big Eight safety on the football team for two years. He went on the tour immediately and quickly established himself as a moneymaker. He shot up to over $99,000 in 1971, his fourth year, and to more than $130,000 and seventh place on the money list in 1973. Irwin's two victories prior to the U.S. Open both came, oddly, in the Heritage Classic, in 1971, 73. As the U.S. Open champion he was an automatic selection for the 1975 Ryder Cup team. Irwin agrees with others who have played both games that golf is tougher than football "because in golf there is no way to blow off your emotions." Accurate iron play has been the strongest part of Irwin's game. A very good year was 1974, when he won $152,529. The year 1975 saw Irwin on the Ryder Cup team and with two more tour victories, the Atlanta and the Western. And as evidence of his match play ability, he won the Picadilly World for the second year in a row. His official tour earnings through 1975 were $762,000. In the winter of 1976, Irwin won twice, the Los Angeles and Florida Citrus Opens.

IVERSON, DONALD B. 10/28/45, LaCrosse, Wisc. 5'10", 185. Iverson turned pro in 1968, went on the PGA tour in 1969, and battled until 1975 before he won his first tournament. That victory came in the B.C. Open and was worth $35,000. This was almost $13,000 more than he made in prize money in all of 1974. Iverson was graduated from the University of Wisconsin in 1968, with a bachelor of science degree in economics. He tied for sixth in the PGA Championship in 1973.

JACKLIN, TONY B. 7/7/44, Scunthorpe, England. 5'9½", 173. The first Englishman to win the USGA Open Championship in 50 years. This momentous event came in 1970 at Chaska, Minn. From cold and high winds the first day, through the whole range of weather conditions, Jacklin scored 281 and won by 7 strokes. He led the field after every round, which only Walter Hagen, Jim Barnes, and Ben Hogan had done in this championship, and his margin of victory was the largest since Barnes won by 9 shots in 1921. The last previous English winner was Ted Ray in 1920. Jacklin came to this country with the British Ryder Cup team in 1967. In 1968 he made the American tour and won the Jacksonville Open. In 1969 he won the British Open. He was the first English pro to take it in 18 years and was honored by the Queen with the Order of the British Empire. He won again at Jacksonville in 1972. Previously, in 1967, Jacklin had won the New Zealand PGA and the Dunlop Masters. He turned pro at age 18, and his career earnings on the PGA tour are in excess of $260,000. In recent years he has played infrequently in this country. He was a member of the British Ryder Cup team in 1967, 69, 71, 73, 75.

JACKSON, MRS. H. ARNOLD (Katherine Harley) B. 11/13/1881, Fall River, Mass. D. 5/2/61, Pinehurst, N.C. Mrs. Jackson was a two-time winner of the USGA Women's Amateur Championship. As Kate Harley from Fall River, Mass., she reached the quarterfinals twice, in 1903, 04, before she broke through for the first time in 1908. She defeated the ever-dangerous Margaret Curtis in the third round and Mrs. T. H. Polhemus in the final, 6 and 5. In 1913 she married, and in 1914 she won for the second time. She defeated Miss Elaine Rosenthal, a persistent challenger, 1 up, in the final. Mrs. Jackson won the Women's Eastern in 1914, 21.

JACKSON, JAMES G. B. 11/19/22, Mulberry, Ark. D. 5/2/61, Pinehurst, N.C. Jackson was the low amateur in the 1952 USGA Open, tying for 19th the year Julius Boros won at Dallas. There were, in fact, only two other amateurs among the 52 finishers: Stan Mosel and Billy Joe Patton. In 1951 Jackson reached the fourth round of the USGA Amateur and in 1952 the fifth round. He played on the Walker Cup teams of 1953, 55 and was unbeaten in his matches. In 1954, 55 he won the Trans-Mississippi and took the Missouri Amateur in 1951, 54, 59. He also was runner-up in the Missouri four times from 1950-70.

JACKSON, JOHN G. B. 2/12/1880, Middletown, N.Y. D. 4/27/59, New York, N.Y. Jackson was at one time former-President Eisenhower's personal lawyer. He was president of the United States Golf Association in 1936, 37. During this period he was instrumental in condensing and clarifying the rules of the game. He also served as the organization's vice president, Rules Committee chairman, and general counsel. Jackson's interest in golf began early, before he played for Columbia University on the intercollegiate level in 1901. He was a life trustee of Columbia. As president of the New York State Bar Association, Jackson worked to prevent court abuses and to keep the judiciary clear of underworld influence.

JACOBS, K. THOMAS (Tommy) B. 2/13/35, Denver, Colo. 5'10", 160. Jacobs started early, being a semifinalist in the USGA Junior at age 15. He turned pro five years later, in 1956, and went on the tour the following season. He won four tournaments: the Denver, San Diego, and Utah Opens and the Bob Hope Classic. The latter victory came in 1964, which was also his best money year with checks worth $48,000. He was selected for the Ryder Cup team in 1965. His greatest chance for enduring fame came in 1966 when he, Jack Nicklaus, and Gay Brewer tied for first in the Masters. In the playoff his 72 was 2 shots behind Nicklaus. He was a member of the PGA Tournament Committee in 1964, 66 and chairman of it the latter two years. He plays the tour infrequently now.

JACOBUS, GEORGE R. B. 6/2/1899, Glen Ridge, N.J. D. 7/22/65, Oradell, N.J. Jacobus had two marks of distinction. He served the PGA as its president longer than anyone else, from 1933-39, and he was the professional at the prestigious Ridgewood (N.J.) Country Club for 52 years, one of the longest stretches on record. While PGA president, he worked for a standardized method of teaching, albeit without success. He saw the tournament circuit as the show window of golf and strove to promote it. Jacobus also started the Baseball-Golf Tournament in 1932. Although not a tournament player, he was capable of hot streaks, attested by his eight consecutive birdies during a round at Ridgewood. Byron Nelson was Jacobus's assistant during the mid-1930s.

JAMES, LOUIS N. B. 9/1882, Chicago, Ill. D. 6/7/35, Chicago, Ill. James was only 19 years, 10 months old when he won the USGA Amateur at Chicago in 1902. He defeated Eben Byers in the final, 4 and 2. The USGA went to a match-play field of 64 that year for the first time. In the qualifying round James shot a 94 and was one of 13 players who set out in a playoff for the last two places in the match-play draw. He won his early matches without much difficulty, while Byers was knocking out Walter Travis, the medalist and defending champion, and H. Chandler Egan, two of the strongest players. Heavy rain fell before the semifinal, and by the next morning the Skokie River had overflowed and inundated the first nine at the Glen View course. So the 36-hole final was played four times around the second nine. Defending his title the next year, James was beaten in the first round.

JAMESON, ELIZABETH (Betty) B. 5/9/19, Norman, Okla. Like many of the other girls, Betty Jameson started early, winning the Southern Amateur when she was only 15. She reached her peak, however, when she won the USGA Amateur Championship two years running, in 1939, 40. In the first she defeated Dorothy Kirby, 3 and 2, in the final, and in the second, Jane Cothran, 6 and 5. Previously she had taken the Texas State Championship four years in a row, 1935-38, and the Trans-Mississippi in 1937, 40. After winning the Western Women's Open and Amateur in 1942, and with women's golf on the dormant side during the war, she turned pro in 1945. In 1947 Betty won the Women's National Open, although it was not then sponsored by the USGA. She had been runner-up to Patty Berg the previous year. In 1952 she won the so-called World Championship and in 1954 the Western. In 1955 she made the Babe Zaharias Open one of her four victories that year.

JAMIESON, JIM B. 4/21/43, Kalamazoo, Mich. 5'10", 210. Jamieson has won only once in the six years he has been on the tour, but he made that victory a big one. It came in 1972 when he took the Western Open, oldest of the tour tournaments and high on the prestige ladder, with a score of 271, which put him 6 strokes in front of the field. Jamieson had been knocking at the door before that and he still is. He has tied for third in both the Masters and the Western, for second in the PGA, for fifth in the Tournament of Champions, and has been sixth in the World Open. His big year was 1972 with his victory and purse winnings of $109,532. Jamieson attended Oklahoma State University.

JANUARY, DONALD (Don) B. 11/20/29, Plainview, Tex. 6'0", 165. Playing much less than he used to, January was long one of the most consistent players on the tour. From the time he joined the circuit in 1956 through 1970, he was never worse than 47th on the money list. He won 11 tournaments including the Dallas and Apple Valley Opens in his rookie year. He also won the Valencia, St. Paul, Tucson (twice), Philadelphia, Greater Jacksonville, Tournament of Champions, and San Antonio-Texas. Biggest of all, however, was his victory in the PGA Championship of 1967. He won it in a playoff with Don Massengale, after having been nosed out of it six years earlier by Jerry Barber's spectacular finish. January's biggest bonanza, however, came when he made a hole-in-one in the Palm Springs in 1961. Don didn't win (the winner's prize was $5,300), but he got $50,000 for the ace. January is a product of North Texas State College, which has turned out so many fine players. He was on the school's NCAA Championship teams of 1950, 51, 52, then went into the Air Force and turned pro while still in service. He has long been easily identified by his deliberate gait and turned-up collar, the latter to protect his neck from sunburn. Don was a member of the Ryder Cup team of 1965. His career earnings are about $645,000. In early 1976, he won the Mony Tournament of Champions.

JENKINS, DAN THOMAS B. 12/2/29, Fort Worth, Tex. Jenkins has been writing golf for close to three decades and is best known now for his articles in *Sports Illustrated.* He started with a newspaper, the *Fort Worth Press,* in 1948. He moved to the *Dallas Times Herald* in 1960 and after two years there went to *Sports Illustrated.* He writes football as well as golf. Jenkins also has written six books, the last two of which were novels, *Semi Tough* and *Dead Solid Perfect* which is about the golf tour. He says that with some practice he can play to a handicap of 6.

JENKINS, THOMAS B. 12/14/47, Houston, Tex. 5'11", 180. Jenkins became a winner for the first time on the PGA tour when he took the IVB-Philadelphia Classic in 1975. This was a tournament which wound up with a double round on a Monday because of a postponed first round. Tom shot himself into a 5-stroke lead in the second round and then hung on through the final 36 holes to edge out Johnny Miller by 1 shot. Jenkins was graduated from the University of Houston with a bachelor of arts degree in 1971. He qualified for the tour in 1972. Until his victory, his best finish was a tie for second in the USI Classic in 1973. In 1974 Jenkins won nearly $31,000. His win at Philadelphia was worth $30,000.

JESSEN, MARY RUTH B. 11/12/36, Seattle, Wash. 5'7", 135. A veteran of the LPGA tour who has won 11 tournaments in spite of physical disabilities which would have stopped a less determined competitor. As an amateur she was a three-time winner of the Seattle City title, twice of the Pacific Northwest, and once of the Washington State. She was also medalist and semi-finalist in the National Junior. In 1956 she turned pro and in 1959 won her first on the tour, the Tampa Open. Victories followed in subsequent years until 1964, when she had the best campaign of her career. That year she won five: the Zaharias, Flint, Omaha, Santa Barbara, and Phoenix Opens. Then after four operations for ailments ranging from a thyroid condition to tendonitis, Miss Jessen came back to win the rich Sears in 1971. A characteristic of her play is her extremely wide putting stance. Her career earnings were more than $142,000 through 1975.

JOHNSON, HOWARD (Howie) B. 9/8/25, St. Paul, Minn. 6'2", 195. A man who apparently gets better with age, Johnson had his best year financially in 1970, when, at age 45, he won $66,508. That year he played in 31 tour tournaments and missed the cut only once, an amazing performance. This consistency accounted for his purse money, for he did not win that year. His two tour victories came in 1958, 59, in the Azalea and Baton Rouge Opens. A one-time University of Minnesota golf team captain and later an insurance salesman, Johnson turned pro on a dare, at age 30. This came after what he calls "a pretty good round" in Houston. So he took the dare and doesn't regret it.

JOHNSTON, HARRISON R. (Jimmy) B. 8/31/1896, St. Paul, Minn. D. 11/18/69, Fla. After a long and steady career in Minnesota, Johnston in 1929 won one of the two USGA Amateur Championships which Bobby Jones did not win from 1924-30. Jimmy had won the Western Amateur in 1924 and had taken the Minnesota Amateur seven years in a row, 1921-27. In 1927 he had startled the pros by leading the Open at Oakmont after 36 holes, but then had a bad third round. In the 1929 Amateur Jones was beaten in the first round by Johnny Goodman. On his way to the final, Johnston went 39 holes to beat George Voigt and then defeated Francis Ouimet easily. His victim in the final was Dr. O. F. Willing, 4 and 3. He was on the Walker Cup teams of 1923, 24, 28, 30, winning the two singles matches in which he played and three of the four foursomes.

JOHNSTONE, ANN CASEY B. 2/14/21, Mason City, Ia. Mrs. Johnstone is one of the select few who have played on three or more Curtis Cup teams against the British women. She made the team in 1958, 60, 62, played in five matches, and won four of them. In 1957 she went to the final of the USGA Women's, losing to JoAnn Gunderson. In 1960 she was a semifinalist, bowing to Jean Ashley. Playing competitively for more than 20 years, Mrs. Johnstone won the Trans-Mississippi and the North and South in 1959, the Western in 1960, and the Iowa State six times. She also was runner-up in the Western and North and South once and in the Trans-Mississippi twice. In 1959 she teamed with Marlene Streit to win the Women's International Four-Ball, an event in which they were runners-up in 1961. The next year she and Deane Beman won the National Mixed Two-Ball title. She was a semifinalist in the French Women's Open in 1960. In 1964 Mrs. Johnstone became a professional and an outstanding teacher, so good that in 1966 she received the LPGA Teacher of the Year award. From 1970-75, she was a staff instructor at the National Golf Foundation's seminar for teachers. Since 1964 she has taught classes at Stephens College in Columbia, Mo., and been coach of the girls' golf team.

JOLLY, JACK B. 4/4/1880, St. Andrews, Scotland. D. 5/19/64, Bloomfield, N.J. Although Coburn Haskell gave us the first rubber-wound golf ball, the man who first put a liquid core in the ball, to give it a proper center of gravity, was Jack Jolly, a man whose story outdoes romance. He went to sea at 13, on various sailing ships, and always carried his golf clubs with him. He played everywhere the British had implanted a course. In the port of New

York he came down with malaria, and his ship sailed without him—to go down in a storm with all hands lost. In 1901 Jolly became the pro at the Forest Hill Field Club in Belleville, N.J. One of the members, Eleazer Kempshall, had a factory nearby which made golf balls, and Jolly soon went to work for him. He knew the golf ball needed a liquid core, but the problem was how to get it there. One day Jolly saw nipples for nursing bottles displayed in a store window. He bought the druggist's whole supply, filled them with water, tied them, and cut off the ends. Jolly had the first basic liquid core. In 1910 the St. Mungo Golf Ball Co. of Scotland bought out Kempshall and put Jolly in as operating vice president of the U.S. company. St. Mungo made the "Colonel" ball, and after the company went out of business in 1932 Jolly continued to make the "Jolly Colonel." After trying many other cores besides water, Jolly went back on a visit to Scotland in 1936 and took lots of his balls with him. He amazed the Scots by throwing handfuls of them out of train windows as samples whenever he passed by a golf course. Jolly was probably the most popular and best known apostle of the game that golf ever has known. He was even made an honorary vice president of the Royal and Ancient.

JONES, ERNEST B. 1888, England. D. 7/31/65, Glen Head, N.Y. Jones was an English pro who lost a leg in battle during World War I. He came to the United States in 1924 and became the professional at the Women's National Club in Glen Head, L.I. The club was closed during World War II, and Jones taught at an indoor establishment in New York City, among other places. He had considerable success with his main theme, "swing the clubhead," which he used as the title of a book. Among his pupils were Virginia Van Wie, a three-time national champion, Mary K. Browne, and Mrs. Fred Austen. Shortly before his death in 1965, Jones was given the Ben Hogan Award by the Metropolitan Golf Writers' Association for success despite a physical handicap.

JONES, GRIER B. Wichita, Kans. 5/6/46. 5'10", 165. Another graduate of Oklahoma State where, in 1968, he won the NCAA, Big Eight, and Oklahoma Championships plus a couple of other tournaments. He promptly turned pro and was the No. 1 qualifier in the Tournament Players' Division qualifying school. In 1969 he took Rookie of the Year honors. Jones's big year came in 1972 when he won the Hawaiian and Robinson Opens, finished second in the National Team Championship with Johnny Miller, tied for second in the Milwaukee, and wound up with $140,177 in prize money. He was fourth on the money list that year. Jones had another good year in 1973, winning more than $83,000, until an ailing back forced him to withdraw late in the season.

JONES, ROBERT TRENT B. 6/20/06, Ince, England. This best-known of American golf course architects was brought to the U.S. by his parents when he was 6 years old, and through his parents he derived United States citizenship. He took up golf early and became a "scratch" player in Rochester, N.Y. He became a partner of Stanley Thompson, a Canadian architect, in 1930 and set up his own practice in 1940. Since World War II Jones has designed more than 400 courses in 40 of the 50 states and in 23 foreign countries. He has built or remodeled many of the courses on which the USGA Open and the PGA have been played, such as Oakland Hills, Baltusrol, Firestone, Bellerive, Oak Hill, Olympic Club, and Hazeltine. His courses are characterized by extensive teeing areas and large greens permitting many pin placements. His principle in designing is that "every hole should be a hard par and an easy bogey." In 1974 Jones was selected to design and build the first course ever planned for the Soviet Union.

JONES, ROBERT TYRE (Bobby) B. 3/17/02, Atlanta, Ga. D. 12/18/71, Atlanta, Ga. 5'8", 160. Incomparable in his era, Jones was the only man to complete the "Grand Slam" of winning the USGA and British Opens and the USGA and British Amateurs in the same year, 1930. At that point, only 28 years old, Jones retired. During a period of eight years, 1923-30, he won thirteen National Championships, something never approached before or since. But Jones, like others, had to go through a period of disappointment before he reached the top. In 1916 (when he was only 14) he lost in the Amateur quarterfinal to Bob Gardner, in 1919 in the final to Davey Herron, in 1920 in the semifinal to Francis Ouimet, in 1921 in the third round to Willie Hunter, in 1922 in the semifinal to Jess Sweetser, and in 1923 in the third round to Max Marston. But earlier in 1923 Jones had broken through. In July he defeated Bobby Cruickshank in a playoff for the USGA Open Championship at Long Island's Inwood course. From then on there was no stopping him. The National Championships became "Jones against the field," and with good reason. He won the Open again in 1926, 29, 30; the Amateur in 1924, 25, 27, 28, 30; the British Open in 1926, 27, 30; and the British Amateur in 1930. A measure of Jones's excellence and consistency is that from 1922-30 he was either first or second in the Open, except for one year. In the Amateur he either won or was runner-up every year from 1924-30, except once. Jones had a full, fluid, graceful swing, was long off the tee, and was an excellent putter. He had a picture swing, although a little loose by today's standards. Little remembered now, but an indication of how Jones dominated the field, was his performance in 1930, just before he set out on the "Grand Slam." After a winter's layoff he entered two tour tournaments. He finished second in the first but won the second, the Southeastern Open, by no less than 13 shots. In his early years of retirement Bobby helped to design the Augusta National course, site of the Masters. A spinal ailment confined him to a wheelchair in his later years and finally caused his death. In 1940 Jones was named as a charter member of the PGA Hall of Fame, and after his death he was elected to the World Hall of Fame.

KAMMER, A. FREDERICK, JR. B. 6/5/12, Brooklyn, N.Y. Kammer was a member of the victorious Walker Cup team of 1947, when the international matches were resumed after World War II. He and Willie Turnesa won their foursomes match, but Kammer was paired against Ronnie White, the talented Englishman who went through four Walker Cup battles before he lost a match. White won that singles encounter. Kammer was a semifinalist in the 1946 USGA Amateur. He was also a semifinalist in the Canadian Amateur. He has twice been second in the Crosby Pro-Am, twice winner of the Seminole Invitation, twice Detroit Amateur champion, twice Junior champion of New Jersey, and winner of the Metropolitan Junior in 1929. In a sport at the opposite extreme, Kammer was a member of the U.S. Olympic ice hockey team in 1936.

KARL, RICHARD B. 9/28/44, Johnson City, N.Y. 5'11", 170. Richie Karl got his start in tournament golf while an amateur in the Army. Stationed in Alaska he won the Alaska State Amateur twice, in 1965, 66. He went on the tour in 1971 and took one of the satellites, the Yuma Open, but through 1973 his best on the big tour was a tie for fifth in the Tucson. But in 1974 he broke the ice. He won the B.C. Open and did it sensationally, too. Finishing in a tie with Bruce Crampton, he holed a 35-foot putt to take the playoff and $30,000.

KAUFFMANN, CARL F. B. 1899, Pittsburgh, Pa. D. 7/8/51, Pittsburgh, Pa. Carl Kauffmann was once referred to as "the poor man's Bobby Jones." This was due to the consistency of his play in winning the USGA Public Links Championship three years in succession, 1927, 28, 29. This streak of three has never been equalled in the USGA Public Links, and it came after Kauffmann, then a clerk in a steel mill in West Homestead, Pa., had been a finalist in the 1928 Championship, losing then to Lester Bolstad. His first victory came only at the 37th hole, over George Serrick, but the next two were easy. Strangely enough, in his bid for a fourth straight crown, Kauffmann disqualified himself by turning in a wrong score in the qualifying round. Carl also won 10 Pittsburgh Public Links titles.

KEELER, OSCAR BAUN (O.B.) B. 6/4/1882, Chicago, Ill. D. 10/15/50, Atlanta, Ga. Keeler came into national prominence for his newspaper coverage of Bobby Jones. He was known as "Jones's Boswell," and with good reason. Keeler went to the *Atlanta Journal* in 1920, after three years with the *Kansas City Star,* just at the time Jones was showing promise of being the superstar he soon became. Also prominent in Atlanta golf at the time were Alexa Stirling and Perry Adair. But Keeler and Jones struck up a close friendship, and Keeler covered every tournament Jones played in. He collaborated with him on books and went on a radio series with him after Bobby's retirement. In fact, he made the first trans-Atlantic sportscast when he described the British Open by radio in 1930. In all, in his 41 years as a reporter, Keeler covered 67 major golf tournaments.

KEISER, HERMAN B. 10/7/14, Springfield, Mo. Keiser's big year in competitive golf was 1946. That was the year he won the first post-war Masters, when the winner was supposed to be Hogan, Nelson, or Snead. But Keiser not only stayed with the leaders, he was 5 shots in front of everybody going into the last round. Then Hogan almost caught him. When Keiser 3-putted the last green he left the door open. Hogan needed only 2 putts to tie. But he also took 3, and Keiser was the winner. Herman also won at Knoxville and Richmond in 1946. In 1942 he teamed with Chandler Harper to take the Miami Pro-Pro tournament, and in 1949 he won the Esmeralda Open. Keiser made the Ryder Cup team in 1947.

KESSLER, KAYE W. B. 12/20/23, Toledo, O. Kessler, writing golf for 30 years for the *Columbus Citizen-Journal,* is known among other things as Jack Nicklaus's Boswell—or Keeler, if you will, to put it in a golf framework. He has covered Nicklaus since Jack took his first lesson at the age of 10 from Jack Grout, the pro at the Scioto Country Club. Kessler was on the tee for the lesson. He went to work for the *Citizen-Journal* in 1941. Besides his paper, for which he covers Ohio State football in the fall and Big Ten basketball and skiing in the winter, he writes regularly for *Golf World* magazine and the *Professional Golfer,* and occasionally for *Golf Magazine* and *Golf Digest.* Kessler plays golf, in a way which has given rise to the line: "Don't ever take that swing out of town, because you can't get parts for it." It can't be that bad, for his handicap, once 7, is now 14.

KIERSKY, ROBERT B. B. 2/28/08, Waco, Tex. Kiersky has a long history of victories, starting with the Texas State Public Links in 1940, 41. He took the Long Island Amateur in 1959, and the American Seniors' Golf Association in 1964, and then crowned the string by winning the USGA Senior in

1965. In this he defeated Robert Beechler in the final, 1 up, at the 19th hole. He has qualified for this championship eight times. In 1967, 73 Kiersky won the United States Seniors' G.A. title. Also, in 1967, he was a member of the USGA team in the World Senior Amateur and had low score for the four rounds in the U.S. victory.

KIMBALL, JUDY B. 6/17/38, Sioux City, Ia. After being Iowa State Champion in 1958 and semifinalist in the Trans-Mississippi and Western Amateurs in 1959, she turned pro in her first year, 1961, and won the American Open. Miss Kimball showed this was no flash in the pan by winning the LPGA Championship the next year. A succession of high finishes followed, including a tie for second in the Titleholders Championship in 1966, until she broke through again to win the O'Sullivan Open in 1971. That year, too, she and Kathy Whitworth teamed to win the Winchester Four-Ball. She was secretary on the LPGA executive board in 1974.

KIRBY, DOROTHY B. 1/15/20, West Point, Ga. This Georgia girl was a model of persistence. She reached the final of the USGA Women's Amateur twice and the semifinal three times before finally winning the big prize. As early as 1937 she won the Southern, and in 1939 she went to the USGA final where she was beaten by Betty Jameson. After the break for World War II she reached the final again, this time bowing to Louise Suggs in 1947. Two years later she got to the semifinal before being turned back by Dorothy Germain Porter, the eventual winner. But in 1951 Miss Kirby went all the way, defeating Claire Doran in the final, 2 and 1. Dorothy was also consistent. Besides the years mentioned, she was a quarterfinalist three times and gained the round of 16 four times. She was good at stroke play too, winning the medal in 1946, 52. And as of this writing Miss Kirby is the only woman to have played on four Curtis Cup teams, 1948, 50, 52, 54. She also won the Southern Women's in 1937, the North and South in 1943, and the Georgia State five times.

KIRKWOOD, JOSEPH B. 3/22/1897, Australia. D. 10/29/70, Burlington, Vt. One of the best-known trick-shot artists in golf, and a partner of Walter Hagen and Gene Sarazen in exhibition tours the world over. Kirkwood learned the trick shots while entertaining soldiers during World War I. "They enjoyed them more than the conventional shots," he said, so he developed them. He came to the United States in 1921 and tied for second in the Canadian Open that year. He won the Canadian in 1922, also the North and South. In 1924 he won tournaments at San Antonio, Houston, and Corpus Christi. He was fourth in the British Open of 1923 and tied for third in 1927. His tours with Hagen and Sarazen, separately, took him all over the world, and he estimated that he had played 8,000 courses—a more conservative estimate was 6,470. At one time he was paid to use a wooden tee, then coming on the market, instead of the customary sand tee. At another time he made a hole-in-one hitting the ball off the face of a watch, in Sioux City, Iowa. For the last five years of his life, Kirkwood was the pro at the Stowe (Vt.) C.C. in the New England ski country.

KIROUAC, MARTHA WILKINSON B. 9/24/48, Los Angeles, Cal. The year 1970 was the big one for the then Martha Wilkinson. That was the season she won the USGA Women's Amateur, defeating Cindy Hill in the final, 3 and 2. That was also the year she was a member of both the Curtis Cup team and the World Cup team, and took the Trans-Mississippi, the Doherty Challenge Cup, and the Harder Hall Invitation. In 1972, after her marriage, she made the Curtis Cup team for the second time. Prior to her big year, Mrs. Kirouac had won the California Junior in 1966, the Women's National Collegiate in 1967, and the Mexican Women's Amateur in 1969. Partnered with Jane Bastenchury Booth, Mrs. Kirouac won the International Four-Ball three times, from 1968-70.

KITE, THOMAS O., JR. B. 12/9/49, Austin, Tex. 5'9", 165. Starting golf when he was 6 years old, Kite developed quickly enough to win the qualifying medal in the Western Amateur of 1970. That same year he reached the final of the USGA Amateur, losing to Lanny Wadkins. In 1972 he tied Ben Crenshaw for the NCAA title and was second low amateur in the USGA Open. He was a member of the 1970 World Amateur Cup team and in 1971 of the Walker Cup team. Kite turned pro in 1972 and went on the tour full-time the next year, distinguishing himself by missing the 36-hole cut only three times. Although he has not won on the big tour, his consistency has earned him more than $220,000.

KNOWLES, ROBERT W., JR. B. 8/16/14, Cambridge, Mass. Knowles was a member of the Walker Cup team in 1951, which defeated the British in Southport, England. While abroad he won the French Amateur Championship. Knowles qualified for the USGA Amateur no less than 16 times, and in 1950 he reached the semifinal, where he was beaten by Sam Urzetta, the ultimate champion. The same year he won the Tri-State Open for the second time and the New England Amateur. He also has won the Maine Open and the South Carolina Amateur twice. Knowles won the Carolina Senior three times, 1965, 66, 67, and the South Carolina Senior twice, in 1965, 66.

KNUDSON, GEORGE B. 6/28/37, Winnipeg, Canada. 5'10", 160. After 14 years on the tour, this Canadian with the smooth, compact swing finally eased off in 1973. He turned pro in 1958, at the age of 21, and went on the tour with some regularity in 1961. He started winning immediately, taking the Coral Gables Open that year. Counting a few victories on the Caribbean circuit, he has won 12 times south of the Canadian border, including the New Orleans, Phoenix, Tucson, Robinson, and Kaiser Opens. To these he added the Canadian PGA in 1964 and was low individual in the Canada Cup Matches in 1966. All told he has won over $500,000. Knudson has two distinctions. One is that he never has lost a playoff on the tour; his record stands at 3-0. One of those was a six-hole effort against George Archer to win the Robinson in 1970. The other distinction is that one of his hobbies is skiing, both snow and water— an activity considered far too risky for most golf pros. He always wears dark glasses on the course.

KOCH, GARY B. 11/21/52, Baton Rouge, La. Koch was something of an infant prodigy. In 1970, when he was 16 years old, he won the USGA Junior Championship. He not only won it but his score of 8 and 6 over Mike Nelms was the highest ever recorded in the Junior. Aly Trompas, the winner in 1969 and trying to repeat, was beaten by Koch in the quarterfinal, 3 and 1. When he entered the tournament Koch already had won the Florida Open and led the local qualifying for the USGA Open by 11 shots. In 1973 he reached the round of 16 in the USGA Amateur and in 1974 the semifinal, where he lost to John Grace. In 1973, 75 Koch played on the Walker Cup team, and in 1974 he was a member of the U.S. World Cup team. Also in 1974 he teamed with Mickey Van Gerbig to win the International Four-Ball. He turned pro in 1975.

KOCSIS, CHARLES (Chuck) B. 1/23/13, Newcastle, Pa. Charley Kocsis had a long career in amateur golf. In 1930 he beat Francis Ouimet in the first round of the USGA Amateur, and in 1958 he reached the quarterfinals of the same championship, losing then to Tommy Aaron. In between he did a lot of things. He reached the quarterfinal of the Amateur in 1935 before bowing to Johnny Goodman, won the NCAA in 1936 while a student at Michigan, and was runner-up in the Western Amateur in 1937. In 1938 he made the Walker Cup team. Then came a lapse until after World War II, when in both 1947, 48 he reached the last 16 in the Amateur and in 1949 again made the Walker Cup team. Following another lapse Kocsis swept to the front by gaining the USGA Amateur final in 1956, losing then to Harvie Ward, 5 and 4, and by making the Walker Cup team for the third time in 1957. He again made the last 16 in the 1957 Championship and, as noted, the quarterfinal in 1958. Kocsis has won the Michigan Amateur six times and the Open three times, beating Tommy Armour in a playoff for that title in 1931. The Kocsis brothers have made Michigan a happy hunting ground. Emerick, an older one, is a former State Open and State PGA champion, and Sam, younger, won the USGA Public Links title in 1958, as well as the State Amateur.

KROLL, THEODORE (Ted) B. 8/4/19, New Hartford, N.Y. 5'8½", 160. This Purple Heart veteran of World War II had his biggest year in 1956, when he won the World Tournament, the Western Open, and the Tucson. Previously Kroll had won the San Diego and Insurance City in 1952, the National Celebrity in 1953, and the Philadelphia in 1955. Then in 1962, at the age of 43, he won the Canadian Open. His best bids in the USGA Open were in 1960 when he tied for third, and in 1956 when he tied for fourth. Kroll was known as the pros' pro; he was the man the others went to see when they were off their games.

LACOSTE, CATHERINE (Mme. De Prado) B. 6/27/45, Paris, France. Catherine Lacoste startled the world of golf when she came to America in 1967 and won the USGA Women's Open Championship. She shot 296 in defeating our best professionals by 2 strokes. Just to show this was no accident, she came in 1969 and won the USGA Women's Amateur, this time beating Shelley Hamlin in the final, 3 and 2. That same year she won the British Women's Amateur. She has won the French International Women's four times, 1967, 69, 70, 72. In 1968 the American Curtis Cup team played a Continental Europe team, headed by Miss Lacoste, and was beaten, 10$^{1}/_{2}$-7$^{1}/_{2}$. She, of course, won both her singles matches. Miss Lacoste married in August 1969. She is the daughter of René Lacoste, the former French Davis Cup tennis star. Her mother was Thion de la Chaume, who won the British Women's Amateur in 1927.

LAFFOON, KY B. 12/23/08, Zinc, Ark. This part-Indian was one of the tour's loudest dressers, as well as one of its best players, during the era of the Great Depression. The year 1934 was his best. During that 12-month span Laffoon won the Atlanta Open, the Eastern, the Hershey, and the Glens Falls. His victories brought him a place on the Ryder Cup team of 1935, and his phenomenal scoring brought him the Radix Cup, precursor of the Vardon Trophy, for the low average score for the season. In 1935 Laffoon won the Phoenix and in 1936 the Inverness Four-Ball with Walter Hagen. He followed with the Miami Four-Ball in 1938, with Dick Metz, and then the Cleveland Open. He was capable of brilliant streaks, which he put together in his big year. Once, furious with a recalcitrant putter, Laffoon "punished" it by tying it to the rear of his car and dragging it for miles between tour stops.

LEITCH, CECIL B. 4/13/1891, Silloth, Cumbria, England. Miss Leitch holds the enviable record of winning the British Women's Amateur Championship four times, more than any other in the tournament's long history. Several women won it three times, including the initial winner, Lady Margaret Scott, and Lady Heathcote-Amory (née Joyce Wethered). Miss Leitch took it first in 1914, again in 1920 when the championship was resumed after World War I, and for a third time in 1921. In that 1921 final she defeated Miss Wethered, 4 and 3. The 1922 final, however, saw Miss Wethered retaliate, 9 and 7. Miss Leitch won her fourth title in 1926. One of the great matches in the Championship's history came in 1925, when Miss Leitch carried the ineffable Miss Wethered to the 37th hole before losing.

LEMA, ANTHONY DAVID (Tony) B. 2/25/34, Oakland, Cal. D. 7/24/66, Munster, Ind. 6'1½", 180. A bright star whose promising career was cut short by a plane crash in which he and his wife were killed. Lema turned pro in 1955 and won several minor tournaments before he won his first PGA-sponsored event, the Orange County Open in 1962, in a playoff with Bob Rosburg. The next year he won the Memphis, and then came his big year, 1964. With almost no practice at St. Andrews he won the British Open with 279, 5 strokes in front of Jack Nicklaus. He also won the Crosby, the Thunderbird, the Buick, and the Cleveland Opens that year. In 1965 Lema took the Buick again and the Cleveland, and in 1966 the Oklahoma City. In June 1966 Tony had tied for fourth in the USGA Open, behind Casper and Palmer. He had tied for fifth in 1963. In 1963 he seemed to have the Masters tied until Nicklaus sank a long putt on the last green to beat him. He played on the Ryder Cup teams of 1963, 65. Before the last round of his Orange County victory Lema told golf writers that if he won he would break out champagne for them. He did, and promptly earned the nickname, "Champagne Tony."

LENCZYK, GRACE (Mrs. Robert Cronin) B. 9/12/27, Newington, Conn. Grace Lenczyk won the USGA Women's Amateur in 1948, and she made it to the top in only three years. In 1946, when the Championship was resumed after World War II, she made her first try and lost in the second round after beating Dorothy Kirby, the medalist. In 1947 she went to the semifinal, losing there to Louise Suggs, the eventual winner. Then she went all the way, wading through six rounds of match play and defeating Helen Sigel in the final, 4 and 3. Miss Lenczyk won the Canadian Women's again in 1948, as she had in 1947. She also won the Intercollegiate in 1948 and was voted Woman Amateur of the Year. In 1949 she shot a 66 to win the qualifying medal in the Western Women's Open but, after losing in the first round of the USGA Women's Amateur in 1949 to Mrs. Joan Barr Tracy, she all but gave up national competition. She married and became a housewife. In 1948, her big year, Miss Lenczyk was selected for the Curtis Cup team and won her singles match decisively.

LEONARD, STANLEY (Stan) B. 2/2/15, Vancouver, B.C., Canada. 5'8½", 160. Although a pro since 1938, Leonard did not hit the U.S. tour until 1955, when he was 40 years old. Still, he won the Greensboro Open in 1957, the Tournament of Champions in 1958, and the Western Open in 1960 at the age of 45. He is the oldest player ever to win the Western. Leonard never won the Canadian Open, which usually was taken by a player from the United States, but, confining most of his activity to north of the border, he won the Canadian PGA title no less than eight times from 1940-61.

LESSER, PATRICIA ANN (Mrs. John Harbottle) B. 8/13/33, Fort Totten, N.Y. Pat Lesser crowned a brilliant career by winning the USGA Women's Championship in 1955 and playing on the Curtis Cup team for the second time in 1956. Miss Lesser got an early start by winning the second USGA Junior Girls' title in 1950, along with the Western Girls' Junior. In the USGA that year, her final round opponent was Mickey Wright, whom she defeated, 4 and 2. In 1952 she won the Women's Intercollegiate and in 1954 the Ormond Beach. Her big year, though, was 1955, when she fought her way to the National title, along with the Western Women's, the Doherty, and the Ormond Beach again. In the National, Pat had two extra-hole matches before downing Jane Nelson in the final, 7 and 6. She reached the last eight in the 1953 USGA, which gave Pat her first Curtis Cup selection. Miss Lesser never turned pro. Her husband, a dentist, is a 2-handicapper, and she is the mother of five children.

LEWIS, JACK W., JR. B. 6/21/47, Florence, S.C. 5'9", 165. Lewis tied for third in the USGA Amateur in 1966, the year Gary Cowan took the trophy to Canada after a playoff with Deane Beman, and thus made the Walker Cup team of 1967 and the World Amateur team in 1968. In the Walker Cup, Lewis won both foursome and four-ball matches teamed with Bill Campbell, and one of his two singles. On the World Amateur team, he was third among the four members with a score of 296. He qualified for the PGA tour in the fall of 1969.

LITTLE, SALLY B. 10/12/51, Sea Point, Capetown, Africa. Miss Little is the only South African on the LPGA tour, which she joined in 1971 after winning everything there was to win in her native country. In 1970, as a member of the South African Women's team in the Women's World Amateur Cup matches, she was the only one to score under 300. As an amateur in the U.S. in 1971, she finished fifth in the Lady Carling. She turned pro that year, joined the tour, and was voted Rookie of the Year. After several high finishes, Miss Little won her first on the tour in May 1976. She did it with a flourish, too, holing out a 75-foot sand shot on the last hole of the Women's International to win by a single shot.

LITTLE, WILLIAM LAWSON, JR. B. 6/23/10, Newport, R.I. D. 2/1/68, Pebble Beach, Cal. 5'9¾", 165. One of the great match players of American golf. In 1934, 35 Little won both the British and USGA Amateur Championships, a feat unheard of before and unapproached since. The son of a colonel in the Army Medical Corps, Little spent his early years at bases all over the United States and in China. Not tall, but burly, with thick, curly, black hair, Lawson was a very long hitter. But he showed no great promise in five previous U.S. Amateurs, although in 1929 he did beat Johnny Goodman the afternoon of the day Goodman ousted Jones. In 1933 he reached the semifinal, there losing to George Dunlap. The fuse was lit. Little started his march to the four national titles by winning the British Amateur, defeating James Wallace in the final, 14 and 13. He had 12 3s that day in 33 holes. In the U.S. Little sliced through the field and crushed Dave Goldman in the final, 8 and 7. He went back to Britain in 1935 and defended his title without much trouble until the final. There he beat Dr. William Tweddell, 1 up. Back again in the U.S., Little completed his "Little Slam" by taking Goodman in the semifinal, 4 and 3, and Walter Emery in the final, 4 and 2. Little had played on the 1934 Walker Cup team, winning by big scores, but turned pro early in 1936. He promptly won the Canadian Open that year, and the Shawnee the next year. In 1940 he capped his career by winning the USGA Open in a playoff with Gene Sarazen. Also in 1940 Little won the Los Angeles Open and in 1941 the Texas Open. He was more than a match player. Lawson became a member of the PGA Hall of Fame in 1961.

LITTLER, EUGENE ALEX (Gene) B. 7/21/30, San Diego, Cal. 5'9½", 165. "Gene the Machine," they call him, for his effortless, smooth, grooved swing. He looks as though he could go on hitting exactly the shot he wanted to from now to eternity. His record shows this isn't far from the truth, even with golf being the baffling, uncertain game that it is. Littler has won 28 tour tournaments since he went on the tour in 1954, a year after he won the USGA Amateur, beating Dale Morey, 1 up, in the final. In his first year he won the San Diego Open and was 28th on the money list—a figure below which he dropped only once until 1972, a remarkable performance. In 1961 he won the USGA Open with 281 and became the eighth person to win both the Amateur and Open. In 1970 he tied Billy Casper for the Masters but lost the 18-hole playoff, 69 to 74. Among his many other triumphs were a remarkable three-in-a-row in the Tournament of Champions, in 1955, 56, 57. Then there were the rich Thunderbird in 1962 and the Canadian Open in 1965. In the spring of 1972, Littler underwent an operation for cancer of the lymph glands, and it seemed that his career might be finished, that the Machine had finally run down. But in October he came back on the tour. That year he played in only 11 events but was in the money six times. Then in 1973 he won the $210,000 St. Louis Children's Hospital Classic, shooting two 66s and two 68s. Recovery was complete, and his earnings shot up from $11,000 in 1972 to $95,308. Seven times Littler has been a member of the Ryder Cup team, from 1961-75. In 1973 he received the Golf Writers' Award for courageous recovery and the Ben Hogan Award from the USGA for distinguished sportsmanship. In 1975 Littler won three tour tournaments and also the $300,000 Japan Masters. His total earnings are more than a million dollars. As a hobby, he tinkers with vintage automobiles.

LLOYD, JOSEPH B. circa 1870, England. D. unknown. Joe Lloyd was an English professional representing the Essex County C.C. in Manchester, Mass., when he won the USGA Open in Chicago in 1897. He actually divided his time, working at Essex County in the summer and at a club in Pau, France, in the winter. At Chicago he shot 83-79—162, to win by a stroke from Willie Anderson, who later was to win the title four times. A 3 on the last hole, 466 yards, brought Lloyd the championship. Golf reporters then were not as sophisticated as they are now, being more familiar with baseball than with golf, as this description of Lloyd's final 3 indicates: "a 250-yard drive, a long brazy shot which put the ball on the green, and a 10-foot putout afforded a spectacle rarely seen in golf." Rare indeed, especially with the old gutta-percha ball. Another newspaper story of the period mentions that one golfer beat another by eight runs. For his efforts Lloyd got a gold medal worth $50 and $150 in cash. This was the last time the Open was played at 36 holes.

LOCKE, ARTHUR D'ARCY (Bobby) B. 11/20/17, Transvaal, So. Africa. This Air Force veteran of World War II established himself as one of the greatest of foreign golfers by winning the British Open four times, in 1949, 50, 52, 57. He had an unconventional swing and an unconventional putting stroke, yet he got the job done in amazing fashion. He was a phenomenal putter. Although he had won everything possible to win in South Africa, first as an amateur and then as a pro, Locke first attracted international attention when he defeated Sam Snead in 12 of 16 matches they played in South Africa. On Snead's urging, Locke came to the United States in 1947 and proceeded to win seven tournaments. Among them were the Canadian Open, the Houston, the Philadelphia Inquirer, and the Goodall. In 1948 he won the Phoenix and the next year the All-America. In all Locke won 15 tournaments in the U.S. His best showing in the USGA Open was a tie for third, 3 shots behind Worsham and Snead in 1947. He was also third in 1951 but well behind Hogan. He was fourth in 1948 and tied for fourth in 1949. Bobby had a decided inside-out swing, with a draw on most shots; the American pros claimed he even hooked his putts.

LONGHURST, HENRY C. B. 3/18/09, Bromham, England. Long a writer of golf in his native country, Longhurst became known to Americans through his accurate and knowledgeable commentary on televised tournaments in the United States. In his college days Longhurst captained the Cambridge University team and later won the German Amateur Championship. He is a writer of long standing, having sent weekly dispatches to the *Sunday Times of London* for more than twenty years. He is the author of several books on golf and a variety of other subjects. Longhurst also served as a Member of Parliament from Acton.

LOONEY, JOSEPH B. 9/18/12, Cambridge, Mass. Looney became golf editor of the *Boston Herald* in April 1946. He continued in that role when the paper became the *Boston Herald Traveller* in 1967 and until it ceased publication in 1972. He was the first to write about the late President Eisenhower as a golfer. This tip he got from Gene Sarazen, whom he interviewed the day after Eisenhower's first election in 1952. Sarazen told him that the General's interest in golf would stir up a wide interest in the game all over the country. It did. Sarazen also mentioned: "The General plays a good game, in the 80s, and is not a whiffer, like most politicians." Looney discovered that Eisenhower had the five-star general's insignia on the back of his iron clubs. In 1953 he founded and ran the Massachusetts Club Champions Tournament. Looney was elected president of the Golf Writers' Association of America in 1954. He is now retired.

LOTZ, RICHARD (Dick) B. 10/15/42, Oakland, Cal. 5'8", 175. Here is a natural left-hander who plays golf right-handed. He came on the tour in 1964 and struggled. Not until 1969 did he win his first tournament, the Alameda County Open. He followed that in 1970 by taking both the Kemper and the Monsanto and by picking up $125,000 in prize money. He thinks the toughest part of the tour is not the playing but the traveling, with weekly changes of food and water, and having to live out of a suitcase. His career earnings are more than $200,000.

LOW, GEORGE B. 1874, Carnoustie, Scotland. D. 4/17/50, Clearwater, Fla. To this Scotsman goes the credit for uttering the most fitting (also undying) appraisal of this sport with his pronouncement that: "golf is a humblin' game." Low followed Alec Smith to America in 1899, part of a general exodus from Carnoustie. That same year Low tied for second behind Willie Smith in the fifth USGA Open. George never won the Open, but he had several high finishes. On May 5, 1903, he was hired by the Baltusrol Golf Club. He remained at that old and prestigious club, as its pro, until September 1925. He won the Metropolitan Open in 1906, defeating Alec Smith. He also won the Florida Open. Low had the distinction of giving lessons to two Presidents: William Howard Taft and Warren G. Harding. He also helped A. W. Tillinghast, one of the great architects of his time, remodel the famed Baltusrol course. A son, George Jr., has gained prominence as a teacher of putting.

LOWELL, DR. WILLIAM B. 10/1/1862, Hoboken, N.J. D. 6/23/54, East Orange, N.J. Insignificant but indispensable in golf today is the little wooden peg we use to tee up the ball. This was not always so. Until about 50 years ago a mixture of sand and water was used to form a mound on which to tee up the ball. Each hole, in fact, had a tee box, with sand in one section and a pail of water in the other. The player molded his tee, placed the ball on top of it and drove off. When Dr. Lowell, a dentist in Maplewood, N.J., took up golf at the age of 60, after being a fine tennis player, he invented a substitute —the wooden peg with a concave top to hold the ball. This was in about 1923. Strangely enough, golfers at first wouldn't use them, even though the doctor handed them out as Rockefeller gave out dimes. Then Dr. Lowell paid Walter Hagen and Joe Kirkwood, who were touring the world, to use them. That did it. Then everybody wanted them. The doctor formed a company, turned out the pegs under the name "Reddy Tee"—they were red and always ready—and made considerable money. Alas, he lost it all in a prolonged court fight to preserve a patent which was not airtight. But the wooden (now often plastic) tee remains as Dr. Lowell originally designed it. Ironically the doctor was a charter member of the Maplewood C.C., but to play tennis, not golf.

LUNN, ROBERT (Bob) B. 4/24/45, San Francisco, Cal. 6'2", 215. Lunn started early by winning the USGA Public Links title when he was 18. After turning pro in 1964 he joined the tour in 1967. He didn't do much that first year, but then he rose like a rocket, winning six times in the next five years. From winning little more than $1800 his first year on the circuit, he shot up to more than $102,000 the next season, winning the Memphis and Atlanta Opens. In 1969 he won the Hartford in a six-hole playoff with Dave Hill. Then, winning once a year, he took the Citrus, the Los Angeles, and the Atlanta again. After that the rocket began to come down, and he slid to 109th place on the money list in 1973. Yet, with two $100,000-plus years in 1968, 70, Lunn has won more than $425,000 in his brief career. His playoff record is 2-0. Bob shares with Lester Bolstad the honor of being the youngest ever to win the USGA Public Links. They were both 18 years, 2 months, and 19 days old.

MacDONALD, CHARLES BLAIR B. 1846, Niagara Falls, N.Y. D. 4/21/39, Southampton, N.Y. MacDonald was one of the major figures behind the popularization of golf in the U.S. He was introduced to it by Old Tom Morris during his studies at St. Andrews University in Scotland. He returned to the U.S. in 1875 and started talking up the game. In 1893 he completed a course at the Chicago G.C., the first 18-hole layout in the U.S. Holes were laid out in a clockwise direction, which some said was to complement his slicing problem. He was involved in founding the United States Golf Association and won the first U.S. Amateur in 1895. He designed the National Golf Links of America, beginning in 1901 when he traveled to Britain to study great courses and use them as a basis for his course. This was the first time any course was designed to have *all* great holes. He also designed Yale Golf Course, Piping Rock in Long Island, and Mid-Ocean in Bermuda. He was a strong-minded self-promoter; the same qualities showed in his career as a stockbroker. He was known as a speculator. In 1928 he wrote a book, *Scotland's Gift: Golf.*

MacDONALD, PAUL B. 6/30/25, Evanston, Ill. Vice president of Marketing, Dunlop Tire and Rubber Co., Sports Division, and 1974-75 president of the National Golf Foundation. He holds a master's degree in literature from Columbia University and was an executive assistant at the United States Golf Association from 1955-60. He is now a member of the USGA Museum Committee and a director of the National Club Association. He plays at a 5 handicap.

MACFARLANE, WILLIAM (Willie) B. 6/29/1890, Aberdeen, Scotland. D. 8/18/61, Miami Beach, Fla. Macfarlane was a strong iron player, who won the 1925 USGA Open, defeating Bobby Jones in the second playoff round by one stroke. Both were even at 433 after 107 holes; on the 108th Macfarlane had a 4 to Jones's 5. Other victories included the 1929 Westchester Open, the 1930 Metropolitan Open, the 1932 New England Open, and the 1925, 28 Shawnee Opens.

MACKENZIE, ADA B. 10/30/1891, Toronto, Canada. D. 1/25/73, Toronto, Canada. Five-time Canadian Women's Open winner, 1919, 25, 26, 33, 35. She was a semifinalist in the USGA Women's Amateur in 1927 and won many other Canadian events, including the Ontario Ladies' Open nine times, the Toronto District Women's Open ten times, and the Canadian Ladies' Senior G.A. Championship eight times. She was named Canada's Outstanding Woman Athlete in 1933 and was the first woman to enter Canadian Golf Hall of Fame. She founded the first all-women's golf club, The Ladies Golf Club of Toronto, in 1924, and managed it for its first five years. It was the only golf club in the world built and owned by women, although now it is also used by men. She operated a women's sportswear shop for 28 years. In 1971 Miss Mackenzie, then nearly 80, played in her last national tournament, the Canadian Ladies' Senior, and won the low gross prize for women over 70.

MACKENZIE, DR. ALISTER B. 1870, Yorkshire, England. D. 1932, Santa Cruz, Cal. This Scottish-born physician turned to golf course architecture after World War I. He wrote one book, *Golf Architecture,* in 1921, giving his views on why course design should follow the natural terrain and place emphasis on strategy, for beginners and experts alike. He was best known for designing the Augusta National with Bobby Jones, but he designed and re-designed many courses around the world, including Cypress Point and Pasatiempo in California, Royal Melbourne in Australia, and the Jockey Club in Buenos Aires.

MAHAFFEY, JOHN B. 5/9/48, Kerrville, Tex. 5'9", 150. A top college player, he was Collegiate All-American in 1969, 70 and won the NCAA Championship in 1970, all while playing on the University of Houston golf team. He tied for low amateur in the 1970 USGA Open. In the spring of 1971, he played a practice round with Ben Hogan which led to a special invitation to play in the 1971 Colonial Invitational, where he finished 12th. He graduated from the University of Houston with a degree in psychology, turned pro, and joined the tour in late 1971. His only pro victory thus far has been the 1973 Sahara, but he has finished in high money positions yearly: 12th in 1973, 16th in 1974 (when he was runner-up in three events), and 8th in 1975 with $141,471. He was runner-up to Lou Graham in the 1975 USGA Open. His career earnings through 1975 are $433,153.

MAIDEN, STEWART B. 1886, Carnoustie, Scotland. D. 11/4/48, Atlanta, Ga. Maiden was the only teacher of the world's best-known golfer, Bobby Jones. He came to the U.S. in 1908 and took a job as pro at East Lake C.C. in Atlanta, succeeding his brother, Jimmy, and his brother-in-law, Alex Smith. At East Lake he taught Jones and Alexa Stirling. Jones patterned his swing after Maiden's who went to the St. Louis C.C. in 1920. In 1930 he opened an exclusive golf studio in New York City. In 1947 Jones brought him back to Atlanta to be the pro at the Peachtree G.C.

MALLORY, LEO B. 11/28/10, Noroton Heights, Conn. An early member of the PGA tour, Mallory came out of golf-oriented southeastern Connecticut. He was a close friend of John Golden, a Ryder Cup member who died as he was nearing the peak of his career. Mallory had one tour victory to his credit and that was on foreign soil, the Nassau British-Colonial Open in 1935. Long retired, Mallory now lives in Florida.

MALTBIE, ROGER B. 6/30/51, Modesto, Cal. 5'10", 175. Maltbie attended San Jose State University and failed to qualify for PGA school in 1973. He qualified in the 1974 school and was one of the surprise successes of the 1975 PGA tour. In two consecutive weeks he won the Quad Cities Open and the Pleasant Valley Classic. He finished the season 23rd in money winnings with $81,035. In May 1976, he was the surprise winner of the Memorial on the course that Jack Nicklaus designed.

MANERO, ANTHONY (Tony) B. 4/4/05, New York, N.Y. After winning various local tournaments and the 1932 Westchester Open, Tony barely made it into the 1936 USGA Open. He had to enter a playoff among qualifiers to get in. But Manero won the Open with a score of 282. Harry Cooper appeared to have the tournament won with a score of 284, 2 strokes under the record set in 1916 by Chick Evans. Yet Manero's 67 on the final round overtook Cooper by 2 shots. Manero was a member of the 1937 Ryder Cup team and won his foursome match with Ralph Guldahl, but bowed in the singles to Henry Cotton. He competed in the New York metropolitan area for another decade but without great success.

MANGRUM, LLOYD EUGENE B. 8/1/14, Trenton, Tex. D. 11/17/73, Apple Valley, Cal. Mangrum turned pro in 1929 and was a major figure on the pro tour in the 1940s and 1950s. He won the 1946 USGA Open, defeating Byron Nelson and Vic Ghezzi in the second playoff round. He lost the 1950 Open to Ben Hogan in a playoff. Handsome, well-dressed, and usually seen on the course with a cigarette hanging from his mouth, he won a career total of 34 PGA tournaments, including 11 events in 1948. In 1951, he was the top U.S. money winner with $26,088.83. He won the Vardon Trophy for his low scoring average in 1951, 53. He was a member of the U.S. Ryder Cup team in 1941, 47, 49, 51 and was captain in 1953, 55. During World War II, he served under General Patton and collected two Purple Hearts. Mangrum was always the focus of a lot of attention, some caused by his flashy manner and reputation for gambling. His life was threatened by anonymous phone calls before the 1951 St. Paul Open, and he played with police protection and won the tournament. He was the first pro golfer to fly his own plane from tournament to tournament. In 1964 he was elected to the PGA Hall of Fame.

Mangrum's 64 set a single-round record for the Masters in 1940. It has since been tied by Jack Nicklaus.

MANN, CAROL ANN B. 2/3/41, Buffalo, N.Y. 6'3", 155. One of golf's most successful and consistent players, always notable for her height as well as her play. She won the Western Junior Championship in 1958 and turned pro and joined the LPGA tour in 1961. Since then she has won 38 tournaments, through 1975, and has accumulated career earnings of $413,301.91. Her victories include the 1964 Women's Western and the 1965 USGA Open. In 1975 she won the Lawson's Open, the Border Classic, the George Washington Classic, and the Dallas Civitan. Her best year on tour was 1968 when she won 10 tournaments; in 1969 she won 8. She was the number one money winner for the LPGA in 1969, and number two in 1968. In 1968 she won the Vare Trophy for her low scoring average. 1971 was her only year without a win since 1964. She shares the 54-hole record of 200 for the LPGA with Ruth Jessen. Mann's was set in the 1968 Lady Carling. She also holds the 36-hole LPGA record of 132, which was also set in the 1968 Lady Carling, and the lowest Vare scoring average of 72.04. She is on the President's Council for Physical Fitness and active in LPGA organizational affairs, serving as president of the LPGA executive board in 1974, 75, a period during which the LPGA actively pursued increased purses and status and brought in a new executive director.

MARR, DAVID (Dave) B. 12/27/33, Houston, Tex. 5'9", 155. Marr became a pro in 1953 but didn't join the tour until 1960. Marr won four PGA tournaments including the 1965 PGA Championship. He was a member of the 1965 U.S. Ryder Cup team and was named 1965 PGA Player of the Year. He was the runner-up in the 1964 Masters and a member of the PGA Tournament Committee from 1963-65. He earned $364,987 on tour. Marr now is a frequent commentator on televised golf tournaments, a job in which his wit and knowledge of the game enliven the programs.

MARSH, GRAHAM B. 1/14/44, Kalgeerlie, Australia. 5'10½", 160. A top world player who has spent little time in the U.S., Marsh turned pro in 1968 but has never won in his native Australia. He did, however, win the 1970 Swiss Open, the 1971 India Open, the 1972 Swiss and German Opens, the 1973 India, Thailand and Scotch Opens, and the 1974, 75 Malaysian Opens. In the latter he was the only one to break par in all four rounds. During 1975, he also won a number of events on the Japanese circuit and was Asian circuit champion in 1972, 73.

MARSTON, MAXWELL R. (Max) B. 6/12/1892, Buffalo, N.Y. D. 5/7/49, Old Lyme, Conn. A Philadelphia investment banker, Marston was one of the top amateurs of his day. He won the USGA Amateur in 1923, defeating Bobby Jones, Francis Ouimet, and, in the final, Jess Sweetser, the defending champion, on the 38th hole. Marston was a reserved, aloof person and at one time was accused of deliberately laying stymies to his opponents. This was ridiculous, of course; any putter who could deliberately lay stymies would have found it easier to putt the ball into the hole. A peculiarity of Marston's iron play was that, like Mac Smith, he never took a divot. Ten years after his victory in the Amateur he went to the final, losing to George Dunlap. He was a member of the Walker Cup team in 1922, 23, 24, 34, and was a three-time winner of the Pennsylvania State Amateur. He had just begun to get involved in senior play when he died.

MARTI, FREDERICK (Fred) B. 11/15/40, Houston, Tex. 6'2", 200. Marti was a top collegiate golfer with many victories while at the University of Houston, including the 1962 NCAA Championship and the 1963 All-America. He was a member of the 1962, 63 All-American College teams and in 1963 was selected Most Outstanding College Player in the U.S. In 1964 he turned pro; although he has no victories yet, he has placed in the top 60 money winners in 1968, 69, 71, 72. His best money year was 1971 with $58,740.

MARTIN, HARRY B. (Dickie) B. 1874, Salem, Ill. D. 4/15/59, New York, N.Y. Martin was a prolific golf writer who wrote for most of the early American golf magazines as well as newspapers. He wrote 17 books on the game, including *50 Years of American Golf* and *Pictorial Golf.* He was an early manager and promoter of Walter Hagen. He organized benefit tournaments for the Red Cross in World War I and developed the idea of charging admission to golf tournaments. His nickname came from a comic strip, "The Dickie Bird," which he started for the *St. Louis Post Dispatch* in 1898. Martin's *50 Years of American Golf* is a storehouse of information about people and events in the game's first half-century here. It is virtually a collector's item today.

MASON, MARGE B. 1/7/18, Paterson, N.J. D. 11/5/74, Teaneck, N.J. The peak of Mrs. Mason's career came when she won the USGA Women's Senior Championship in 1967. A real estate saleswoman in New Jersey, her victories in the state were numerous. She won the Women's State Championship six times and the 54-hole Stroke Play title five times. When another women's organization was formed, the Garden State, she won 14 titles, some at match play, some at stroke play. In 1960 Mrs. Mason won the Women's Metropolitan Golf Association Championship. She was by no means a long hitter, but she was accurate and her chipping and putting were excellent.

MASSENGALE, DONALD (Don) B. 4/23/37, Jacksboro, Tex. 6'1", 195. Massengale turned pro in 1960 after starring on the golf team at Texas Christian University. His successful pro career included over $200,000 in lifetime earnings. Tour victories included the 1962 Beaumont and Motor City Opens. His best money year was 1966 when he won $38,000 and the

Canadian and Bing Crosby Opens. He lost the 1967 PGA Championship to Don January in a playoff. Now he only occasionally plays on the tour.

MASSENGALE, RICHARD (Rik) B. 2/6/47, Jacksboro, Tex. 5'11", 170. Attended Texas University and won the 1968 Western Amateur and 1969 Southwest Conference title. He turned pro in 1969 and joined the PGA tour in 1970. His first victory was the 1975 Tallahassee Open. He finished 1975 as 25th in money winnings with $77,079. He is the younger brother of Don Massengale.

MASSERIO, JAMES (Jim) B. 10/13/48, Pittsburgh, Pa. 6'0", 170. Masserio won the USGA Junior Championship in 1965. In 1969 he won the Pennsylvania Open and was college All-American in 1970. He turned pro and made the tour in the 1973 PGA qualifying school. So far he's had limited success on the tour, winning $7,505 in 1974 and $22,188 in 1975.

MASSEY, DEBORAH (Debbie) B. 11/5/50, Grosse Pointe, Mich. Debbie made a surprising emergence in 1974 as one of the top women amateur players. She won four major events in the U.S. in 1974, plus the Canadian Amateur. She was low amateur in the 1974 USGA Women's Open and played on the 1974 U.S. Curtis Cup and Women's World Amateur teams. In 1975 she won the Women's Eastern and Western Amateurs, adding up to 10 victories in 18 months. In 1975 Miss Massey repeated her victory in the Canadian Women's Amateur. During the winter months she is a ski instructor in Vermont.

MASSY, ARNAUD B. 7/6/1877, Biarritz, France. D. 1958, France. Massy, a successful European player, won the British Open in 1907 and then lost it to Harry Vardon in a 1911 playoff. He won the French Open a number of times and also the Belgian and Spanish Opens. Massy was an outstanding putter, stroking the ball entirely by feel and instinct with no regard for the mechanics of the movement.

MASTERS, MARGARET ANN (Margee) B. 10/24/34, Swan Hill, Victoria, Australia. 5'6", 125. A swimming star in high school, she turned to golf and won the 1956 New Zealand Women's Open, 1957 South African Women's Open, and 1958 Australian Ladies' Open. She also won Australia's Victoria Open in 1959, 60, 61, 62, 63. She came to the U.S. in 1965, shortly after winning the 1964 Canadian Women's Amateur. She was the 1965 LPGA Rookie of the Year. Her victories on tour are the 1967 Waco and the 1968 Four-Ball. Never in top echelons, yet she has had career earnings of $107,700 through 1975, which was an off year with earnings of only $6,619.

MAXWELL, PERRY D. B. 1879, Marion, Ky. D. 11/17/52, Tulsa, Okla. Maxwell designed about 120 golf courses and redesigned some of the nation's best. Among his original designs are Southern Hills, Tulsa, Okla.;

128

Prairie Dunes, Hutchinson, Kans.; Colonial C.C., Fort Worth; and two nines of the Grand Hotel, Point Clear, Ala. He helped Bobby Jones with the Augusta National after Alister Mackenzie died and was involved in redesign work at the Pine Valley, the Westchester C.C., the Philadelphia C.C., and the Saucon Valley C.C. He was a charter member of the American Society of Golf Course Architects.

MAXWELL, WILLIAM (Billy) B. 7/23/29, Abilene, Tex. 5'7½", 165. Billy Maxwell won the USGA Amateur in 1951 and turned pro in 1954. Maxwell's victory came over Joe Gagliardi in the final, 4 and 3, after disposing of Deane Beman in the semifinal and Bo Wininger and Harvie Ward along the way. Maxwell was one of the most consistent tour players in the 1950s and early 1960s. He won eight tour events, although no majors. His top victories were the 1958 Memphis, the 1961 Hope and Insurance City, and the 1962 Byron Nelson. He was a member of the 1963 U.S. Ryder Cup team. Career earnings totalled over $250,000. His best year was 1961, when he finished 10th in U.S. money with $28,335. He finished 12th in 1955, 59, 62, with $31,834 in the latter year.

MAY, GEORGE S. B. 1890, Windsor, Ill. D. 3/12/62, Chicago, Ill. May was important in bringing big prize money to golf through sponsorship of the Tam O' Shanter All-American and World Championships for pro and amateur men and women, from all over the world. He took control of the Tam O' Shanter Country Club in Chicago in 1936. Byron Nelson won the first World Championship in 1941 for $15,000 in war bonds. In the last year it was played, 1957, the total prize money was $250,000, including the first prize of $50,000 for the World Championship, plus the guarantee of 50 $1,000 exhibitions during the year. May also paid the expenses of the world's top players invited to play in events. He sponsored several golfers on the tour, including Lloyd Mangrum. He was founder of the Tournament Sponsors' Association.

MAYER, ALVIN RICHARD (Dick) B. 8/29/24, Stamford, Conn. 5'11", 165. A pleasant, easygoing golfer, Mayer turned pro in 1949 and had his best year in 1957 when he won the USGA Open and the World Championship, was top money winner with $65,835, was a member of the U.S. Ryder Cup team, and was named PGA Player of the Year. Probably the best shot in his career was a 30-yard wedge to win the 1965 New Orleans Open. He also shot a $50,000 hole-in-one during the 1962 Palm Springs Classic. In 1966 he dropped off the tour with a total of seven tournament wins and $185,049 in prize money. Mayer's victory in the Open came in a playoff with Cary Middlecoff after Middlecoff had put on a great spurt and had sunk a 9-foot putt on the final green to tie him. Mayer won the playoff, 72 to 79.

MAYFIELD, SHELLEY B. 6/19/24, Liberty Hill, Tex. 6'0", 175. A consistent PGA competitor of the early 1950s, Mayfield won the 1954 San Francisco, the 1955 Thunderbird, and the 1956 Baton Rouge. In the Thunderbird he defeated Mike Souchak on the second extra hole of a playoff after they had tied in a regulation 18-hole playoff. Mayfield was a member of the PGA Tournament Committee in 1954. In the late 1960s he turned from competitive playing to designing courses.

McALLISTER, MARY H. (Susie) B. 8/27/47, Beaumont, Tex. 5'8", 135. Susie McAllister took up golf at age 15, after playing active tennis. Her interest in golf was the result of meeting golf teacher Vernon Brown while she was ushering at the Houston Astrodome. She turned pro in 1971. Her first big year was 1975, when she won the Wheeling Classic and finished the year with $31,437 for 11th place in money winnings.

McCALLISTER, ROBERT (Bob) B. 5/3/34, Toledo, O. 6'0", 180. McCallister turned pro in 1959 and was sponsored on the tour by Lawrence Welk. He won the 1961 Orange County Open and the 1964 Sunset Camellia Open.

McCORMACK, MARK H. B. 11/6/30, Chicago, Ill. The number one player on the William & Mary golf team when Arnold Palmer was at Wake Forest. McCormack, a young lawyer, became Palmer's business representative in 1960. Since then he has been a major factor in making golf a commercial, big-money sport. His International Management handles Palmer, Gary Player, Tony Jacklin, Doug Sanders, Bob Charles, and many other top golfers and other athletes. He has written a biography of Palmer, as well as a yearly annual on golf. He originated the Piccadilly World Match Play Championship, which has been played yearly since 1964.

McDERMOTT, JOHN J. (Johnny) B. 8/12/1891, Philadelphia, Pa. D. 8/1/71, Yeadon, Pa. 5'8", 130. McDermott was the first native-born American to win, in 1911, the USGA Open; he was also the youngest winner, at age 19. The previous year he had played in the Open but lost in a playoff to Alex Smith. In 1912 he repeated his 1911 win. He was a perfectionist who excelled with a mashie. In 1911 he challenged the Philadelphia area pros to 18 holes for $1,000; he defeated three and no more volunteered. In 1913 he defeated Harry Vardon and Ted Ray at the Shawnee Open. He was the only one to break 300 and he finished 13 strokes better than Vardon. He played in his last U.S. Open in 1913, finishing ninth. In 1915 he suffered a nervous breakdown following a series of personal upsets and depressions, including a 1914 trip on the liner *Kaiser Wilhelm II* returning from Britain. The liner crashed into another ship and McDermott was picked up from a lifeboat. He retired from golf after 1915. He was elected to the PGA Hall of Fame as a charter member in 1940.

McGEE, JERRY B. 7/21/43, New Lexington, O. 5'9½", 160. Turning pro in 1966, McGee joined the tour in 1967. He has had various "almosts" in his career, finally winning a tournament, the Pensacola Open, in 1975. He has had injury problems, including a wrist injury that put him out of action for the second half of 1971. In 1972, he had a hole-in-one in the USGA Open and won, or won use of, four cars for being closest to the hole in four events. His best year was 1975 with earnings of $93,569 to finish 16th. His career earnings through 1975 were $334,707.

McGOWAN, JOHN (Jack) B. 12/18/30, Concord, N.H. 5'9½", 140. Jack McGowan turned pro in 1954 and joined the tour in 1961. His only victory is the 1964 Mountain View Open, but he placed in the money ranks off and on throughout the 1960s.

McINTIRE, BARBARA JOY B. 1/12/35, Toledo, O. Barbara McIntire was runner-up in the USGA Junior Girls' Championship in 1951, 52, and winner of the USGA Women's Amateur in 1959, 64. She was low amateur in the USGA Women's Open in 1964 but had, in 1956, lost that tournament in a playoff. She first played in the U.S. Amateur in 1950, at age 15, defeating Glenna Collett Vare in her first match, losing her second. Barbara won the British Women's Amateur in 1960 and was a member of the U.S. Curtis Cup team in 1958, 60, 62, 64, 66, 72. She now runs a clothing store in Colorado Springs.

McLENDON, BENSON RAYFIELD (Mac) B. 8/10/45, Atlanta, Ga. 6'2½", 185. McLendon graduated from Louisiana State in 1967 with a major in accounting. He turned pro in 1968 and won the first event he entered, the 1968 Magnolia Classic. He was a consistent player. His other victory was in the 1974 Walt Disney National Team Championship; he won with Hubert Green, who also introduced him to his wife. Trouble with asthma has sometimes held back his game. But even without victories, he won $76,971 in 1975, his best money year, to finish 26th in earnings' standings. His career earnings through 1975 were $260,892.

McLEOD, FREDERICK (Freddie) B. 4/25/1882, North Berwick, Scotland. D. 5/8/76, Augusta, Ga. Emigrated to the United States in 1903 and in 1908 won the USGA Open in a playoff. He weighed only 108 pounds at the time, making him the championship's smallest winner. He used only seven clubs to win. He finished in the top 10 eight times in the 20 U.S. Opens he played and was runner-up in 1910, 11, 21. From 1913 to 1965 he was the professional at the Chevy Chase C.C., Columbia, Md. He played in the first Masters tournament in 1934 and, with Jock Hutchison, has been honorary starter in the tournament since 1965. He won the 1938 PGA Senior Championship and was elected to the PGA Hall of Fame in 1960.

McMAHON, THOMAS J. B. 1872. D. 2/7/41, Brooklyn, N.Y. McMahon has the distinction of being the first executive director of the United States Golf Association. He started his career in golf as an official scorer for the Metropolitan Golf Association. Then he held the same position for the USGA. He became the USGA executive director in 1922, and served until 1934 when Joseph Dey took over. He is credited with setting up a regular system for holding USGA tournaments, and with setting up the first public scoreboard and charging admission to tournaments.

McSPADEN, HAROLD (Jug) B. 5/21/08, Rosedale, Kans. Known, with Byron Nelson, as the "Gold Dust Twins" on the PGA tour during the 1940s. His winnings include the 1939 Canadian Open, the 1940 Philippines Open, and many PGA events, including the 1934 National Match Play Championship, the 1943 All-American, and the 1944 Phoenix. He was runner-up in the 1937 PGA Championship. He was second in money winnings on the PGA tour in 1944, 45, and sixth in 1939. When he retired from competition in 1947, he built, and now runs, Dubs Dread G.C., Piper, Kansas, which is considered to be one of the nation's toughest courses with its full length being 8,101 yards and having a USGA rating of 78. McSpaden was not eligible for military service because of an extreme asthmatic condition.

MEHLHORN, WILLIAM (Wild Bill) B. 1898, Elgin, Ill. He was a colorful regular on the early PGA tour and his nickname came from his wearing cowboy hats and being a big talker. He won a variety of events but never made it really big on the tour. He was a member of the first U.S. Ryder Cup team in 1927. Although runner-up to Walter Hagen in the 1925 PGA Championship, he won the Oklahoma Open in 1920, 23; the San Antonio Open in 1928, 29; the Los Angeles Open in 1921; the Western Open in 1924; and the Mid-Continent Open in 1922. He is known as a good shotmaker, but poor putter, and as a card player.

MELNYK, STEVEN NICHOLAS (Steve) B. 2/26/47, Brunswick, Ga. 6'1¾", 215. His very successful amateur career has not yet been matched by his pro career. While attending the University of Florida he was a member of the Collegiate All-American Golf Team in 1967, 68, 69. He won the 1969 USGA Amateur and the 1971 British Amateur. He was a member of the U.S. Walker Cup team in 1969, 71 and was low amateur in the 1971 Masters. After college, he went into the insurance business rather than on the pro tour but turned pro in late 1971. He had no victories on the pro tour through 1975, but had career earnings amounting to $165,091.

MENNE, ROBERT (Bob) B. 2/19/42, Gardner, Mass. 6'0", 175. Menne turned pro, but failed in the PGA's 1967 qualifying school. He made it on the tour in 1969. He failed to do well on the tour until 1974 when his victory in the Kemper Open—and its $40,000 check—kept him on the tour. In 1975, he had another off year, earning only a little more than $10,000. His career earnings through 1975 were $132,000.

METZ, RICHARD (Dick) B. 5/29/08, Arkansas City, Kans. Metz turned pro in 1929 and was active on the PGA tour in the late 1930s and 1940s. His victories include the 1937 Thomasville and Hollywood Opens, the 1938 International Four-Ball, the 1939 Asheville and St. Paul Opens, and the 1940 Chicago Open. He was second in the 1938 USGA Open, and was runner-up in the 1946 Canadian Open. In 1939 he was the No. 5 money winner on the PGA tour.

MICKLEM, GERALD HUGH B. 8/14/11, Burgh Heath, Surrey, England. A major British golfing personality both on the course and behind the scenes. Micklem won the British Amateur in 1947, 53 and played on the British Walker Cup team in 1947, 49, 53, 55. He was captain of the Royal and Ancient Golf Club in 1968, 69 and chairman of the Royal and Ancient Rules of Golf Committee from 1960-63. Also, he was president of the English Golf Union from 1965-66 and of the European Golf Association from 1967-69. The USGA honored him with the Bob Jones Award for distinguished sportsmanship in 1968.

MIDDLECOFF, CARY (Doc) B. 1/6/21, Halls, Tenn. 6'2", 185. This golfing dentist won the Tennessee Amateur from 1940 through 1943 and turned pro in 1947. During a very successful pro career, he won 35 PGA events including the USGA Open in 1949, 56 and the Masters in 1955. The highlight of his Masters win was an 82-foot putt on the 13th green in the final round for an eagle. He lost the 1957 Open in an 18-hole playoff to Dick Mayer. His best year was 1955 when he won the Masters, the Western Open, and four other tournaments for a total of $39,567. In 1949 he won six tournaments and was No. 2 money winner, as he was in 1951, 52, 55. A slow and meticulous player, he was in the top 10 money winners from 1950-56. He won the Vardon Trophy in 1956 and was a member of the U.S. Ryder Cup team in 1953, 55, 59. He was chairman of the PGA Tournament Committee, 1954-55, and elected to the PGA Hall of Fame in 1975. Middlecoff shares with Lloyd Mangrum the distinction of playing the longest sudden-death playoff in PGA history. After tying at 273 in the Motor City Open in 1949, this tenacious pair went 11 extra holes before halted by darkness. They were declared co-champions and split the first money of $5,000.

MILLER, ALLEN L., III B. 8/10/48, San Diego, Cal. 5'10", 175. His successful amateur career began with his 1965 Junior Orange Bowl victory. He was a member of the 1969 U.S. Walker Cup and 1970 World Amateur teams. In 1970 he won six amateur tournaments, including victory by 10 strokes in the Canadian Amateur. In 1971 he turned pro and since then has often been referred to as the "other Miller." His only pro win through 1975 was the 1974 Tallahassee Open. His career earnings through 1975 were $133,761.

MILLER, JOHN B. 4/29/47, San Francisco, Cal. 6'2", 178. Probably the most important golfer to emerge in the 1970s. Miller won the USGA Junior Championship in 1964, and as a 19-year-old, finished eighth in the 1966 USGA Open. A practicing Mormon, Miller graduated from Brigham Young

University in 1969 and turned pro. He has always finished in the top 60. Through 1975 he won 15 PGA events, including the 1971 Southern Open, the 1972 Heritage Classic, and the 1973 USGA Open; in the latter he had a final round record of 63. He had an incredible 1974 season, winning a record $353,021 and eight events, the most for any player in a single year since Arnold Palmer in 1960. He won the first three events of the year—the Bing Crosby, the Phoenix, and the Tucson—a first for the PGA tour. He also won the Tournament of Champions, the World Open, the Westchester Classic, the Heritage Classic, and the Kaiser International in 1974 and was PGA Player of the Year. He finished the year with a win in Japan's Dunlop Phoenix Open and in 1975 started the season by winning the Phoenix Open by 14 strokes, the largest margin since Ben Hogan won the 1945 Portland Open by 17. His 260 Phoenix score was the best since Mike Souchak's record 257 in the 1955 Texas Open. Miller also won the Tucson, the Bob Hope, and the Kaiser. In 1973 Miller won the World Cup championship for the U.S. and in 1975 played on the U.S. Ryder Cup team. He had total earnings through 1975 of $947,152. He finished 1975 second in the year's earnings to Jack Nicklaus.

MILLER, SHARON KAY B. 1/13/41, Marshall, Mich. 5'3½", 130. An all-around athlete who graduated from Western Michigan University with a degree in physical education. Sharon Miller taught for four years before becoming a golf pro. As an amateur, she won two Michigan Women's titles and the 1965 Trans-Mississippi. She joined the LPGA tour in 1966 and played consistently, finishing several times as runner-up before her first victory in 1973, the Corpus Christi Open. She also won the 1974 Borden Classic and has career earnings through 1975 of $116,443. Miller added two more victories in early 1976, the Tucson and Bob Hope Classics.

MILLS, MARY B. 1/19/40, Laurel, Miss. 5'8", 134. Mary Mills' amateur career included eight straight victories in the Mississippi Women's Championship, 1954-1961, among other successes. A philosophy major at Millsaps College in Jackson, Mississippi, she graduated in 1962, and turned professional. She joined the tour and was named first LPGA Rookie of the Year in 1962. A very consistent player, she has won eight LPGA events through 1975, including the 1963 USGA Women's Open, the 1964, 73 LPGA Championship, the 1964, 65 Eugene Ladies' Classic, the 1965 St. Louis Women's Open, the 1970 Immke Buick, and the 1973 Lady Tara. She finished in the top 20 every year from 1963-74. In 1973, she finished in the top ten 15 times, despite hand surgery in 1972. Her career earnings were $226,566 through 1975.

MITCHELL, ABRAHAM (Abe) B. 1887, East Grinsted, Sussex, England. D. 6/11/47, St. Albans, England. Abe Mitchell was a top British player who never won a national tournament. He was runner-up in the 1912 British Amateur, which he lost on the 38th hole. After that tournament he turned pro. He never won the British Open, though he was close several times.

134

Match play was his forte, and he won the British Professional Match Play Championship in 1919, 20, 29, and was a member of the British Ryder Cup team in 1929, 31, 33. He was private pro to Samuel Ryder, the man who donated the Ryder Cup in 1925. Mitchell had powerful hands and was a long hitter, though with a short, controlled swing.

MITCHELL, ROBERT (Bobby) B. 2/23/43, Chatham, Va. 6'0", 185. Mitchell dropped out of high school at age 15 and became a golf pro. He joined the tour in 1966 and has complained of being its "invisible man." He won the 1971 Cleveland Open and the 1972 Tournament of Champions. In the latter, he was 2 strokes behind Jack Nicklaus going into the last round, tied him at 280, and beat him on the first playoff hole. 1972 was his best money year, finishing 11th, with $113,719. His career earnings through 1975 were $393,768.

MOE, DONALD (Don) B. 11/14/09, Portland, Ore. A regular amateur competitor during the 1920s and 1930s, especially in the Pacific Northwest. His victories include the Oregon Amateur in 1928, 37 and the Western Amateur in 1929, 31. He was runner-up in the Canadian Amateur in 1953 and a member of the U.S. Walker Cup team in 1930, 32. Moe's most notable feat was his rally against Bill Stout in the 1930 Cup matches. Seven down with 13 to play, Don won seven holes in a row and finally won the match, 1 up, with a birdie on the last hole. "That was not golf," said Stout. "That was a visitation from the Lord."

MOLINA, FLORENTINO B. 12/30/38, Rio Cuarto Cordoba, Argentina. 6'2", 175. Molina turned pro in 1957 and had a successful career in South America before trying the U.S. circuit. His South American victories include the Argentine Open in 1971, 73; the Argentine PGA in 1970; the Maracaibo Open in 1970, 74; and the 1973 Bogotá Open. He was first in the Argentine PGA Order of Merit in 1971. He played on the 1967 Argentine World Cup team and qualified for the U.S. PGA tour in the 1974 school on his first try. In 1975, however, he earned only $8,669 on the tour.

MONTAGUE, JOHN D. (Mysterious Montague) B. 1906. D. 5/26/72, Studio City, Cal. His real name was LaVerne M. Moore. He was a big hitter and good trick-shot artist. He got his nickname because of his extreme avoidance of photographers on golf courses. He even avoided tournaments where photographers were likely to be. A photo of him in 1937 revealed the reason: he was wanted in New York for a 1930 robbery. He stood trial and had depositions from such people as Bing Crosby, Oliver Hardy, and Andy Devine. He was acquitted. After that he stayed in Hollywood, depending more on trick-shot skills than on playing prowess.

MONTI, ERIC B. 12/6/18, Pekin, Ill. 5'10", 156. Monti turned pro in 1943 and, though most pro victories were local California tournaments, he did win the 1955 Miami Beach Open, the 1959 Hesperia Open, and the 1961

Ontario Open. His best money finish was 36th in 1955. He's now a Los Angeles club pro.

MOODY, ORVILLE (Sarge) B. 12/9/33, Chickasha, Okla. 5'10", 200. After 14 years in the U.S. Army, Moody emerged in 1967 as a sergeant with a good record in service tournaments, including the 1965 All-Service Championship and three Korean Opens. He went on pro tour full-time and made a big splash in 1969 when he won the USGA Open in spite of remarks of "Orville Who?" Moody's victory, with a score of 281, was by a single stroke over Deane Beman, Al Geiberger, and Bob Rosburg. He had played in the Open only once before and had failed to survive the 36-hole cut. He went on to win the 1969 World Series of Golf and with Lee Trevino won the 1969 World Cup. In 1969, his best year, he won $79,176 and was named PGA Player of the Year. His second best year was 1973 with $74,286 earned. In the years since 1969 he has spent a lot of time playing in the Far East and in Europe with some success. He earned over $250,000 on the U.S. pro tour through 1975.

MOREY, DALE B. 12/1/18, Martinsville, Ind. An active amateur player for over two decades, Morey has won more than 220 amateur tournaments. His victories include the Southern Amateur in 1951, 64, the Western Amateur in 1953, the North and South Amateur in 1964, and the Mid-Atlantic Amateur in 1972. Morey was a member of the Walker Cup team for the U.S. in 1955, 65; runner-up in the 1953 USGA Amateur Championship; and a member of the U.S. Americas Cup team in 1954, 65. He won the 1974 USGA Senior Championship in his first year as a senior. He also won the North and South Senior Four-Ball with Harry Welch that year. In 1975, he won the U.S. Seniors' Golf Association Championship. A director of the Carolinas Golf Association from 1962 to 1975, he has also served as director of the Southern Golf Association since 1960, and as president of that organization from 1973-75. When not playing golf, Morey is a furniture manufacturer's representative.

MORRIS, THOMAS (Old Tom) B. 6/26/1821, St. Andrews, Scotland. D. 5/24/08, St. Andrews, Scotland. One of the game's most legendary founding fathers. He was apprenticed to Allan Robertson and was later greenskeeper at St. Andrews, from 1865-1904. He competed in every British Open from 1861 to 1896 when he was 75 years old. He won the British Open in 1861, 62, 64, 67. Brilliant "Young Tom" Morris was his son. He designed one of Scotland's top courses, Muirfield, and another, Lahinch, in Ireland. His death was the result of a brain concussion caused by falling down a flight of stairs at the Saint Andrews clubhouse.

MORRIS, THOMAS, JR. (Young Tom) B. 1850, St. Andrews, Scotland. D. 12/25/1875, St. Andrews. The greatest player of his day. He won his first British Open in 1868 at age 18, and won again in 1869, 70, 72 (the Open was not played in 1871). With his 1872 victory, he retained the Championship Belt permanently. He scored the first recorded hole-in-one in the 1868 British Open at Prestwick and won the British Opens by an average margin of nine shots. His career was short: it began when he entered his first tournament at age 13 and ended with his sudden death at age 25, apparently caused by the shock of the sudden death of his wife a few months earlier. He was elected to World Golf Hall of Fame in 1975.

MORSE, SAMUEL FINLEY BROWN B. 7/18/1885, Newton, Mass. D. 5/10/69, Monterey, Cal. Morse is credited with developing the Monterey Peninsula area for tourists, homeowners, and golfers. In 1910 he went West and in 1914 bought 8,400 acres in Monterey with a group of businessmen, and in 1915 formed Del Monte Properties. He added to and sold properties over the years, planning roads in the area to maintain its beauty. He had a personal say on each building that was put up and each tree that was cut. At age 80, his company had about 8,500 acres. He commissioned the Pebble Beach Golf Links which opened in 1918. He was a grandnephew of the inventor of the telegraph and Morse Code and had been captain of the 1906 Yale football team. In 1965, he was honored with the Outstanding Citizen of the Monterey Peninsula award.

MOZLEY, DANA OLIVER B. 6/4/16, Lowell, Mass. Mozley is the long-time golf writer for the *New York Daily News,* the paper with the largest daily circulation in the United States. A graduate of Colgate University, where he ran the news bureau for three years, Mozley went to the *Daily News* in 1939 after a stint with the *Lowell Courier-Citizen.* He has reported on every sport at the *Daily News* and has covered golf steadily since 1948. During the off season he covers track and field. He is a former president of the Golf Writers' Association of America and is a member of its board of directors and its Hall of Fame board. He has twice won the GWAA prize for the best golf story of the year.

MURPHY, ROBERT (Bob) B. 2/14/43, Brooklyn, N.Y. 5'10", 210. A consistently successful player—as a pro and an amateur. Murphy attended the University of Florida on a baseball scholarship and turned to golf after an injury. He won the 1965 USGA Amateur and 1966 NCAA Championship. He was a member of the 1967 U.S. Walker Cup team. Also in 1967 he turned pro and in 1968 had an extremely successful rookie year, winning the Philadelphia and Thunderbird Opens, on successive weekends, and $105,595, a record for a rookie at that time. He's been in the top 50 money winners every year since joining the pro tour. Other victories have included the 1970 Hartford Open, the 1975 Inverrary Classic, and the 1972 Australian Wills Masters. He was a member of the 1975 U.S. Ryder Cup team and finished 1975 11th in earnings with $127,471. His career earnings through 1975 were $708,392.

NAGLE, KELVIN DAVID GEORGE (Kel) B. 12/21/20, Sydney, Australia. 5'10½", 190. Although Nagle is one of Australia's most successful golfers, he has rarely played in the U.S. He turned pro in 1946 and won the Australian Open in 1959; the Australian Professional Championship in 1949, 54, 58, 59, 65; the New Zealand Open in 1957, 58, 62, 64, 67, 68, 69; and the Canadian Open in 1964. In 1965 he lost the USGA Open to Gary Player in a playoff. With Peter Thomson, he won the Canada Cup (later the World Cup) for Australia in 1954, 59. He has also had a successful senior career, including three victories in the British Senior PGA Championship and two in the World Professional Senior Championship, in 1971, 75.

NELSON, JOHN BYRON, JR. (Byron) B. 2/4/12, Fort Worth, Tex. 6'1", 179. Nelson turned pro in 1932 and was the top golfer of the late 1930s and 1940s, winning 49 PGA tournaments. He won the USGA Open in 1939, and was runner-up, losing in a playoff, in 1946. He won the PGA Championship in 1940, 45 and the Masters in 1937, 42. He was the top U.S. money winner in 1944, 45; won the Vardon Trophy for a low scoring average in 1939; was elected to the PGA Hall of Fame in 1953; and was elected to the World Golf Hall of Fame in 1974. He was a member of the U.S. Ryder Cup team in 1936, 47. In 1945, his only full-time year on the tour, he set an amazing number of records, winning 18 official and one unofficial tournament and winning 11 tournaments in a row. Both records still stand. Nelson had 17 consecutive rounds under 70 that year and no four-round scores over par. His scoring average for the 30 tournaments he played was 68.33, but no Vardon Trophy was awarded during that war year. The war, and the fact that some top players were not in contention that year, has been used to downplay Nelson's achievement, but his scores tend to make him stand on his own record. Nelson was exempt from military service during World War II because he was a free bleeder; his blood did not coagulate normally. His play was so consistent and powerful throughout his career that he was sometimes called a "mechanical" golfer. He retired almost completely from tournament golf after 1945, devoting most of his time to his ranch in Texas. He is now a TV golf commentator and sometime golf magazine instruction writer.

NEVIL, DWIGHT B. 8/25/44, Alton, Okla. 5'8", 178. Nevil joined the PGA tour in 1971, having won the World Wide Air Force Championship in 1969. As a pro, he won the Magnolia Classic (played opposite the Masters) in 1973, 74. His best money year was 1974 when he won $49,610 for 57th on the money list. Career earnings through 1975 total $214,929.

NEVILLE, JOHN FRANCIS (Jack) B. 7/1/1891, St. Louis, Mo. He won the first California State Amateur Championship, then won the event again in 1913, 19, 22, 29, the latter two times on the Pebble Beach Golf Links Course, which he co-designed with Douglas Grant and which opened in 1918. He also designed nine holes of the Pacific Grove Municipal Golf Course in 1932. In 1914 he won the Pacific Northwest Amateur. He played on the Walker Cup team of 1923. Neville still lives in California and was employed by Del Monte Properties until his recent retirement at age 80.

NICHOLS, ROBERT (Bobby) B. 4/14/36, Louisville, Ky. 6'2", 195. Nichols turned pro in 1959 and joined the tour in 1960 for a very successful career, which he combines with a club pro job at Firestone C.C., Akron, O. He finishes in the top 60 every year and has won 12 PGA tournaments including the 1964 PGA Championship. He also won the 1968 PGA Team Championship with George Archer and was runner-up in the 1968 Masters. In 1970 he won the Dow Jones Classic, at $300,000 the biggest purse then ever offered on the tour; Nichols took home $60,000. His most recent victories were the 1974 Canadian Open and the 1974 Andy Williams-San Diego Open. He won the 1962 Ben Hogan trophy for fine play after recovery from a physical disability which resulted from an auto collision at age 16 that left him with a broken pelvis, a brain concussion, and spinal damage. He was a member of the 1967 U.S. Ryder Cup team. He holds a degree in business administration from Texas A & M University. Through 1975 his career earnings were $906,276.

NICKLAUS, JACK WILLIAM B. 1/21/40, Columbus, O. 5'11¾", 185. One of the greatest golfers of all time. Nicklaus took up golf at age 10, won his first USGA Amateur in 1959, and played on the U.S. Walker Cup team that year. In 1961 he won the NCAA Championship, won the USGA Amateur again, played on the U.S. Walker Cup team, and set a record 282 for an amateur in the USGA Open, finishing second to Arnold Palmer. He won a record 16 major championship titles through 1975, including the two USGA Amateurs, five Masters (1963, 65, 66, 72, 75), three USGA Opens (1962, 67, 72), two British Opens (1966, 70), and four PGA Championships (1963, 71, 73, 75). He played on the U.S. Ryder Cup team in 1969, 71, 73, 75; was a member of the winning U.S. World Cup team in 1963, 64, 66, 67, 71, 73; and was an individual winner in 1963, 64, 71. Nicklaus is still in the process of setting records while at the peak of his career. Through 1975 Nicklaus had won 58 official PGA events, including five in 1975—Doral-Eastern, Heritage, Masters, PGA, World Open. In 1974, considered an "off" year, he won two tournaments and $238,178 for second place money winnings, and finished 13 times in the top 10. He was the top money winner on the tour in 1964, 65, 67, 71, 72, 73, 75. Through 1975 he won a record $2,541,772 in official money. He also likes to play out of the U.S. and has won the Australian Open four times through 1975. In 1976 he won the Tournament Players' Championship, worth $60,000. He was named PGA Player of the Year in 1967, 72, 73, 75, and elected to the World Golf Hall of Fame. He's the only player to win all four major events at least twice, for his record of 16 through 1975. He's known for aiming at the big events and playing in selected others, often as a buildup for majors. In recent years, Nicklaus has become a crowd favorite, although he was rather stolid and overweight as a young man and was often unpopular as the contender against the popular favorite, Arnold Palmer. In the 1970s Nicklaus lost weight, let his hair grow, relaxed without losing his famed concentration, and saw popularity equal his success. He also took up golf course design in the 1960s; his work includes the Harbour Town course at Hilton Head Island, S.C., which he designed with Pete Dye. On his own, he has designed in and out of the U.S., including the Muirfield Village G.C., Dublin, Ohio—his own favorite, and the site of the Nicklaus sponsored Memorial Tournament beginning in 1976. Nicklaus also has been selected to design the permanent home of the Canadian Open. He is expected to add to the records he has set through the 1980s.

NIEPORTE, THOMAS (Tom) B. 10/21/28, Cincinnati, O. 6'1", 185. He was the 1951 NCAA champion and also won the 1953 All-Army Championship. He joined the tour in 1957 and played regularly through 1961, winning the 1959 Rubber City Open and the 1960 Azalea Classic. In a rare appearance he won the 1967 Bob Hope Desert Classic. He's the father of nine children.

NORTH, ANDREW (Andy) B. 3/9/50, Thorp, Wisc. 6'2", 210. As a high school basketball star, he was also winning many local and Wisconsin golf titles. He was College All-American in golf at the University of Florida in 1970, 71, 72, and won the 1971 Western Amateur. North joined the PGA tour in 1973 and, although he has yet to win a major event, he finished in the top 60 in 1974, 75. He won the Little Crosby in 1973 and has career earnings of more than $190,000.

NOVAK, JOSEPH (Joe) B. 8/9/1898, Butte, Mont. A top teaching professional, he was the first, in 1924, to give a full golf instruction course on radio. He also wrote four books, put out a golf instruction record, and served as president of the Professional Golfers' Association from 1948-52. While PGA president, he initiated its junior program.

OEHMIG, LEWIS W. (Lew) B. 5/11/16, Cincinnati, O. Oehmig won the USGA Senior Amateur in 1972, defeating Ernie Pieper in the final on the 20th hole. This was his third extra-hole match, following a victory over William Hyndman on the 20th hole in the semifinal and Eddie Meister on the 19th. Oehmig is a former president of First Flight Golf Company, now owned by ProGroup, Inc., of which he is a director. He says he escaped "Yankee influence" early in life by moving south, where he now views the passing scene from Lookout Mountain, Tenn. He has won the Tennessee Amateur eight times and has been elected to the Tennessee State Sports Hall of Fame.

OLIVER, EDWARD (Porky) B. 9/6/16, Wilmington, Del. D. 9/20/61, Wilmington, Del. An affable, colorful player, he got his nickname as a result of his portly build. He weighed 225 pounds. In 1940 he turned pro and has won eight tournaments during his career. He gained the reputation of being runner-up in major championships such as the 1946 PGA Championship and the 1953 Masters. He played on the 1947, 51 Ryder Cup teams and was named honorary non-playing captain of the 1961 team when it was learned he was suffering from cancer. He died a month before the matches were played. Probably the worst hole of his career was the 222-yard 16th at Cypress Point during the 1954 Crosby; he hit four balls into the ocean and took a 16 on the hole. Oliver is perhaps best remembered for a penalty which prevented him from tying Gene Sarazen and Lawson Little in the 1940 USGA Open. He drew the penalty because he started his last round ahead of his scheduled time.

OOSTERHUIS, PETER B. 5/3/48, London, England. 6'5", 200. After being a member of the 1967 British Walker Cup team, he turned pro in 1968. A true world player, with his base in England, his victories include the French Open in 1973, 74 and the Italian Open in 1974. He won the British Vardon

Trophy for his low scoring average in 1971, 72, 73, 74 and the British PGA Order of Merit in 1971, 72, 73, 74. He has also won tournaments throughout Britain, Australia, South Africa, and Rhodesia. He was a member of the British Ryder Cup team in 1971, 73, 75 and the British World Cup team in 1971. After failing in the U.S. PGA qualifying school in 1973, he made it in 1974 and played regularly in the U.S. in 1975. No victories, but he won $59,935 to finish 34th in money winnings for the year.

ORCUTT, MAUREEN B. 4/1/07, New York, N.Y. A golfer and golf writer, Maureen has won over 65 championship events in a long career. Her first victories came in the Metropolitan Junior in 1922, 24. She won 10 Women's Metropolitans between 1926-68; 3 North and South Championships; 7 Women's Easterns between 1925-49; 10 New Jersey Women's 54-Hole Medal titles between 1926-59; and 6 New Jersey State Championships. She also won the Canadian Women's Amateur in 1930, 31 and was runner-up in the USGA Women's Amateur in 1927, 36. She won the Metropolitan Brother-Sister four times with her brother Bill, and four times with her brother Sinclair. In 1932, 34, 36, 38, she played on the Curtis Cup team. As a senior in 1962, she won her first USGA Women's Senior Championship, and again in 1966; she also won three North and South Seniors, and six Metropolitan Women's Seniors. Her father held major editorial positions with the *New York Times, Herald-Tribune,* and *Wall Street Journal.* She started covering golf in the 1920s for New York papers and golf magazines, and in 1937 started in the *New York Times* sports department, working there until 1972 when she retired to Durham, N.C. Maureen was elected to the Ladies' PGA Hall of Fame in 1966. In 1969 she received the Tanqueray Award for 50 years of contributions to golf.

ORLICK, WARREN B. 7/9/12, Detroit, Mich. One of the nation's most active golf pros. He served as president of the national Professional Golfers' Association in 1971, 72. He had previously been treasurer, secretary, and a member of the National Tournament Policy Board Committee. He was selected as 1960 PGA Professional of the Year. He was chairman of the PGA Championship in 1968, 69, 70, and chairman of the Ryder Cup Rules Committee in 1955, 59, 63, 67, 73. He was the first professional to serve on the USGA Rules Committee, from 1968-73, and had been a member of the Masters Rules Committee since 1955. He was also rules chairman of Shell's Wonderful World of Golf and a member of the PGA rules seminar panel, 1974-76. He has been a lifetime sponsor of the World Golf Hall of Fame. Active in Michigan golf, he has been head pro at Tam O'Shanter C.C., Orchard Lake, Michigan, since 1953.

OUIMET, FRANCIS DE SALES B. 5/8/1893, Brookline, Mass. D. 9/2/67, Newton, Mass. 6'2", 175. One of the greatest figures in golf history in the United States, the former caddie from working class background came out of nowhere, at age of 20, to win the 1913 USGA Open, defeating English greats Harry Vardon and Ted Ray in a playoff. He had failed to qualify for the U.S. Amateur in 1910, 11, 12, each year by 1 stroke. He qualified in 1913 and was eliminated in the second round. He considered his 1914 U.S. Amateur victory his most important; he also won that event in 1931. Ouimet was the first native son to make it big in the golfing world, and his youth, his calm on the course, his less than affluent background, and his unquestioned success were considered responsible for the spreading popularity of the game in the U.S. A member of the first U.S. Walker Cup team in 1922 and a member or the non-playing captain of the team every year through 1949, he played in more Walker Cup matches than any other player—eight straight through 1934. The USGA suspended his amateur status in 1916 because he opened a sporting goods store in Boston, which was ruled as profiting from his golf game. The great furor that ensued was interrupted by World War I, in which Ouimet served. After the war, the incident was forgotten and Ouimet was reinstated as an amateur. In 1951 he was the first non-Britisher to be elected captain of the Royal and Ancient Golf Club of St. Andrews. In 1955 he was the first recipient of the USGA's Bobby Jones Award for distinguished sportsmanship. The 1963 USGA Open at The Country Club, Brookline, Mass., the site of Ouimet's Open victory in 1913, was played in his honor 50 years after his triumph. In the playoff with Vardon and Ray, Ouimet scored 72 to Vardon's 75 and Ray's 78. Ouimet was known as one of the great putters the game has known.

PACE, ROY B. 6/21/41, Runge, Tex. 6'1", 160. Pace graduated from Louisiana Tech in 1964 with a degree in mechanical engineering and joined the tour. He had limited success, with his only victory being the 1971 Magnolia Classic. Pace still plays regularly and won $130,810 on the tour through 1975.

PAGE, ESTELLE LAWSON B. 3/22/07, East Orange, N.J. Mrs. Page won the 1937 USGA Amateur, defeating Patty Berg, was runner-up in 1938, and semifinalist in 1941, 47. She was a member of the Curtis Cup team in 1938, 48. She won many amateur championships, including the North and South in 1933, 36, 38, 40, 41, 46, 47, 49 and was runner-up in 1942, 43.

PALMER, ARNOLD DANIEL B. 9/10/29, Latrobe, Pa. 5'11", 185. Starting at the age of 3 under his only teacher, his father, "Deacon" Palmer, Arnold established one of the most phenomenal and popular careers in the history of golf. His successful amateur career culminated with a victory in the 1954 USGA Amateur; he turned professional that year. By 1956 he was making his mark on the PGA tour with a bold, charging game that became his trademark. He was the leading money winner in 1958, 60, 62, 63 and won the Vardon Trophy for the lowest scoring average in 1961, 62, 64, 67. In his first big year, 1960, he won the Masters and USGA Open, plus six other tournaments and the World Cup, and set a record at that time with earnings of $75,262.85. He also set his "charge" pattern as in the U.S. Open, where he was 7 strokes behind Mike Souchak going into the final round and birdied six of the first seven holes, made 30 on the first nine and 65 for the round to win. "Arnie's Army" emerged as a large dedicated group of fans around the world who stuck with him even when his game fell on bad times. His skill and popularity are often credited with helping to popularize the sport. His face is always very expressive, win or lose. Through 1975 he won 61 U.S. official events (No. 3 all-time record, after Snead and Hogan) plus 18 foreign victories. His career earnings through 1975 of $1,623,113 are second only to Nicklaus's. Of major events, he has won the USGA Open in 1960, the Masters in 1958, 60, 62, and the British Open in 1961, 62. He is still trying for his first PGA Championship. He was a member of the Ryder Cup team in 1961, 63, 65, 71, 73, and was captain in 1975. His World Cup victories came in 1960, 62, 63, 64, 66, 67. In recent years, his game has fallen off. 1972 was the first year he had no victories on the PGA tour. His last win on the tour was the 1973 Bob Hope Classic, although he came close in the 1975 Hawaiian, which he lost with a bogie on the 71st hole and finished third. He finished 1975 as 36th money winner with $59,017. In 1975, he had his first win in two years, the Spanish Open, which he won with an eagle on the last hole. He also won the 1975 British PGA Championship.

PALMER, JOHN (Johnny) B. 7/3/18, Eldorado, N.C. 5'10", 170. Palmer turned pro in 1938 and had a successful career on the PGA circuit in the 1940s and 1950s. He won six PGA events, including the 1947 Western Open, 1949 World Championship, 1949 Houston Open, and 1954 Colonial Open. He also won the 1952 Canadian Open and 1954 Mexican Open. He was runner-up in the 1949 PGA Championship, losing to Sam Snead, 3 and 2. He was in the top 15 money winners in 1949, 50, 52, 54 and a member of the 1949 Ryder Cup team.

PALMER, RAYMOND B. 1/11/12. A successful amateur player in the early 1950s, he was sidelined from the game from 1955-63 as a result of calcium deposits on his spine. He came back as a senior, winning the USGA Senior Amateur in 1967, the first year he was eligible to play. He defeated Walter Bronson, 3 and 2. He also won the American Senior Championship in 1974.

PALMER, SANDRA JEAN B. 3/10/41, Fort Worth, Tex. 5'1½", 117. One of the LPGA's top players. She graduated from North Texas State University in 1963, where she was cheerleader and homecoming queen, with a degree in physical education. She joined the LPGA tour in 1964 and didn't really make it big until 1971. That year she made an eagle out of the sand on the final hole in the Sealy Classic to beat Donna Caponi Young and to win $10,000 and a new car, her biggest prize up to that time. Through 1975 she won 14 LPGA events: the 1971 Sealy and Heritage Classics; the 1972 Four-Ball and Title-holders; the 1973 Pompano Beach, Angelo's Four-Ball, St. Paul, and National Jewish Hospital Opens; the 1974 Cameron Park Open; the 1974 Burdine's and Cubic Classics; the 1975 Dinah Shore Colgate Winners Circle (for $32,000 first prize); and the 1975 USGA Women's Open. In 1973 she finished in the top ten 23 times and finished No. 3 in earnings. In 1974, she had 25 top 20 finishes out of 30 tournaments played. In 1974 Sandra finished No. 1 in money winnings with $76,374.51. Her career earnings through 1975 were $331,292.37.

PARK, WILLIE, SR. B. c.1844. One of the most famous members of the Park family which was associated with golf in Scotland for 400 years. He won the first British Open in 1860 and won the event again in 1863, 66, 75. His brother, Mungo, won the British Open in 1874 and his son, Willie Jr., won it in 1887, 89. Willie Sr. was always willing to play matches with anyone who would play him, and he often played with Old Tom Morris.

PARK, WILLIE, JR. B. 1864. D. 5/24/25. This great early British player was a son and nephew of British Open winners. He won the British Open in 1887, 89 and came to the U.S. in 1895 at request of the founders of St. Andrews G.C., Yonkers, N.Y. Here he played in a series of matches to promote and popularize the game in America. In early money matches against Willie Dunn, three matches were played at $200 each, winner take all, and Park won all three.

PARKS, SAMUEL McLAUGHLIN (Sam) B. 6/23/09, Hopedale, O. This surprise winner of the 1935 USGA Open learned golf from Gene Sarazen, when Gene was at Highland C.C. in Pittsburgh. Parks graduated from the University of Pittsburgh, where he was captain of the golf team in 1930, 31. He turned pro in 1933 and played a few tournaments, entering the 1935 Open because the site, Oakmont C.C., was close to home. Parks was the only one who broke 300 in the tournament with his winning 299. In 1942 he quit pro golf and went to work for U.S. Steel. He is still a member and regular player at Oakmont.

PATE, JEROME KENDRICK (Jerry) B. 9/16/53, Macon, Ga. 6'0", 165. Took up golf at the age of 6 and attended the University of Alabama because of the presence there of golf coach Conrad Rehling. Pate was the surprise winner of the 1974 USGA Amateur. He also won the 1973 International Intercollegiate, the 1974 Florida Amateur, the 1974 Buckeye Intercollegiate, and the 1974 All-American Sun Bowl. He shared medalist honors in the 1974 World Amateur Team Championship, was runner-up in the 1975 NCAA Championship, and played on the 1975 U.S. Walker Cup team. In the 1974 Amateur, Pate defeated John P. Grace in the final, 2 and 1. He was a member of the World Cup team in 1974. In 1975 he turned pro and was the best finisher in the 1975 PGA qualifying school.

PATTON, WILLIAM J. (Billy Joe) B. 4/19/22. This Wake Forest graduate was one of the best amateurs to play in the 1950s. In 1954, his first Masters appearance, he had the best amateur score. He was low scorer in the first round, took first place in the pre-tournament driving contest, and had a hole-in-one with a five iron on the 6th hole in the last round, to finish 1 stroke behind Snead and Hogan who tied for first. He was also the top amateur in the Masters in 1958 and a member of the Walker Cup team in 1955, 57, 59, 63, 65; non-playing captain in 1969. He was a member of the U.S. World Amateur team in 1958, 62, and on the Americas Cup Team in 1954, 56, 58, 63 (as captain in last two years). Patton is a North Carolina lumber broker. He has also won many amateur tournaments, including the North and South in 1954, 62, 63. He was a popular gallery favorite in his tournament days.

PEARCE, EDWARD (Eddie) B. 3/16/52, Fort Myers, Fla. 6'0", 175. Pearce took up golf at age 4 and won his first tournament at age 7. In 1968 he won the USGA Junior and lost the 1969 Junior only in the final. In 1968 he also won the Future Masters and played in the USGA Amateur and Open. Pearce attended Wake Forest University on an Arnold Palmer golf scholarship. He was runner-up in the 1971 Amateur. He turned pro in 1973, lost part of the 1974 season due to a broken collar bone, but still won $56,384. That year he was runner-up to Jack Nicklaus in the Hawaiian Open. Pearce, a very long driver, won $54,595 in 1975.

PENNA, TONEY B. 1/15/08, Naples, Italy. A regular on the PGA circuit in the 1930s and early 1940s, he got his training serving as assistant professional to Tommy Armour and Alex Smith. He won the 1938 Kansas City Open and 1947 Atlanta Open. A consistent player, he finished in the top 20 money winners in 1938, 44, 45, 47, 49. After leaving the tour, he founded the Toney Penna Golf Company, now a part of ATO Inc.

PENNICK, HARVEY B. 10/23/04, Austin, Tex. Pennick is an important American golf teacher, who spent 33 years as golf coach at the University of Texas, during which time the team won 20 conference championships. Golfers he coached there included Ben Crenshaw and Tom Kite. A popular teacher among women pros, he has coached, among others, Kathy Whitworth, Betsy Rawls, and Betty Jameson. He served as golf pro at the Austin Country Club for 48 years and is now a pro *emeritus* there. He has served as instructor at many PGA seminars and workshops.

PERSON, CURTIS, SR. B. 9/13/10, Mount Pleasant, Tenn. One of the most active competitors among seniors, he won the Mississippi Amateur in 1941, 45 and the Tennessee Open in 1953, 57. In all he has won over 65 senior championships, including the USGA Senior in 1968, 69; the International Senior in 1969, 71; and the U.S. Senior in 1968. In 1968, 69 Person won 69 of 72 competitive matches played, including 38 in a row. He was ranked as top senior by *Golf Digest*, 1966-70, named Tennessee Athlete of the Year in 1968, and inducted into the Tennessee Sports Hall of Fame in 1971. In 1969 he was presented the Golf Writers' Association's Ben Hogan trophy. He came back from apparent multiple sclerosis in the early 1960s and a ruptured disc in 1965, winning the Southern Senior three months after an operation. He was co-founder, and often chairman, of the Danny Thomas Memphis Classic. Captain of the winning 1969 U.S. World senior team, he was also past president and director of the Tennessee and Southern Golf Associations. Person is active in many golf organizations, including the Memphis Golf Association, Eastern Seniors' Golf Association, and International Seniors' Golf Tournament. He is a director of the National Golf Foundation and a member of the PGA Advisory Board and probably one of golf's biggest boosters.

PHILP, HUGH B. 1782, St. Andrews, Scotland. D. 1856. In 1819 Philp was named official clubmaker to the Society of St. Andrews Golfers. His specialty was wooden putters. He was important in popularizing hickory, rather than ash, in golf club shafts. Clubs he made are valuable collectors' items today.

PICARD, HENRY B. 11/28/07, Plymouth, Mass. One of the best PGA players of the 1930s, he won 30 tournaments in his career. He is the only player to defeat Walter Hagen in a playoff, in the 1932 Carolina Open. He won six PGA tournaments in 1936 and in 1937 was No. 2 U.S. money winner. He also won the Argentine Open in 1937. He won the 1938 Masters and was No. 3 money winner that year. In 1939 Picard won five tournaments including the PGA Championship and was No. 1 U.S. money winner with $10,303. In 50 out of 54 tournaments he entered between August 1934 and April 1935, he broke par on all but three, when he equalled it. A member of the U.S. Ryder Cup team in 1935, 37, Picard was elected to the PGA's Hall of Fame in 1961. He cut back on tournament play in 1940 due to illness.

PLATT, J. WOOD B. 4/16/1899, Philadelphia, Pa. D. 12/9/59, Philadelphia, Pa. An executive of Equitable Life Assurance Society, Platt was also the top Philadelphia area golfer. He won the Philadelphia Amateur seven times and was president of the Philadelphia Golf Association, which established a caddie scholarship in his name. He was a member of the first U.S. team, in 1921, to meet a British team, before the establishment of the Walker Cup. In 1955 he won his first USGA Senior Championship. One of Platt's most notable achievements was the spectacular start he made at the murderous Pine Valley course one day in a friendly round. Par on the first four holes at Pine Valley is 4, 4, 3, 4. Platt started 3, 2, 1, 3. It was utterly incredible. Platt thought so too, for he walked into the clubhouse, hard by the 4th green, and never came out to finish the round.

PLAYER, GARY JIM B. 11/1/36, Johannesburg, South Africa. 5'8", 159. Since taking up golf at age 15, he has set many golfing records while traveling more than a million miles around the world. He won the South African Open nine times through 1975 and is one of only four men in history to have won the U.S. and British Opens, the PGA Championship, and the Masters. Player was the first foreigner to win the USGA Open in 45 years when he won in 1965. He is the only foreign player to win the Masters, in 1961, 74. He won the British Open in 1959, 68, 74, and the PGA Championship in 1962, 72. He has won seven Australian Opens, three World Series of Golf, five Piccadilly World Championships, and was individual champion in the 1965 World Cup. Player is a natural athlete and physical fitness devotee, who jogs, lifts weights, exercises, and eats natural foods. He usually dresses in black and has learned to cope well with demonstrators in the U.S. and Australia who protest South African policies toward blacks by harassing

Player on the course. He brought Lee Elder to South Africa to play with him. A world golfer, his nine victories in 1974 were the Masters and Memphis Classic in the U.S., the British Open, the Australian Open, the Brazil Open, and three South African tournaments—all after hardly playing in 1973 due to surgery. He won 18 PGA events in the U.S. through 1975 and $1,163,153, was elected to the World Golf Hall of Fame, and was awarded the 1975 Golf Writers' Association of America Richardson Award for outstanding contributions to golf.

PORTER, DOROTHY GERMAIN (Mrs. Mark) B. 5/3/24. Dorothy Porter first qualified for the USGA Women's Amateur in 1939 at age 15. She won the event in 1949 and became a member of the U.S. Curtis Cup team in 1950 and captain in 1966. Her many amateur victories include the Philadelphia City Championship seven times and the Women's Western in 1943, 44, 67. She won the USGA Senior Women's Championship by 17 strokes in 1974, her first year as a senior player. She is a member of the USGA's Women's Committee and a former member of the Trans-Mississippi and Western Golf Association boards. She has also played and coached field hockey and now referees field hockey and basketball and is the mother of three children.

PORTER, MARY BEA B. 12/4/49, Everett, Wash. 5'7", 135. Mary Porter studied golf with Betty Hicks and was 1972 Collegiate All-American at Arizona State, from which she graduated in 1973. She turned pro that year and won her first LPGA event in the 1975 Golf Inns of America Mixed Pro tournament. In 1975 she won $11,665.08.

POST, SANDRA B. 6/4/48, Oakville, Ontario, Canada. 5'4", 120. She took up golf at age 5 and was Canadian Junior Champion three times. She came to the U.S. and joined the LPGA tour in 1968 when she was named Rookie of the Year. She won the LPGA Championship in 1968 by defeating Kathy Whitworth in an 18-hole playoff. She did well again in 1969, but fell off in 1970-71 and had back problems in 1972. In 1973 she earned $25,500 and in 1974 won the Colgate Far East tournament. Without any victories, she finished 1975 fifth in money winnings with $34,840.88 and has career earnings of $121,435.29.

POTT, JOHN (Johnny) B. 11/6/35, Cape Girardeau, Mo. 6'1", 195. Pott graduated from Louisiana State and was a member of its 1955 NCAA championship team. He turned pro in 1956 and in the course of his career won five tournaments and almost $400,000. He was often found in playoffs; his first victory, the 1960 Dallas Open, was won in a playoff over Ted Kroll and Bo Wininger. He lost the 1962 San Diego and Colonial in playoffs as well as the 1965 Memphis and Insurance City, and 1966 Buick. He was a member of the 1963, 65, 67 Ryder Cup teams. His best year was 1965: he won $50,896 for 14th place. He was in the top 60 money winners from 1958-69.

PRENTICE, JO ANN ("Fry") B. 2/9/33, Birmingham, Ala. 5'5½", 122. She turned pro and joined the LPGA tour in 1956, after some amateur successes, and was on tour eight years before her first victory, the 1965 Jackson Open. Since, she has won the 1967 Dallas Civitan, the 1972 Corpus Christi, the 1973 Burdines, the 1974 Colgate-Dinah Shore, and the 1974 American Defender. She won the 1972 Corpus Christi in a 10-hole playoff with Sandra Palmer. Her best year was 1974 when she had 20 finishes in the top 20, won two tournaments, and won $67,227 in official money to finish fourth for the year. Her career earnings through 1975 were $279,630.10.

PREUSS, PHYLLIS (Tish) B. 2/9/39, Detroit, Mich. A successful amateur player, she was runner-up in the 1961 USGA Women's Amateur and low amateur in the USGA Women's Open in 1963, 68. She was a multiple winner of many major amateur championships, including the North and South, and Southern and Eastern. She was a member of the U.S. Curtis Cup team in 1962, 64, 66, 68, 70.

PRICE, CHARLES B. B. 9/26/25, Philadelphia, Pa. Original editor-in-chief of *Golf Magazine* (1958), now a columnist, Price has written for other golf and general interest publications. He has written a number of books: *The World of Golf, Golf, Bobby Jones on Golf,* and *The Natural Way to Better Golf* (with Jack Burke), and was editor of *The American Golfer.* He won three second-place awards in the Golf Writers' Association of America writers' contest, the magazine division. He is a member of the board of directors of the World Golf Hall of Fame and the PGA Hall of Fame. He also wrote for Shell's "Wonderful World of Golf" TV series, wrote radio scripts for Gene Sarazen, and produced a record for Arnold Palmer and Chris Schenkel. A good golfer, Price was medalist in the 1951 USGA Amateur, Mid-Atlantic sectional qualifying, and was the Golf Writers of America Association's champion in 1962. He has had three holes-in-one, a double eagle, and a best score of 65.

PROBST, OTTO (Col.) B. 11/21/1889, South Bend, Ind. Probst had the largest and most complete collection of golf literature, art, equipment, programs, magazines, novelties, postcards, etc., totalling over 18,000 items, including clubs made by Old Tom Morris. He graduated from Notre Dame in 1911 with a degree in electrical and mechanical engineering and was employed by a local utility from 1912-54. He served in World War I and II. He took up golf in 1922 and purchased his first golf book, *Golf Fundamentals* by Seymour Dunn. His collection was maintained at his home in South Bend, "The Golf Library," until 1974, when it was transferred to warehousing while waiting for the PGA to build a special museum for it.

PUNG, JACQUELINE (Jackie) B. 12/13/21, Hawaii. Jackie Pung won the Hawaiian Women's Amateur in 1937, 38, 39, 48 and became the USGA

Women's Amateur Champion in 1952, in her third try. She was the first Hawaiian champion and was employed as a saleswoman in a department store at the time of her victory. As a professional, she won two LPGA events in 1953, two in 1955, and one in 1958. She's most well known for what she almost won: the 1957 USGA Women's Open. She lost as a result of signing an incorrect scorecard. Spectators, officials, and members of the Winged Foot C.C., where the tournament was played, contributed over $3,000 to her to make up for losing the $1,800 purse. In recent years, 1965-70, she has worked as a teaching pro at Mauna Kea in Hawaii. Since 1971 she has been the head professional at Waikoloa Village, Hawaii. Her awards include the LPGA Teacher of the Year in 1967 and the Ben Hogan Award in 1974.

QUAST, ANNE DECKER, WELTS, SANDER B. 8/31/37, Everett, Wash. One of the top woman amateurs for almost two decades. She won the USGA Women's Amateur in 1958, 61, 63 and was runner-up in 1965, 68, 73. Her first victory in the Amateur came before her marriage. In 1961 she won as Mrs. Jay D. Decker and in 1963 as Mrs. David Welts. The year 1973 marked the 14th time in the last 19 that she had reached at least the quarterfinal round in this championship. She first entered the event at age 14 and won for the first time one week before her 21st birthday. She won the Western Amateur in 1956, 61, and was low amateur in the USGA Women's Open in 1958, 59 and finished fourth in 1973. In 1957 she was runner-up to Patty Berg in the Titleholders Championship, a member of the U.S. World Amateur team in 1966, 68, and a member of the Curtis Cup team in 1958, 60, 62, 66, 68, 74.

QUICK, LYMAN (Smiley) B. 3/19/07, Centralia, Ill. Nicknamed Smiley as a boy because of his grin, he officially adopted the name as an adult. He won the 1946 Public Links Championship, was runner-up in the 1946 USGA Amateur, and tied for low amateur in the 1946 USGA Open. He played on the 1947 U.S. Walker Cup team and turned pro in 1948, but never lived up to his amateur promise.

RAGAN, DAVID WILLIAM, JR. (Dave) B. 8/7/35, Daytona Beach, Fla. 5'11", 185. Ragan turned pro in 1956 and won five PGA tournaments: the 1959 Eastern Open, the 1961, 63 Haig & Haig Scotch Foursome, and the 1962 Beaumont and Palm Beach Opens. He was runner-up to Jack Nicklaus in the 1963 PGA Championship and a member of the 1963 U.S. Ryder Cup team. His best money year was 1962: he finished eighth in the U.S. with $37,327.

RANKIN, JUDITH TORLUEMKE (Judy) B. 2/18/45, St. Louis, Mo. 5'3½", 110. Judy Rankin won her first National Pee Wee Championship in 1953 at age 8 and won it again in 1954, 55, 56. She was the youngest ever Missouri State Champion, at age 14 in 1959, and the low amateur in her first try in the USGA Women's Open in 1960. In 1962, at age 17, she turned pro and joined the LPGA tour. A consistent winner, she has won 15 tournaments through 1975, including three in 1970 and four in 1973 (Raleigh, Carling, Columbus, GAC). In 1973 Judy was second in money with $74,900, finished in the top ten 25 times, and was named LPGA Player of the Year and winner of the year's Vare Trophy for the tour's low scoring average of 73.08. In 1975 she won the National Jewish Hospital Open after six runner-up finishes since her last win. She was vice president of the LPGA Governing Board in 1972. Her husband "Yippie" and son "Tuey" often accompany her on the tour. She finished 1975 as fifth in money winnings with $50,174 and sixth in all-time money winnings with $327,164. Judy got off to a fast start in 1976, winning three times in three months. She took the Burdine's in February, and the rich Colgate-Dinah Shore and the Karsten-Ping in April. The Colgate-Dinah Shore was worth $32,000 and the Karsten-Ping $14,000.

RANSOM, HENRY B. 2/25/11, Houston, Tex. 5'10¼", 180. This smooth swinger turned pro in 1933 and was on and off the tour throughout his career, serving as club pro till 1945 and later as golf coach at Texas A & M University. He won four tournaments in 1950 including the 1950 World Championship and was fourth in money winnings that year. In 1955 he won the Rubber City Open defeating Doug Ford, Jack Burke, and Jackson Bradley in a sudden-death playoff. He won the 1948 Illinois PGA by birdieing 8 of the last 11 holes. He was a member of the 1951 U.S. Ryder Cup team. After winning the 1950 World Championship, he cut down on his golf play because of an allergy to grass.

RAVENSCROFT, GLADYS (Mrs. Temple Dobell) B. 1888, Rock Ferry, England. D. 1960, Wirral, England. The winner of the 1913 USGA Women's Amateur and the 1912 British Women's Amateur. Miss Ravenscroft defeated Marion Hollins in the final, 2 up, and became the third woman to take the championship out of the country. That year, 1913, two of the four semifinalists were English, the other being Muriel Dodd, the reigning British champion, who lost to Miss Ravenscroft.

RAWLINS, HORACE J. B. 8/5/1874, Isle of Wight. D. c. 1940. Horace Rawlins was the winner of the first USGA Open, in 1895. A British pro, he had come to the U.S. to be assistant professional at Newport C.C., where the tournament was played. He was 21 at the time and he won $150. It was the third tournament he'd ever played in; the following year he played again and was runner-up. He played for over a decade more, but never again approached victory. It was thought for many years that he was only 19 years old at the time he won and was the youngest winner ever, but thorough checking of birth dates in subsequent years proved he was 21.

RAWLS, ELIZABETH EARLE (Betsy) B. 5/4/28, Spartanburg, S.C. Betsy Rawls is the winner of 55 LPGA tournaments, the third all-time highest number of wins. She took up golf at age 17 and in 1950, as an amateur, placed second in the USGA Women's Open. She graduated from the University of Texas as a Phi Beta Kappa in physics. Her tour victories include the USGA Women's Open in 1951, 53, 57, 61; and the LPGA Championship in 1959, 69. She won at least one tournament every year from 1954-65. She was the tour's leading money winner in 1952, 59, winning $26,744 in the latter year, a record at the time. She won 10 tournaments that year and over $300,000 in her career. She was named *Los Angeles Times'* Woman Golfer of the Year in 1953, won the Vare Trophy for the lowest scoring average in 1959, and was named LPGA Golfer of the Year in 1963. She was elected to the LPGA Hall of Fame in 1960. She was twice president of the LPGA. Her last victory was at Tucson in 1972. In 1975 she was named LPGA tournament director.

RAY, EDWARD (Ted) B. 3/28/1877, Isle of Jersey, England. D. 8/28/43, London, England. One of Britain's top players in the early part of the 20th century, Ray's golf career spanned four decades. He won the British Open in 1912 and was second twice and in the top ten 15 times over 25 years. Big, cheerful and calm, he was a long driver with a slow, easy swing and identifiable on the course by his big moustache and always present pipe. He was an excellent putter. With Vardon he helped spark U.S. interest in golf when they toured this country giving golfing exhibitions in 1913 and 1920. Ray won the 1920 U.S. Open at age 43, and remains the oldest Open winner. His last recorded victory was in 1935 in the Herts Open in England, when he was 57. He was pro at Oxney C.C. in Hertfordshire, England, from 1912 until his retirement in 1941.

REES, DAVID JAMES (Dai) B. 3/31/13, Barry, Glamorgan, Scotland. One of Britain's top players for many years, his victories include the British PGA Match Play in 1936, 38, 49, 50. He was runner-up in the British Open in 1953, 54, 61 and won Britain's Vardon Trophy for his low scoring average in 1955, 59. He won the Swiss Open in 1956, 59, 63. He was the mainstay for years of Britain's Ryder Cup team: a member in 1937, 47, 49, 51, 53; captain in 1955, 57, 59, 61; and non-playing captain in 1967.

REGALADO, VICTOR B. 4/15/48, Tijuana, Mexico. 5'10½", 182. A native Mexican, he had many successes in Mexico before trying the U.S. He won the 1962 Pan Am Junior at age 14, the 1970 Mexican Amateur, the 1972 Mexican PGA, and the 1972, 73 Mexican Masters. He played for Mexico on the 1968, 70 World Amateur teams and 1972, 73 World Cup teams. In 1972 he joined the PGA tour in the U.S. and, in 1974, was the surprise winner of the Pleasant Valley Open. He won $61,848 on the U.S. tour in 1974, but in 1975 made only $31,000.

REHLING, CONRAD B. 2/6/20, Peru, Indiana. Rehling, a top golf coach, learned the game from Paul Runyan and did his masters thesis on *An Analysis of the Techniques of the Golf Drive.* As golf coach at the University of Florida, he produced such golfers as Tommy Aaron, Frank Beard, Steve Melnyk, Bob Murphy, Doug Sanders, and Dan Sikes. After a short coaching stint at the University of West Florida, he went to his current post at the University of Alabama, a school chosen by the 1974 USGA Amateur champion, Jerry Pate, because of Rehling.

REID, JOHN B. 1840, Dunfermline, Fife, Scotland. D. 10/7/16, Yonkers, N.Y. Considered the father of American golf, he was the prime mover behind what is generally acknowledged as America's oldest permanent golf club, St. Andrews of Yonkers, N.Y. The club was formed by Reid and the "Apple Tree Gang" on November 14, 1888, and incorporated in 1894. Apple trees were the principal hazards, with three holes built first, then six. The club moved its locale to Hastings-on-Hudson in 1893. Reid was the club's first president, serving nine years. He was also one of the founders of the United States Golf Association. His son John won the club championship three times and won the 1898 Intercollegiate. His son Archie won the club championship 11 times and became a president of the USGA in the 1930s.

Reid was a close friend of Andrew Carnegie and one followed the other as president of the St. Andrews (Scotland) Society. Reid, who was married in the unlikely town of Volcano, W. Va., was not accustomed to losing, and the story goes that he once played a mixed foursome with a Mrs. Ten Eyke against his wife and Mr. Ten Eyke, lost the match, and never would play with a woman again.

REID, STEVEN (Steve) B. 7/27/36 Santa Barbara, Cal. 6'0", 185. Reid turned pro in 1956 and joined the tour in 1965. He had some success on the tour with one victory, the 1968 Azalea Open, where he defeated Gary Player. He was so obscure at the time that he wasn't even listed in the PGA's player book. His best money year was 1969, with $29,000.

RENNER, JACK B. 7/6/56, Palm Springs, Cal. 6'0", 165. Renner was the winner of the 1973 USGA Junior Championship and 1972 World Junior, and runner-up in the latter event in 1971, 73. With his brother Jim, he won the 1975 U.S. Amateur Team Championship. Playing against professionals, he made the cut in the 1974 Andy Williams Open and lost the 1974 Guadalajara Invitational in a playoff. He is now a member of the golf team at the College of the Desert in Palm Desert, California.

REVOLTA, JOHN (Johnny) B. 4/5/11, St. Louis, Mo. A top PGA player of the 1930s whose major strength was his short game. His many tournament victories include the 1935 Western Open, the International Four-Ball (with Henry Picard) in 1935, 36, 37, and the 1944 San Antonio and Texas Opens. He won the 1935 PGA Championship and was top money winner that year with $9,543. In 1938 he was the No. 2 U.S. money winner. He was a member of the 1935 U.S. Ryder Cup team. In 1963 he was elected to the PGA Hall of Fame. Today he is a respected teacher of men and women, pros and club players, at Mission Hills Golf and C.C. in Palm Springs, California.

RICE, GRANTLAND B. 11/1/1880, Murfreesboro, Tenn. D. 7/13/54, New York, N.Y. Rice was one of the greatest sports writers of all time. He had a special interest in golf, which he played and followed avidly. After 19 years of sportswriting for various newspapers, he became editor of the *American Golfer* in 1920, an early golf magazine. He wrote two golf books, *The Duffer's Handbook* and *The Winning Shots,* and a volume of verse. A graduate of Vanderbilt University, Rice first went to the *Atlanta Journal,* then, in 1914, to the *New York Tribune.* In 1930 his popular column, "The Sportlight," was syndicated and used in a large number of papers. He was also active for several years in selecting the football All-American for *Collier's* magazine. Rice died at his desk in the *Daily Mirror* office.

RICHARDSON, WILLIAM DUNCAN B. 4/18/1885, Milwaukee, Wisc. D. 8/8/47, Cornwall, N.Y. This *New York Times* sportswriter joined the paper in 1921. Golf became his specialty beginning in 1922, and he covered the game until his death. He also edited the annual golf guides. Richardson became the first president of the Golf Writers' Association of America in 1946, and the Association gives an award in his name yearly for outstanding contributions to the game. A New York area amateur tournament named for him is played annually.

RICHTER, BENJAMIN (Ben) B. 4/22/1895, St. Louis, Mo. Richter promoted and sponsored the first left-handed golf tournament in 1936, at the Triple A G.C. in St. Louis where he was pro. The National Association of Left-Handed Golfers was formed as a result, and he served it as promoter.

RIDLEY, FREDERICK S. (Fred) B. 8/16/52, Lakeland, Fla. The surprise winner of the 1975 USGA Amateur. In the final of the Amateur Ridley defeated Keith Fergus, 2 up. Ridley had played with limited success on the University of Florida golf team but had had no significant amateur wins when he won the major event. He is a law student at Stetson University.

RIEGEL, ROBERT HENRY (Skee) B. 11/25/14, New Bloomfield, Pa. Skee Riegel didn't take up golf until 1938. In 1947 he won the USGA Amateur, in 1948 the Western Amateur, and in 1949 was low amateur in the USGA Open. He played on the U.S. Walker Cup team in 1947, 49. In 1950 he turned pro. He finished eighth in the U.S. money winners list in 1951 and was runner-up in that year's Masters, two shots behind Ben Hogan. When he won the Amateur, Riegel defeated John Dawson, 2 and 1, in the final.

RILEY, POLLY ANN B. 8/27/26, San Antonio, Tex. An active and energetic amateur, she has won over 100 tournaments so far in her career. Her victories include the Southern Amateur in 1948, 50, 51, 53, 54, 61, the Western Amateur in 1950, 52, and the Trans-Mississippi in 1947, 48, 55. She was runner-up in the 1953 USGA Women's Amateur. She played on the U.S. Curtis Cup team in 1948, 50, 52, 54, 56, 58 and was non-playing captain in 1962. She is a director of the Women's Western Golf Association and the Women's Southern Golf Association and served as assistant tournament director for the PGA's San Diego Open in 1958, 59, 60.

RISCH, ROBERT (Bob) B. 8/4/47, Los Angeles, Cal. 6'1½", 195. This 1970 USGA Public Links Champion turned pro in 1970 but failed to qualify for the tour in the 1971, 72, 73 qualifying schools. He won three mini-tour events before qualifying for tour in 1974 but has yet to be truly competitive on the circuit.

ROBBINS, HILLMAN, JR. B. 4/22/34, Memphis, Tenn. Robbins won the 1954 National Collegiate Championship and while in the service won the All-Air Force Championship in 1956 and the All-Services Tournament in 1957. In 1957, as a lieutenant on leave from the Air Force, Robbins won the USGA Amateur Championship. His victim in the final was Dr. Frank M. Taylor, 5 and 4. Robbins was a member of the Walker Cup team in 1957, and the Americans Cup team in 1956, 58. In 1958 he turned pro but had little success.

ROBBINS, THOMAS C. B. 1893. D. 6/26/70, Pinehurst, N.C. Tom Robbins took up golf at age 31, switched from left- to right-handed play, and scored in the 70s within a month of his first lesson. He won the 1951, 52 U.S. Seniors' G.A. Championship, the 1951 American Senior Championship, and the 1958 USGA Senior. Robbins defeated John Dawson in the final, 2 and 1. At 65 he is still the oldest winner of the Senior Championship.

ROBERTS, CLIFFORD B. 3/6/1893, Morning Sun, Ia. Roberts has run the Masters tournament since its inception. He helped Bobby Jones select the property for the Augusta National Golf Course in 1931, helped set up the tournament, and was its chief organizer during Jones' lifetime and since his death. A very private individual, Roberts was awarded the Golf Writers' Association of America 1964 Richardson Award for contributions to golf and the 1975 Metropolitan Golf Writers' Gold Tee Award for "outstanding impact on the game."

ROBERTS, SUSAN (Sue) B. 6/22/48, Oak Park, Ill. 5'6", 140. Sue Roberts worked as a telephone operator for two years to earn enough money to go on the LPGA tour. She turned pro in 1969. Her first big year was 1974 when she won the Niagara Frontier, and was co-winner of the Southgate Open, had 12 top ten finishes, and won $26,745. In 1975 Sue won $5,000 for a hole-in-one in the Dinah Shore Colgate. She also won the San Isidro Open, leading all three rounds. She finished 1975 as 18th on the money list with $21,154. In May 1976, Sue picked up another victory, the American Defender.

ROBERTSON, ALLAN B. 1815, St. Andrews, Scotland. D. September 1858, St. Andrews, Scotland. Robertson was an early golfing star and the maker of feathery balls. He was the first great professional golfer whose forte was iron play. He supposedly produced 2,456 feather balls in 1844. Old Tom Morris served as his apprentice; they never played each other but were partners in many matches. Robertson fired Old Tom when he found him playing with a gutta-percha ball. There is a memorial to him in the St. Andrews churchyard.

ROBINSON, CLINTON E. B. 4/18/07, Montebello, Quebec, Canada. A Canadian golf course architect whose work in Canada, the United States, Mexico, and South America includes design of 75 courses and redesign and modernization of another 50. His courses include the Cape Breton Highlands in Nova Scotia and the Mill River on Prince Edward Island. He was president of the American Society of Golf Course Architects in 1961, 71 and a member of the association's board of governors and ethics committee. The Ontario Golf Association, on its 50th anniversary, honored him for outstanding service to golf in the province.

RODGERS, PHILLIP (Phil) B. 4/3/38, San Diego, Cal. 5'8″, 175. Rodgers had a top amateur career beginning with the 1955 International Jaycee Junior Championship. He attended the University of Houston and was a member of the 1958 All-America team and winner of the 1958 NCAA Championship. He turned pro in 1961 and has won five pro events: the 1962 Los Angeles and Tucson, the 1963 San Antonio, and the 1966 Doral and Buick. At one time he used a very long-shafted putter, with his right hand far down on the shaft. He had a couple of "almosts" in major events, losing the 1963 British Open to Bob Charles in a 36-hole playoff. In the 1962 USGA Open, he finished behind only Palmer and Nicklaus, despite shooting an 8 on one hole in the first round. Rodgers was on the losing side in a match that set the extra-hole record for the PGA tour. He was beaten by Dick Hart on the eighth extra hole in a sudden-death playoff for the Azalea Open of 1965. He was an infrequent tour player for a few years in the early 1970s, but in 1974 and 1975 he has been trying to make a comeback. His career earnings on tour through 1975 were over $450,000.

RODRIGUEZ, JUAN (Chi Chi) B. 10/13/35, Bayamon, Puerto Rico. 5'7½″, 125. Rodriguez has had an up-and-down career since turning pro in 1960, at least partially a result of various physical ailments. He's always a crowd favorite because of constant good humor, generosity, jokes, and hat tossing. He has won seven tournaments during his career—1963 Denver, 1964 Lucky International and Western, 1967 Texas, 1968 Sahara, 1972 Byron Nelson, and 1973 Greater Greensboro. In 1973 he was a member of the U.S. Ryder Cup team. He had a bad year in 1975, winning only $13,955. His career earnings through 1975 were $650,969.

ROMACK, BARBARA B. 11/16/32, Sacramento, Cal. 5'4″, 99. Barbara Romack won the 1954 USGA Women's Amateur and was runner-up in 1958. She also won the Canadian Women's Amateur in 1953, was low amateur in the 1954 LPGA Titleholders Championship, and played on the U.S. Curtis Cup team in 1954, 56, 58. She was four-time California State Champion and the 1954 *Los Angeles Times'* Woman Athlete of the Year. She turned pro in 1958, after selling life insurance to help finance amateur play, and has played consistently but has won only the 1963 Rock City Open. She was named Best Dressed LPGA Pro in 1965 and was on the first plane hijacked to Cuba in 1968. She devotes much of her time to clinics and personal appearances.

ROSBURG, ROBERT (Bob) B. 10/21/26, San Francisco, Cal. 5'11″, 185. On and off the tour since he turned pro in 1953, Rosburg has been a consistently successful contender. He has won seven events: the 1954 Brawley and Miami; the 1956 Motor City and San Diego; the 1959 PGA Championship; the 1961 Crosby; the 1972 Hope. He won the latter at age 47. He also won the 1970 Club Pro Championship. A very outspoken player and sometimes temperamental, Rosburg has come close to real stardom, beginning with a hole-in-one made at age 7 at the Stanford University golf course. He graduated from Stanford, where he was a basketball player, in 1948. He is one of few tour pros to use a baseball grip. He was winner of the 1958 Vardon Trophy with a 70.11 stroke average and a member of the 1959 Ryder Cup team. He avoids long practice sessions, but comes through under pressure, as in the 1959 PGA Championship, where he came from 6 strokes back to win. He was chairman of the PGA Tournament Committee 1959-62 and player-director of the Tournament Players' Division Policy Board 1972-73. His career earnings total over $435,000 through 1975.

ROSS, ALEXANDER (Alex) B. 1881, Scotland. D. 6/25/52, Miami, Fla. Alex Ross emigrated to the United States from Scotland and won the 1907 USGA Open. He also won various lesser U.S. tournaments and the Swiss Open in 1923, 25, 26. He is the brother of the famous golf course architect, Donald Ross. He served as professional at the Detroit (Mich.) C.C. for over 30 years.

ROSS, DONALD J. B. 1873, Dornoch, Scotland. D. 4/26/48, Pinehurst, N.C. One of the greatest golf course architects. Ross came to the U.S. in 1899 after serving a brief apprenticeship to Old Tom Morris at St. Andrews. He was the first U.S. architect to really design courses; he worked on over 500 in the U.S. He came to Pinehurst in 1901 and was based there till his death. There he designed and built the Pinehurst Nos. 2, 3, and 4 courses. He also designed Oakland Hills, Seminole, Inverness, Scioto, Skokie, Interlachen, Whitemarsh Valley, and Oak Hill. A fine golfer, he won his first North and South Open in 1903 and won again in 1905, 06. He finished fifth in the 1903 U.S. Open. At the time of his death he was president of Pinehurst C.C. and honorary president of the American Society of Golf Course Architects. Ross's No. 2 course at Pinehurst is regarded as one of the world's finest.

ROSS, JOHN B. 10/17/22, Brooklyn, N.Y. John Ross is the current editor-in-chief of *Golf Magazine,* a position he has held since 1972 and previously held from 1961-67. His past positions include sports writer for the *Brooklyn Eagle,* editor for *American Lawn Tennis Magazine,* and editor for MacFadden Publications. He served as director of public relations for the PGA tour. He is a member of the boards of directors of the World Golf Hall of Fame and of governors of the Golf Writers' Association of America, and a charter member of the American Society of Magazine Editors. In 1975 he was the president of the Metropolitan Golf Writers' Association. In 1957 he won the Christopher Award for the best magazine story of the year.

ROSSI, DONALD A. (Don) B. 6/2/18, Detroit, Mich. Executive director of the National Golf Foundation since 1970. His past activities include officiating in the National Football League, serving as general manager for an American Football League team, and serving as worldwide chief of sports for the U.S. Air Force during the Korean War. He is a graduate of Michigan State University, 1940.

ROYER, HUGH B. 8/19/36, Eastman, Ga. 6'3", 197. Royer joined the tour in 1966 and had a major moment of glory when he won the 1970 Western Open. The $26,000 first prize was more than his total earnings for the entire previous year. He's had no victories since, through 1975.

RUDOLPH, MASON B. 5/23/34, Clarksville, Tenn. 5'11", 180. Rudolph has had a long, successful career, beginning with the 1950 USGA Junior Championship victory. As an amateur he played on the 1957 Walker Cup team and the 1958 U.S. Americas Cup team. He was named 1959 Rookie of the Year and won the 1959 Golden Gate Open in his 12th start as a touring pro. Six victories also include the 1962 Haig & Haig; the 1963 Fig Garden Village; the 1964 New Orleans; the 1966 Thunderbird; and the 1970 Green Island, the latter won on his 12th wedding anniversary for a $12,000 check. He was a member of the 1971 U.S. Ryder Cup team. In 1959-67 he was in the top 60 money winners, again in 1973. His career earnings through 1975 were $538,128.

RULE, JACK, JR. B. 11/13/38, Mason City, Ia. 5'10", 180. Rule won the 1956 National Jaycee tournament, defeating Jack Nicklaus in the playoff. After graduating from the University of Iowa, he turned pro in 1961. His off-and-on career on the tour included winning the 1963 St. Paul Open, the 1965 Oklahoma City Open, and the 1966 Haig & Haig Mixed Foursome.

RUNYAN, PAUL SCOTT B. 7/12/08, Hot Springs, Ark. 5'7½", 142. One of the top players of the 1930s, although he was small and not a strong hitter. Sometimes known as "Little Poison," he turned pro in 1922 and won over 50 PGA tournaments. He won the 1934 PGA Championship, defeating his old teacher, Craig Wood, on the 38th hole, and the 1938 PGA Championship, defeating Sam Snead, 8 and 7. His 8-and-7 victory over Snead was a record for the PGA Championship final. Other victories include four Arkansas Opens, four Metropolitan Opens, and five Westchester Opens. He won seven tournaments in both 1933 and 1934 and was top money winner both years. He was a member of the 1933 and 1935 Ryder Cup teams and was elected to the PGA Hall of Fame in 1959. In 1961, 62 he won the PGA Senior Championship; he had been runner-up in 1959. One of the game's finest putters, Runyan is still sought by pros who are in trouble on the greens. He also had a peculiar, very unorthodox swing, with a decided sway.

RUSSELL, CLINTON F. B. 1896. D. 9/5/61, Duluth, Minn. Russell was the founder of the U.S. Blind Golfers' Association in 1935. He lost his sight in 1923 when a tire that he was changing blew out in his face. In 1941, 48 he won the Blind Golfers' Championship and in 1957 received the Ben Hogan Award.

RYDER, SAMUEL B. 1859. D. January 1936, London, England. Donor of the Ryder Cup, for which matches are played every other year between teams of the best U.S. and British professionals. He made his fortune by implementing the idea of selling seeds to the public in small packages. He started the Ryder Cup matches in 1927 and was a major contributor to meeting expenses of PGA players in Britain.

SANDERS, DOUGLAS (Doug) B. 7/24/37, Cedartown, Ga. 5'11", 165. One of golf's more colorful players, Doug Sanders is known for his flashy wardrobe and short backswing. He won the 1956 International Junior Championship and was the first amateur ever to win the Canadian Open, when he took it in 1956. He turned pro later that year and has been a regular competitor on the U.S. tour since. He has won 20 pro events, including the 1958 Western Open, and the 1961 Colonial. In 1961 he won five tournaments—the New Orleans, Colonial, Hot Springs, Eastern, and Cajun; and three in 1966—the Hope, Greensboro, and Jacksonville. He was runner-up in the British Open in 1966, 70, the latter year losing to Nicklaus in the playoff, and a member of the 1967 U.S. Ryder Cup team. Injury prone, Sanders has been on and off the tour in recent years. His most famous "injury" was a hit on the head from then Vice President Spiro Agnew's golf ball in the 1970 Bob Hope Classic. He was in the top 60 money winners every year from 1958-68, and again in 1970, 72. His best money finishes were No. 3 in 1961 and No. 4 in 1965, 66. His best money year was 1967 with $109,455 for sixth place. In 1975 he was elected to the Georgia Athletic Hall of Fame. His career earnings through 1975 were $767,434. Pros have joked that Sanders's swing is so short he could take it in a phone booth.

SANDERS, GARY B. 10/16/49, Lunwood, Cal. D. 8/1/75, Buena Park, Cal. Sanders won the USGA Junior Championship in 1966 and enjoyed a successful amateur career. While a student at Southern California, he won the Pacific Eight Conference title in 1968, the Mexican Amateur in 1971, and the Western Amateur in 1972 among others, and made college All-American in 1969, 71. He joined the PGA tour in 1973 and in 1974 earned $22,665. While undergoing treatment for cancer in 1975, he died of a stroke at his home.

SANOK, CHESTER B. 12/22/18, Belleville, N.J. Sanok was the first amateur in the history of the Metropolitan (N.Y.) Open to win the event, which was first played in 1905. Sanok won it in 1952, beating Jim Turnesa and Dick Mayer by 2 strokes with a 289 total. Previous winners of this venerable championship included such stars as the Smith brothers, Walter Hagen, Gene Sarazen, Johnny Farrell, Tommy Armour, and Craig Wood. Only one other amateur ever has won it, Jerry Courville, 15 years after Sanok. Sanok also won the New Jersey State Open twice, 1951, 56; the State Amateur five times, 1947, 50, 54, 74, 75; the State Seniors twice, 1974, 75; and the Ike, named for the late President Eisenhower, also in 1975.

SARAZEN, EUGENE (Gene) B. 2/27/02, Harrison, N.Y. 5'5½", 162. One of golf's all-time greats, with one of the longest careers. A former caddie from a poor family, Gene won the 1922 USGA Open at age 20. His major tournament victories include the U.S. Open in 1922, 32, the British Open in 1932, the PGA Championship in 1922, 23, 33, and the Masters in 1935. Early success was followed by a long dry spell in which tournament wins eluded him, and he tried many different approaches to the game before coming back to the top with major wins in 1932. During this period, he developed the sand wedge. He played on the Ryder Cup team in 1927, 29, 31, 33, 35, 37. Not especially active as a senior golfer, but he did win the PGA Senior Championship in 1954, 58. He is perhaps most famous for his double eagle on the 15th hole at the Augusta National in the 1935 Masters. He needed three birdies to tie leader Craig Wood in the last round when he knocked the ball in on the 15th with a four wood. He won the tournament. He is one of only four golfers in history to have won the U.S. and British Opens, the Masters, and the PGA Championship. He has always worn knickers on the course. A fast player, Sarazen, with George Fazio, played the final round of the 1947 Masters in 1 hour and 57 minutes; Sarazen scored a 70. He officially retired from tournament golf at the 1973 British Open, where he scored a hole-in-one on Troon's 126-yard 8th hole. He still plays, while dividing his time between his Florida and upper New York State homes.

SARGENT, GEORGE B. 1880, Dorking, England. D. 6/18/62, Atlanta, Ga. Sargent, winner of the 1909 USGA Open, served as assistant to Harry Vardon in England before emigrating to the U.S. In 1912 he won the Canadian Open with 295, the first in that championship to break 300. He served as third president of the Professional Golfers' Association, from 1921-26. In that position he raised $10,000 in 1921 through *Golf Illustrated* magazine to send 10 U.S. professionals to play in Britain. He was also the organizer of the PGA Senior Championship. In 1930 he introduced the use of motion pictures for golf instruction, using Harry Vardon and Bobby Jones as models.

SARGENT, HAROLD B. 1913, Bethesda, Md. An active PGA official, Harold Sargent served as the organization's vice president, secretary, and, from 1958-60, president. He was also chairman of the PGA Ryder Cup Committee from 1958-65. During his term as PGA president, he remodeled the PGA merchandise program and signed its first TV contract. He is the son of former PGA president George Sargent. Sargent is currently a golf professional at the Atlanta Athletic Club.

SCHLEE, JOHN B. 6/2/39, Kremling, Colo. 6'3", 165. Schlee turned professional in 1964 and was graduated valedictorian of the first PGA qualifying school in late 1965. He was Rookie of the Year in 1966, winning $21,442 and finishing the year in 47th place. Despite consistent play, Schlee has won only one tournament, the 1973 Hawaiian Open. Also in 1973, he lost the Kaiser Open in a playoff to Ed Sneed and was runner-up in the USGA Open. He is very interested in astrology. His career earnings were $409,677 through 1975.

SCHROEDER, JOHN B. 11/12/45, Great Barrington, Mass. 5'10", 160. Schroeder turned pro in 1966, joined the tour in 1969, and was the surprise winner of the 1973 U.S. Match Play event. He finished 42nd in money winnings for that year. His career earnings through 1975 were $204,811. John is the son of tennis professional Ted Schroeder.

SCOTT, LADY MARGARET B. 1875. D. 1938. One of the first women players to emerge in British golf. Lady Margaret won the first British Ladies' Championship, played in 1893. She won again in 1894, 95, and then retired from competition.

SEAGLE, JANET B. 3/29/24, Spokane, Wash. Miss Seagle is the librarian and museum curator for the United States Golf Association. In her keeping are the records of all acquisitions in the library, museum, and film collections of the USGA. Miss Seagle is also the art editor for the organization's publications. Operating at Golf House, the USGA's home in Far Hills, N.J., she is a veritable gold mine of information about everything in her custody.

SEITZ, NICHOLAS JOSEPH B. 1/30/39, Topeka, Kans. Seitz, who had been 10 years in the newspaper business, went to work for *Golf Digest* magazine in 1968. In 1972 he was made its editor. He plays a good game of golf, with a handicap of 12. He won low net in the 1974 World Cup Pro-Amateur and has been included in the E. P. Dutton annual *Best Sports Stories* several times. Seitz also enjoys tennis, which he says is "legitimate" now, since the *New York Times*, which bought *Golf Digest* in 1969, also publishes *Tennis* magazine.

SEMPLE, CAROL KEISTER B. 10/27/48, Sewickley, Pa. Carol Semple won the 1973 USGA Women's Amateur, was runner-up in the event in 1974, and won the 1974 British Women's Amateur. In the final of the USGA Amateur, Miss Semple defeated Mrs. Anne Quast Sander, 1 up, and in the British final she downed Angela Bonallack, 2 and 1. She was a member of the 1974 U.S. World Amateur team and of the 1974 Curtis Cup team. She was runner-up in the National Women's Collegiate Championship in 1968, winner of the Western Pennsylvania Women's Championship in 1965, 67, 71, 73, and a member of the Women's Western Golf Association board. She is the daughter of USGA president, Harton Semple.

SEMPLE, HARTON B. 12/19/20, New York, N.Y. Harton Semple was president of the United States Golf Association in 1974-75 and chairman of its Management Committee. He formerly served the USGA as general counsel and as chairman of the Rules, Amateur Status, and Bob Jones Award Committees and as a member of the Championship, Sectional Affairs, Finance, and Implements and Balls Committees. He was co-chairman of the USGA Women's Championship in 1954, 66 and is a member of the Masters tournament Rules Committee. He was also president of the Pennsylvania Golf Association in 1965, president of the Western Pennsylvania Golf Association in 1958, a member of the Western Pennsylvania Sports Hall of Fame, director of the International Mixed Four-Ball Championship Association, and a member of the Yale golf team 1939-42. He has won many local tournaments, including the Hot Springs, Va., three times; the Sea Island Championship four times, and the Wilcoma Cup (Hot Springs) 11 times. He qualified for the USGA Amateur in 1947, 48, 49, 51, 56, 60, 61, 62. His wife was runner-up in the 1974 USGA Senior Women's, and his daughter Carol was a U.S. and British Amateur champion.

SHARKEY, HAROLD S. (Hal) B. 6/2/1895, Plainfield, N.J. D. 3/27/39, Montclair, N.J. Sharkey was, in a way, the original organizer of the PGA tour. He started covering golf for the *Newark (N.J.) Evening News* in 1920 and for health reasons took leaves of absence during the winter months and spent them in California. Most of the pros were congregating there too, and Sharkey began rounding up chambers of commerce and other organizations for tournament purses. Until he took charge, tournaments were hit-or-miss propositions, the pros seldom knowing much in advance about a tournament —if it would be played, where, or whether they would get paid. Sharkey gradually worked out a schedule for them, the first they ever had. He had to give up this connection with the pros when he became sports editor of the *News* in 1933, a position he held until his death.

SHARP, WILLIAM W., JR. (Bill) B. 7/12/08, Madison, N.C. D. 12/14/74, Greensboro, N.C. A former professional baseball player, Sharp became president of the National Association of Left-Handed Golfers in 1936, organized its 27 divisions in the U.S. and Canada, and promoted its three major annual events. In 1955, he was made the Association's executive vice president, a position he held till death. He was also owner and manager of a hosiery company and a colonel in the National Guard.

SHAW, ROBERT (Bob) B. 12/24/44, Sydney, Australia. 6'0", 200. Bob Shaw turned pro in 1965 and joined the U.S. tour in 1969. Since then, he has divided his time between the U.S. and world circuits. His victories include the 1972 Tallahassee Open in U.S. and the 1968 New Zealand PGA Championship.

SHAW, THOMAS (Tom) B. 12/13/42, Wichita, Kans. 5'10", 180. Tom Shaw turned pro and joined the tour in 1963, after graduating from the University of Oregon. He was a streak player whose best years were 1969, when he won the Doral and Avco Opens and finished 16th in the top money winners with $83,332; and 1971, when he won the Crosby and Hawaiian Opens and finished the year 15th with $96,220. Shaw broke his back in a car accident on his way to the Bob Hope Classic in 1966, and it took him until 1969 to come back from that. He has been struggling for a comeback during the last few years, with limited success. His career earnings through 1975 were $327,478.

SHEPARD, ALAN B., JR. B.11/18/23, East Derry, N.H. An Apollo 14 astronaut, he was the first man to drive a golf ball on the moon, on February 6, 1971. He used a ball he had smuggled into space and a six iron head he had secretly put on his moon pick. Shepard undoubtedly had the greatest "gallery" of anyone who ever struck a golf ball, for television sets all over the world were tuned in on the moon landing.

SHUTE, HERMAN DENSMORE (Denny) B. 10/25/04, Cleveland, O. D. 5/13/74, Akron, O. 5'10½", 190. Shute took up golf at age 3 and turned pro in 1928. A consistent winner on the PGA circuit, he won the PGA Championship in 1936, 37 and was the last golfer to win it two years in a row. He was excellent in match play and on the green. In 1933 he won the British Open with 73-73-73-73, defeating Craig Wood with a 74 in a playoff. He lost the 1939 USGA Open in a playoff and was runner-up in that tournament in 1941. In 1937 he lost to Henry Cotton, 6 and 5, for 72 holes in a challenge for the unofficial world title. The favorite shot of his career was a three wood off the 18th fairway at Pinehurst in the final of the 1936 PGA Championship; the shot stopped four feet from the pin to give Shute an eagle and a win. He tied for second in the 1955 PGA Senior. He served as pro at the Portage C.C., Akron, Ohio, from 1948 till his retirement in 1971, and was elected to the PGA Hall of Fame in 1957.

SIDEROWF, RICHARD B. 7/3/37, New Britain, Conn. A consistent amateur player, he has won over two dozen titles in his career, including the 1973 British Amateur, 1971 Canadian Amateur, and 1961 New England Amateur. He was low amateur in the 1968 USGA Open. He was a member of the U.S. Walker Cup team in 1969, 73, 75 and a member of the U.S. World Cup team in 1968. In 1975 he won the Gold Key Award. He is currently a stockbroker in Connecticut.

SIFFORD, CHARLES B. 6/2/22, Charlotte, N.C. 5'7", 185. Sifford turned pro in 1944, joined the PGA tour in 1954, and was the first black to achieve success on the PGA circuit with his 1967 Hartford Open win. Prior to going on the PGA circuit, he played the Negro United Golfers' Association tour and was singer Billy Eckstine's private golf tutor from 1947-52. A cigar is his trademark. He won the 1969 Los Angeles Open and became the first black to win the PGA Senior Championship, in 1975 in a sudden death playoff. Sifford won $334,964 through 1974 on the PGA tour and in 1975 signed as club pro at Sleepy Hollow G. & C.C. in Cleveland, Ohio.

SIKES, DANIEL (Dan) B. 12/7/30, Jacksonville, Fla. 6'1½", 195. The pro tour's only practicing lawyer, Sikes is a member of the Florida Bar Association and a 1953 graduate of the University of Florida Law School. He won the 1955 All-Army Championship and the 1958 USGA Public Links. In 1960 he turned pro and in 1961 joined the PGA tour, at the age of 30. A long hitter, he has won six pro events: the 1963 Doral, the 1965 Cleveland, the 1967 Jacksonville and Philadelphia, the 1968 Florida Citrus and Minnesota. He was a member of the 1969 Ryder Cup team. His best overall year was 1967 with two victories, one runner-up, and earnings of $111,508 for a fifth place finish. His career earnings through 1975 were $773,508.

SIKES, RICHARD H. B. 3/6/40, Paris, Ark. 6'1", 150. Sikes won the USGA Public Links Championship in 1961, 62, carrying his own bag. In 1963, he won the NCAA Championship and was runner-up in the USGA Amateur. He turned pro in 1964 and was named Rookie of the Year. He's won two tournaments, the 1964 Sahara and the 1966 Cleveland Open. 1966 was his best money year, finishing eighth with $67,348. He was in the top 60 money winners, 1964-70. Now he plays less frequently; he has career earnings totaling over $300,000.

SIMONS, JAMES B. (Jim) B. 5/15/50, Tequesta, Fla. 5'10", 175. A top junior and amateur player, he lost the 1971 British Amateur to Steve Melnyk in the final. He was low amateur in the 1971 USGA Open, leading for three rounds, and finishing tied for fifth. At 21, he was the youngest member of the 1971 Walker Cup team. While attending Wake Forest, he was All-American in 1971, 72. Simons joined the PGA tour in 1972 after graduation from Wake Forest. While he has no victories yet, 1975 was his best season, finishing 50th in money winnings with $47,724.

SKALA, CAROLE JO KABLER B. 6/13/38, Eugene, Ore. Carole Jo Skala won the USGA Junior Girls' Championship in 1955 and made the semifinals in the USGA Women's Amateur in 1957. She is a seven-time winner of the Oregon State Championship (1955-61) and winner of many other amateur events. She graduated from Portland State, is married to an eye surgeon and is now mother of three; she and her family live off the fifth fairway at the Cameron Park C.C. in Sacramento, and her husband Michael was general chairman of the Sacramento Union Classic, played there in 1974, which Carole Jo won. She turned pro in 1970 and has played on a limited schedule.

In 1973 she won the George Washington Classic; in 1974 the Sacramento Union, the Peter Jackson, the Wheeling Ladies, and $47,691 (eighth top money winnings) for her best year on the tour. In 1975, with no wins, she finished 13th in money with $29,493.

SLINGERLAND, GEORGE B. 3/10/04, Brooklyn, N.Y. From the Bay Ridge section of Brooklyn, where he caddied at the old Marine and Field Club, Slingerland went all the way to Georgia to win a tournament on the PGA tour. That was the Southeastern PGA Open, which he won in 1935 with a score of 294. This was 4 shots better than Tony Manero, who won the USGA Open the following year. Henry Picard was third. Slingerland was the pro at the Greensboro Country Club for 18 years and while there established the Greensboro Open, still a regular tour stop, when one of his club members put up a purse of $5,000. The purse at the Greater Greensboro in 1976 was $230,000. In 1938 Slingerland organized the Carolinas PGA. George later moved to New Jersey, where he still teaches.

SMITH, ALEX B. 1872, Carnoustie, Scotland. D. 4/20/30, Baltimore, Md. He came to the United States in 1898 and was one of the more versatile pros of his time as a player, clubmaker, greenskeeper, and teacher. He won the USGA Open in 1906, defeating his brother Willie by 7 strokes. He won that event again in 1910, defeating brother Macdonald and Johnny McDermott in a playoff. A fast player, his other victories included the 1903 and 1906 Western Open. Smith was the first to break 300 in the USGA Open when he won in 1906 with 295. He was much admired as an instructor. His pupils included Glenna Collett and Jerome Travers. Alex was elected to the PGA Hall of Fame in 1940.

SMITH, HORTON (The Joplin Ghost) B. 5/22/08, Springfield, Mo. D. 10/15/ 63, Detroit, Mich. An excellent putter, Horton was one of the major figures of his day, winning 29 PGA tournaments in his career, after turning pro in 1926. He won the French Open on his 20th birthday. In 1929, he won eight tournaments in and out of the U.S. and was top money winner for the year. He won four tournaments in 1930. He continued to be a top player into the 1940s, finishing 10th in money in 1939, 40; 8th in 1941. Smith won the first Masters tournament in 1934 and won again in 1936. He was a member of the Ryder Cup team in 1929, 33, 35 and was elected to the PGA Hall of Fame in 1958. He was president of the PGA in 1952, 53, 54 and honorary president in 1955. He died of Hodgkin's disease which he'd had for six years; he collapsed while watching Ryder Cup matches. Since 1964 a trophy has been given in his name by the PGA to the professional who has made the most outstanding contribution to golf professional education.

SMITH, KENNETH B. 4/27/01, Westport, Mo. Smith got his start in clubmaking at age 16, while still in high school, working at the Mission Hills C.C. in Kansas City. He continued through college and, after doing work for area pros, made the first Kenneth Smith clubs in 1925. He started in the custom club business in 1927 on a full-time basis and got a big break when Horton Smith (no relation) used his clubs to become the top U.S. money winner in 1928-29. Working out of a Kansas City plant that has its own golf course for employees, he has made about two million clubs, all custom made, to nine base measurements.

SMITH, LOMA MOULTON (Mrs. Hulet P.) B. 8/15/13, Pasadena, Cal. Loma Smith took up golf in 1944 after winning four U.S. National Badminton titles and being elected to that sport's Hall of Fame. She has won many California golf titles including the 1958 Southern California Championship and the 1964, 65 USGA Senior Women's titles of which she was runner-up in 1967, 68. She is a member of the Northern California Golf Association Rating Committee.

SMITH, MACDONALD (Mac) B. 1880, Carnoustie, Scotland. D. 8/31/49. Glendale, Cal. A member of a famous golfing family, he won many tournaments but never a national. He was the youngest brother of Willie and Alex who came to the U.S. in the early 1900s. In 1910 he lost the Open to brother Alex in a playoff. In 1930 he finished second to Bobby Jones in the Open, the year of Jones's Grand Slam. He was runner-up in the British Open in 1930, 32. In 1925 Smith went into the last round of the British Open with a 5-stroke lead and took an 82 and lost the tournament; he blamed the loss on distractions of a very unruly gallery. Smith won many tournaments in the U.S. including the Western Open in 1912, 25, 33 and the Los Angeles Open in 1928, 29, 32, 34. He was sometimes known as the "Silent Scot," probably partly because of his personality and partly due to a hearing injury sustained during World War I. Smith had one of the smoothest swings the game has ever known and never took a divot with his iron shots. He was voted into the PGA Hall of Fame in 1954.

SMITH, MARGARET (Wiffi) B. 9/28/36, Redlands, Cal. 5'6", 160. Wiffi Smith learned to play golf in Mexico, where she moved at age 11, and won the Women's Championship of Mexico in 1952 at age 16. She won the USGA Junior Girls' Championship in 1954, the World Women's Amateur in 1955, the British and French Women's Amateur in 1956, and the Trans-Mississippi in 1956. A long and accurate hitter, she played on the 1956 Curtis Cup team. She turned pro and was runner-up in the 1957 Ladies' PGA Championship and won the 1957 Dallas Open.

SMITH, MARILYNN LOUISE B. 4/13/29, Topeka, Kans. 5'8", 142. She won the Women's Intercollegiate tournament in 1949, turned pro, and joined the LPGA tour later that year. She has won 22 LPGA tournaments and been a consistent performer through the years. Her first victory was the Fort Wayne Open in 1954, and her most recent was the Pabst Classic in 1972. She also won the Titleholders Championship in 1963, 64. Her best year was 1963, with four tournament victories and a third-place money finish. Her best money year was 1972 when she finished eighth and won $29,910. A very personable golfer, Marilynn Smith frequently gives clinics around the country and was selected as a member of the President's Physical Fitness Council. She was president of the LPGA in 1958, 59, 60.

SMITH, WILLIAM (Willie) B. c.1875, Carnoustie, Scotland. D. 1915, Mexico City, Mexico. Willie Smith won the 1899 USGA Open by 11 strokes, the largest margin in the history of the tournament. He also won the first Western Open in 1899. He served as pro at the Mexico City Country Club, one of the first courses in that country, from 1907 till his death in 1915. Willie was a younger brother of Alex Smith, and together they are the only brothers ever to win the United States Open Championship.

SNEAD, JESSE CARLYLE (J.C.) B. 10/14/41, Hot Springs, Va. 6'2", 200. After a try at a career in baseball, Sam Snead's nephew turned golf pro in 1964 and joined the PGA tour in 1968, after twice failing the PGA qualifying school. He's had a very successful career since he broke through in 1971. He won the Tucson and Doral Opens that year, the Philadelphia Classic in 1972, and the San Diego in 1975, the latter in a playoff. He was runner-up in the 1973 Masters and played on the U.S. Ryder Cup team in 1971, 73, 75. He was in the top 25 money winners in 1971, 72, 73, 74, 75. His best money year was 1974; he had no wins but won $164,486 and finished eighth in rankings. He had career earnings through 1975 of $530,692. In early 1976, he won the Williams-San Diego Open.

SNEAD, SAMUEL JACKSON (Sam) B. 5/27/12, Hot Springs, Va. 5'11", 185. One of golf's all-time greats and probably the longest-lived successful career in the sport. Snead has a picture-perfect swing and is amazingly limber even in his 60s, often proving it by kicking his foot up to the ceiling to show his agility. He has won 84 PGA tournaments since he joined the pro tour in 1937, far more than anyone else. He is believed to have hit over 1.6 million golf balls in over 10,000 rounds played and has been credited with 134 total tournament wins. His many tournament victories include the Masters in 1949, 52, 54; the PGA Championship in 1942, 49, 51; and the British Open in 1946. He is still trying for his first USGA Open win, although he placed second four times. He was the top PGA money winner in 1938, 49, 50, and Vardon Trophy winner in 1938, 49, 50, 55, with his scoring average of 69.23 in 1950 still a record; he is co-holder of PGA scoring records for 18 holes— 60, and 36 holes—126, and the oldest man to win a PGA event, the 1965 Greater Greensboro Open at age 52. He also holds the record for the most wins in a single event, eight in the Greater Greensboro between 1938-65. In 1953 he was elected to the PGA Hall of Fame. He was a member of the U.S. Ryder Cup team in 1937, 47, 49, 51, 53, 55, 59; playing captain in 1959 and non-playing captain in 1969. He was on the U.S. Canada Cup (now World Cup) team in 1956, 60, 61, all winning years for the U.S., and won the individual title in 1961. Snead is known worldwide for his straw hat. He still plays golf almost daily and is known to be willing to play with anyone anytime, if the money is right. His major problem over the years has been his putting. He still competes periodically on the PGA tour, playing against pros young enough to be his grandsons and occasionally topping them, as in his tie for second in the 1974 Los Angeles Open. He had career earnings of $611,886 through 1975, although most of his play was in days when purses were very small. Sam is also an active senior competitor. He won the PGA Senior Championship in 1964, 65, 67, 70, 72, 73 and the World Senior Championship in 1964, 65, 70, 72, 73. In 1959 Snead shot a 59 at Greenbrier, the lowest recorded score made on a standard-size course.

SNEED, EDGAR (Ed) B. 8/6/44, Columbus, O. 6'2", 190. Ed Sneed graduated from Ohio State in 1967 after being the top player on the school's golf team. He joined the pro tour in 1969, taking it on full-time in 1971. He has won the 1973 Kaiser Open in a sudden-death playoff and the 1974 Milwaukee Open. In the latter, he led all four rounds. He had no wins in 1975 but he still earned $46,634. His career earnings through 1975 were $191,113.

SOLHEIM, KARSTEN B. c. 1910. Solheim designed the forerunner of the current heel-and-toe-weighted investment cast clubs in 1954 as a special putter with an enlarged sweet spot. In 1959 he began to manufacture and sell them on a small scale as the Ping Putter, while still employed as a mechanical engineer for General Electric. Later he formed the successful Karsten Manufacturing Company. He continues to produce clubs and now sponsors the LPGA Karsten-Ping Championship.

SOMERVILLE, CHARLES ROSS (Sandy) B. 5/4/03, London, Ontario, Canada. Somerville was the first Canadian to win the USGA Amateur, in 1932. He defeated Jesse Guilford in the semifinal, 7 and 6, and Johnny Goodman in the final, 2 and 1. He is a six-time Canadian Amateur Champion and was runner-up four times. He won the Canadian Senior Championship twice and was joint holder of the title twice. In 1957 he was president of the Royal Canadian Golf Association.

SOMMERS, ROBERT T. B. 8/6/26, Baltimore, Md. Sommers is the public information director of the United States Golf Association. He is a graduate of the University of Maryland and served in the Coast Guard during World War II. Prior to coming to the USGA Sommers worked in the sports departments of the *Baltimore Sun* and the *Washington Star* and covered all sports, including golf. He came to the USGA in 1966. Before becoming information director he was the editor of *The Golf Journal*, the organization's monthly magazine.

SORENSON, CAROL (Mrs. William Flenniken) B. 11/15/42, Janesville, Wisc. Carol Sorenson took up golf at age 6. She won the Women's Western

Junior Championship and the USGA Junior Girls' Championship in 1960 at age 17. In 1960 she won the Women's National Collegiate, while attending Arizona State, and the Western Amateur in 1962. In 1964 she won the British Women's Amateur and the Trans-Mississippi. She played on the U.S. Curtis Cup team in 1964, 66 and on the U.S. World Cup team in 1964. She currently lives in Colorado and plays in events there.

SOUCHAK, MICHAEL (Mike) B. 5/10/27, Berwick, Pa. 5'10", 200. After turning professional in 1952, Souchak became one of the top players of the decade. He won 16 PGA events, including three in 1955 and four in 1956. He was one of the top 10 money winners in 1955, 56, 59, 60, 64. He was a member of the Ryder Cup team in 1959, 61. He holds the PGA 72-hole scoring record of 257 (60-68-64-65) at Brackenridge Park C.C., San Antonio, in the 1955 Texas Open; the nine-hole record of 27 for the second nine of the first round in that event; and is co-holder of the 18-hole record of 60 for that round. In the 1960 Open, Souchak led the field after 54 holes but was overtaken when Arnold Palmer shot a 65 on the last round to Mike's 75. He comes from a football family; Mike once starred for Duke University and his brother Frank for Pittsburgh.

SPRAY, STEVEN (Steve) B. 12/16/40, Des Moines, Ia. 6'1", 170. Steve Spray joined the tour in 1965. His only win so far is the 1969 San Francisco Open. His career earnings through 1975 were around $140,000.

SPUZICH, SANDRA ANN B. 4/3/37, Indianapolis, Ind. 5'6". A former bowler who bowled a 289 game at age 17. She took up golf at age 16, graduated from the University of Indiana in 1959 with a degree in physical education, and turned pro in 1962. Sandra won four tournaments through 1975—the 1966 Haig & Haig, 1968 Buckeye, 1966 USGA Open, and 1974 Lady Tara. In the 1966 Open, she defeated Carol Mann by 1 stroke to win; in the 1970 Open, she lost by 1 stroke to Donna Caponi Young. Her best money year was 1974, when she won $33,645 for 14th place and had 20 finishes in the top 20.

STACKHOUSE, WILBURN ARTIST (Lefty) B. 1911, Oklahoma. D. 12/3/73, Seguin, Tex. One of the more colorful personalities in golfing history, Stackhouse played the pro tour in the 1930s and 1940s but never met with much success. He did once defeat Byron Nelson in an exhibition. He was known more for his drinking prowess, his short temper, club-breaking, and other eccentricities. He was a promoter of junior golf.

STACY, HOLLIS B. 3/16/54, Savannah, Ga. Stacy won the 1969, 70, 71 USGA Junior Girls' Championships, a record number of victories in that event. She won the 1970 North and South and played on the 1972 U.S. Curtis Cup team. She dropped out of Rollins College to turn pro in 1974, playing in 12 LPGA events, with her best finish being a tie for second in the

Bill Branch Classic. In 1975, she won $14,409 in official earnings. She finished second in the rich Japan Classic and picked up $11,000 more.

STADLER, CRAIG B. 6/2/53, San Diego, Cal. 5'10", 210. Stadler won the 1971 World Junior Championship. His major victory, however, was the 1973 USGA Amateur. In the final he defeated David Strawn, 6 and 5. This was the year the USGA returned the Amateur Championship to match play after eight years of stroke play. In the semifinal he ousted Vinny Giles, the defending champion, 3 and 1. As a student at the University of Southern California, he was a 1973, 74 All-American, winning 11 college tournaments from 1971-74. He also won the 1974 Guadalajara Invitational and finished sixth in the 1974 Los Angeles Open. In 1975 he was a member of the Walker Cup team. In late 1975, he failed to qualify for the PGA tour in the year's qualifying school.

STANDISH, JAMES D. B. 5/30/1891, Detroit, Mich. D. 5/2/67, Detroit, Mich. One of golf's most active boosters, Standish was president of the United States Golf Association from 1952-57. He was a member of the USGA Executive Committee from 1921-27 and from 1946-51, and chairman of the first USGA Public Links Committee, which started the annual championship. He donated the individual cup which bears his name. Investment broker by profession, he was also president of the Intercollegiate Golf Association in 1912-13, vice president of the Western Golf Association from 1923-25, and president of the Detroit District Golf Association from 1935-46. A good amateur golfer as well, he won the Michigan Amateur Championship in 1909, 12, 15, 24; the Austrian Amateur in 1907, 08; and the North and South Amateur in 1909.

STEELSMITH, JERRY B. 11/26/35, Peoria, Ill. He turned pro in 1957 and often finished in the money in the early 1960s. He won the 1961 Hesperia Open, the 1962 Azalea Open, and the 1963 Frank Sinatra Open.

STEPHENSON, JAN B. 12/22/51, Sydney, Australia. After winning the new South Wales Junior Championship four times, and the Australian Junior three times, Miss Stephenson turned pro in 1972 and played the Australian LPGA tour in 1973 before joining the U.S. tour full-time. She won the Australian LPGA title in 1973 by 5 strokes and won four other events. In 1974 she was named Rookie of the Year on the U.S. tour, and it was only a question of when she would win in the U.S. She settled that by winning twice in 1976, taking the Sarah Coventry in February and the Birmingham in April, the latter by four shots.

STETSON, MRS. HELEN B. 9/23/1887, Media, Pa. A top Philadelphia area golfer, she won the USGA Women's Amateur in 1926 and was a semifinalist in 1928. She also won the 1926 Women's Eastern. Beginning in 1915, Mrs.

178

Stetson was a major factor in local women's golf, winning numerous local titles, including the Whitemarsh Cup in 1925, 27, 33, 34, 36, 37 and the Philadelphia Women's Championship in 1924, 28. She represented the Huntingdon Valley C.C. in interclub matches for over 30 years. She was a member of the Executive Committee of the Women's Golf Association of Philadelphia from 1929-33. Her father-in-law was the founder of Stetson Hats. Never an active senior competitor, she got involved in racing homing pigeons in later years. She still lives in Philadelphia, but no longer plays golf.

STEWART, EARL, JR. B. 10/15/21, Dallas, Tex. 5'10", 153. Stewart won the 1941 NCAA Championship and served in the Army Air Corps in World War II. He turned pro in 1950 and won the 1953 Greensboro Open in a four-way playoff with Sam Snead, Doug Ford, and Art Wall. He won the 1953 Ardmore Open and the 1961 Dallas Open at Oak Cliff G.C. Also at Oak Cliff, he had two holes-in-one in the same nine-hole round in 1955.

STILL, KENNETH ALLAN (Ken) B. 2/12/35, Tacoma, Wash. 6'1", 170. Ken Still turned pro in 1953 at age 18 but didn't join the PGA tour until 1960. An avid sports fan, he has a special fondness for baseball, which he follows closely. He has three tournament wins: the 1969 Florida Citrus, 1969 Milwaukee, and 1970 Kaiser, the latter in a sudden death play-off. In 1969 he was a member of the Ryder Cup team. 1974 was the first year in nine that he failed to finish in the top 60 money winners; he also fell below that in 1975. He has career earnings through 1975 of $453,140.

STOCKTON, DAVID (Dave) B. 11/2/41, San Bernardino, Cal. 5'11½", 185. Dave Stockton learned golf from his father, Gail, and as an amateur he won 14 tournaments which his father had also won. A college All-American at the University of Southern California, he turned pro in 1964 and has been one of the tour's top players since. He's been in the top 40 every year since 1967. He has won 10 tournaments, including the 1967 Colonial and Haig; the 1968 Cleveland and Milwaukee; the 1970 PGA Championship; the 1971 Massachusetts; the 1972 Milwaukee; and the 1974 Glen Campbell-Los Angeles, Quad Cities, and Sammy Davis Hartford. In his PGA victory he nosed out Arnold Palmer and Bob Murphy, who tied for second. He was a member of the 1971 Ryder Cup team and is a two-time winner of the televised CBS Classic, with Al Geiberger. He tied for second in the 1974 Masters. He doesn't have a picture swing but is usually a strong clutch putter. His career earnings through 1975 were $815,483.

STONE, ELIZABETH (Beth) B. 5/15/40, Harlingen, Tex. She was the first girl to earn a varsity letter at the University of Oklahoma for being on the men's golf team; she attended the school on a golf scholarship. She turned pro in 1961 and has been a steady player but has had no wins. She's been active in the LPGA and served as its treasurer. She tied for runner-up in the

USGA Open in 1967, 74. She and Susie Maxwell were two shots behind Catherine Lacoste in 1967, and she and Carol Mann finished 1 stroke behind Sandra Haynie in 1974. Her best money year was 1973 with $22,842.

STRANAHAN, FRANK R. B. 8/5/22, Toledo, O. 5'10", 175. One of the country's top amateur players, he won the 1948, 50 British Amateurs, and was top amateur in the British Open in 1947, 49, 50, 51, 53 (runner-up in 1947, 53). He won the Tam O' Shanter All-American Amateur in 1948, 49, 50, 51, 52, 53. His best amateur year was 1948, when he won the British, Canadian, Mexican, Brazilian, North and South, and All-American Amateurs, plus the Delaware, Ohio, and Miami Opens. He played on the 1947, 49, 51 Walker Cup teams. He turned pro in 1954 and won the 1955 Eastern Open and the 1958 Los Angeles Open. Stranahan's strongest bid for the USGA Amateur came in 1950, when he lost the final to Sam Urzetta on the 39th hole. He is an avid weight lifter.

STRANGE, CURTIS NORTHRUP B. 1/30/55, Norfolk, Va. Chandler Harper was instrumental in developing his game. Strange was awarded the Arnold Palmer golf scholarship to Wake Forest. As a freshman at Wake Forest, he led the team to the 1974 NCAA Championship and won individual honors, with a 65 in the third round that tied the NCAA record. Other amateur victories include the 1973 Southeast Amateur, 1974 Western Amateur, 1975 North and South Amateur, and Eastern Amateur (the latter won by his late father in 1957). He was a member of the 1975 U.S. Walker Cup team and the 1974 World Cup team.

STREIT, MARLENE STEWART B. 3/9/34, Cereal, Alberta, Canada. 5'1", 115. A top Canadian woman amateur who won the Canadian Women's Open in 1951, 54, 55, 56, 58, 59, 63. She won the USGA Women's Amateur in 1956 and was low amateur in the 1961 Women's Open. She defeated JoAnne Gunderson, 2 and 1, in the U.S. Amateur. She won the British Women's Amateur in 1953, the Australian Women's Amateur in 1963, and the World Women's Amateur in 1966. In 1956, the year she graduated from Rollins College in Florida, she won seven tournaments. She was named Canadian Woman Athlete of the Year in 1951, 53, 56, 60, 63; and Canadian Outstanding Athlete of the Year in 1951, 56. In 1962 she was elected to the Canadian Sports Hall of Fame.

SUGGS, LOUISE B. 9/7/23, Atlanta, Ga. 5'5½", 132. A top amateur player who won the 1947 USGA Women's Amateur and the 1948 British Women's Amateur, plus three North and South Amateurs and three Western Amateurs. She was a member of the 1948 U.S. Curtis Cup team. She turned pro in 1948 and won four tournaments in her first two years on the tour. In 1961 she was elected to the LPGA Hall of Fame. One of golf's best players, Miss Suggs won 50 LPGA events, including the 1949, 52 USGA Women's Opens, the 1957 LPGA Championship, and the 1954, 56, 57 Titleholders Championship. She was the top LPGA money winner in 1953, 60. In 1957, she won the

Vare Trophy for her low scoring average. In 1966, she was the first woman elected to the Georgia Athletic Hall of Fame. She is now semi-retired.

SULLIVAN, CYNTHIA JAN (Silky) B. 9/15/37, Harrisburg, Pa. Although she never won an LPGA event, Miss Sullivan was important in developing the organization. She turned pro in 1959 after graduation from Coker College with a degree in social sciences. She served as LPGA president in 1969, 70, 72, 73 and devoted more of her time to the behind the scenes activity. She won a new car in the 1971 Sealy tournament for the closest-to-hole contest.

SULLIVAN, THOMAS DESMOND (Des) B. 2/28/13, Brooklyn, N.Y. Des Sullivan was the *Newark Evening News* golf reporter from 1944-69, and is now a columnist for the *Myrtle Beach, (S.C.) Sun-News*. He was president of the Golf Writers' Association of America in 1956-57 and winner of the Golf Writers' Association Championship in 1956, 68, 69, 71, 72, 73. He won the Carolinas Golf Association Senior Championship in 1973 and was low amateur in the Carolinas PGA Senior Open in 1973, 74. In 1975 Sullivan again won the Carolinas Senior title and was second low amateur in the Carolinas Senior Open, these after a second serious operation in January. He holds the amateur course record at the Essex Fells C.C. in New Jersey, a 64, and now plays to a handicap of 2.

SWEETSER, JESS W. B. 4/18/02, Cobb, Ky. A Yale graduate, he was one of the U.S. amateur stars during the 1920s. He won the 1920 Intercollegiate Championship and in 1922 won the USGA Amateur. He defeated his first four opponents by a total of 29 holes before beating the veteran Chick Evans in the final, 3 and 2. One of his victories was an 8-and-7 beating of Bobby Jones in the semifinal. In 1923 Sweetser went to the final again but lost to Max Marston. In 1926 Sweetser became the first native-born American to win the British Amateur. He played on the Walker Cup team six times, in 1922, 23, 24, 26, 28, 32, and was non-playing captain in 1967, 73, and non-playing captain of the 1966 U.S. World Amateur team. When he won the 1926 British Amateur he was suffering from the flu, an injured knee, and a wrist sprained during the semifinal. He managed to finish the tournament but was carried off the boat returning to the U.S. and put in an ambulance. It was more than a year before he could play tournament golf again. Sweetser was at his best in match play.

SYKES, GAIL (Mrs. Clayton) B. 3/22/48. The winner of the 1965 USGA Junior Girls' Championship. In 1968, she won the Women's National Collegiate Championship. She didn't participate in golf events for some years after college, but won the Ohio Women's Amateur in 1975.

SYMS, NANCY ROTH B. 3/30/39, Elkhart, Ind. This Colorado resident has won two dozen major amateur events, including the 1975 British Women's Amateur, where she defeated a 17-year-old girl in the final. Other victories include the Doherty Challenge Cup in 1963, 64, 66; the North and South in 1963, 66; the Southern Amateur in 1964, 66; the Eastern Women's Amateur in 1963, 64, 65; and the Broadmoor Invitational in 1972, 75. She was the medalist in the 1975 USGA Women's Amateur and was a member of the Curtis Cup team in 1964, 66.

TAIT, FREDERICK GUTHRIE B. 1/11/1870, Edinburgh, Scotland. D. 2/7/ 1900, South Africa. Tait, a personable golfer, won the 1896 British Amateur but lost on the 37th hole of a playoff in the 1899 Amateur to John Ball. At age 20 he broke the St. Andrews' course record with a 77. He was killed in action in the Boer War. A Freddie Tait Cup is given annually in his honor to the best amateur in the South African Open. Tait was highly regarded as one of the best British amateurs of his day.

TALLMADGE, HENRY OVERING B. 10/3/1862, Westchester, N.Y. D. 9/3/ 48, Bar Harbor, Me. One of the prime movers behind the growth of golf in the United States. He was one of the original "Apple Tree Gang" which founded the St. Andrews Golf Club in Yonkers, N.Y., in 1888. He was a prime organizer of the United States Golf Association, serving as its first secretary for three terms in 1894, 95, 96. He brought Willie Park Jr. to the U.S. in 1895 to play exhibitions and to help in laying out early courses. He was a member of the Sons of the American Revolution.

TAYLOR, JOHN HENRY (J.H.) B. 3/19/1871, North Devon, England. D. 2/ 10/63, Devonshire, England. One of Britain's great early golfers, Taylor was, along with Harry Vardon and James Braid, a member of what was called the "Great Triumvirate." They dominated golf at the turn of the century. A long driver, his favorite club was the mashie, which he popularized. He won the British Open in 1894, 95, 1900, 09, 13, and was runner-up five times, including a loss to Vardon in a playoff in 1896. He also was runner-up to Vardon in the 1900 USGA Open. He was founder and chairman, in 1901, of the first professional golfers' association. He had 10 holes-in-one during his career. He was a resident pro at Royal Mid-Surrey Golf Club for 47 years, retiring in 1946, and was elected to life membership in the Royal and Ancient Golf Club of St. Andrews in 1950.

TAYLOR, RICHARD STARK B. 1/22/25, Indianapolis, Ind. Dick Taylor is editor-in-chief and vice president of *Golf World*, which is the only golf news magazine that is published weekly and gives the complete scores of all the outstanding tournaments. Taylor worked on the *Palm Beach Post-Times* from 1948-62 when he joined *Golf World* as managing editor. In 1965 he was named editor-in-chief and in 1972 vice president. He has been secretary of the Golf Writers' Association of America from 1969, is a member of the British Golf Writers' Association, and is on the board of the National Golf

Day Fund. Taylor has a 12 handicap at his home course, Pine Needles Lodge and Country Club, Southern Pines, N.C.

THOMSON, JAMES (Jimmy) B. 10/29/08, North Berwick, Scotland. This long hitter was a frequent competitor in the 1920s and 1930s. He averaged 280 yards off the tee and was considered the longest driver of that era. In 1937 he hit a 386-yard drive from an elevated tee at Lookout Point C.C. He came to the U.S. from Scotland in 1920 and was a periodic winner, with victories including the 1927 Virginia Open and 1938 Los Angeles Open. He was runner-up in the 1936 Canadian Open and PGA Championship and once won $5,000 in an Australian Open. He was the No. 10 money winner on the PGA tour in 1937. Because of the length of his drives, he spent much of his time touring and giving exhibitions.

THOMSON, PETER W. B. 8/23/29, Melbourne, Australia. Australia's top golfer, he has won three Australian Opens and has distinguished himself in the British Open, winning in 1954, 55, 56, 58, 65 and runner-up in 1952, 57. He has also won nine New Zealand Opens over a 16-year period from 1950-65; three Hong Kong Opens; one German, Philippine, Spanish, and Italian Open; and two Indian Opens. He's won one event in the U.S., the 1956 Texas Open, during one of his brief visits to this country. He has been very outspoken on his preference for the shorter, but, to him, more challenging, courses of the United Kingdom to those of the United States. He won the World Cup with Kel Nagle in 1954, 59. Thomson has spent the past several years as an active proponent of a true world tour; as such, he spends a great deal of time playing tournaments in the Far East. One of golf's more literate personalities, he also writes a golf column for an Australian newspaper, often covering tournaments he is also playing in. Thomson's five British Open victories put him in a niche with J. H. Taylor and James Braid, one behind Harry Vardon.

THOMPSON, ALVIN CLARENCE (Titanic) B. 1892, Arkansas. D. 5/19/74, Euless, Tex. A legendary golf hustler, he was renowned for betting on anything, particularly in golf. His various stunts included sinking a 25-foot putt using his instep as a putter and throwing a playing card over a clubhouse roof. He was a left-hander. He was part of the poker game in progress when gambler Arnold Rothstein was shot and killed in New York. Reportedly he shot a caddie who once tried to rob him of substantial winnings. In later years he ran a driving range and restaurant in Texas.

THOMPSON, LEONARD B. 1/1/47, Laurinburg, N.C. 6'2", 200. Thompson joined the tour in 1972 on a full-time basis after playing on the Wake Forest golf team. He's had many high finishes in the past few years, with his only victory being the 1974 Gleason Inverrary, when he donated $10,000 of the $60,000 first prize to the Boys' Club of America. His best year was 1974, with earnings of $122,349 for 15th place. His career earnings through 1975 were $296,365.

TILLINGHAST, ALBERT WARREN (A.W.) B. 5/7/1875, Frankfort, Pa. D. 5/19/42, Toledo, O. An early amateur golfer, golf course architect, and golf writer. Tillinghast designed many great courses, including Winged Foot in Mamaroneck, N.Y.; the four courses at Bethpage, Long Island; and Baltusrol in New Jersey. He learned golf on a visit to Scotland in 1898. He wrote a syndicated feature on golf in the years before World War I and many articles later in his career and was editor of *Golf Illustrated* from 1933-35. He designed courses in the U.S., England, Scotland, Germany, and South America. One of his trademarks was small, tightly trapped greens. He was the consulting architect to the PGA from 1934-37; he visited over 700 courses during those years, giving advice. The PGA said he saved clubs $320,000 through his work. He said he recommended removal of 7,427 unnecessary sand traps.

TODD, HARRY B. 11/6/16, Dallas, Tex. One of the many fine players who have come out of Texas, Todd started as an amateur, and in the USGA Open of 1941 he was the low amateur in the field, tying for 13th place as Craig Wood won. In 1947, then a professional, Todd was tied for the lead after the first round of the Open, with a 67, but then slipped back. In 1946 Todd won the Orlando Open, his one victory on the tour.

TOLLEY, CYRIL JAMES HASTINGS B. 1896, London, England. Tolley was a successful British amateur contender in the 1920s and 1930s. He spent 13 months in a German POW camp during World War I. He won the British Amateur in 1920, 29, the Welsh Amateur in 1921, 23, and the French Open in 1924, 28. When Tolley won the British Amateur in 1920 he turned back a strong American threat, beating Bob Gardner in the final, on the 37th hole. In 1930 Tolley met Bobby Jones in the fourth round of the British Amateur, which was the first leg of Jones's Grand Slam. It was a close match all the way, with Jones finally winning when he laid Tolley a stymie on the 37th hole. He was a semifinalist in the British Amateur in 1950 at age 55. He was a member of the British Walker Cup team in 1922, 23, 24, 26, 30.

TOSKI, ROBERT (Bob) B. 9/18/27, Haydenville, Mass. 5'7", 135. Toski turned pro in 1945 and waited seven years for his first win. He won five PGA tournaments, four in 1954 when he was leading money-winner. One of his 1954 wins was the George S. May World Championship for a $50,000 first prize and $1,000 each for 50 guaranteed exhibitions during the year. He left the tour in 1957 after serving in 1955, 56 on the PGA Tournament Committee. Today Toski is one of the top teaching pros, giving lessons to men and women professionals as well as to club players. He estimates he has taught over 50,000 golfers. He's the author of *The Touch System for Better Golf.*

TRAVERS, JEROME D. (Jerry) B. 5/19/1887, New York, N.Y. D. 3/29/51, East Hartford, Conn. One of the top players of his day, he was one of only five amateurs in history to win the USGA Open, in 1915. He also won the USGA Amateur in 1907, 08, 12, 13. He played in his first Amateur in 1902, at age 15. Travers had a running competition with Walter Travis, which began when they faced off in the 1904 Nassau Invitation when Travers was only 17. Travers used Travis's trademark, the Schenectady putter, for the first time when the two met in the final of that tournament; Travers won on the third extra hole. He developed his game around the irons, even using them from the tee, and he was an excellent putter. After losing to Walter Travis in the 1915 Metropolitan Amateur, he decided not to play anymore, claiming it was impossible to make a living and compete in amateur golf. He did play in a series of benefit matches for the War Relief Fund in 1917 and later turned pro, but his game was not good enough to sustain a career. During the last 10 years of his life he was an inspector at Pratt & Whitney Aircraft. Travers was voted into the PGA Hall of Fame in the original group in 1940.

TRAVIS, WALTER J. (The Old Man) B. 1/10/1862, Malden, Victoria, Australia. D. 7/31/27, Denver, Colo. Travis got his nickname as a result of taking up golf in his 30s and winning the 1900 USGA Amateur at age 38. He also won the Amateur in 1901, 03 and was medalist in 1900, 01, 02, 06, 07, 08. He was the first foreign golfer to win the British Amateur, in 1904, at age 42, much to the dismay and humiliation of the British, who treated Travis coldly during and after the tournament. Travis used his famous Schenectady putter in that tournament, and the British ruled it illegal as a result, rescinding the ruling quite a bit later. Much embittered, Travis never returned to Britain, but continued winning tournaments in the U.S., his last recorded win being at age 54. Because he took up golf at a late age, he concentrated and practiced constantly on his short game and was said to virtually never miss a holeable putt. He was active in other areas of golf, including the founding and editing of the *American Golfer* magazine in 1905, one of the top early golf publications. He also designed golf courses and lost his amateur status in 1910 when the USGA ruled such activities illegal for amateurs. The decision was later rescinded, but Travis, angry, limited much of his subsequent tournament play to invitations and sectionals, rather than major tournaments, and was quite successful. He was generally a dour figure on the course, usually smoking a cigar, often bearded, and always a stickler for the rules. He once received a letter from President Taft, telling how much he enjoyed using the Schenectady putter and how much it helped his game. The Schenectady was a center-shafted putter with a mallet head, similar to many in common use today. Travis was named to the PGA Hall of Fame in 1940, along with his rival, Travers.

TREVINO, LEE B. 12/1/39, Dallas, Tex. 5'7", 180. One of the tour's most colorful players and also one of its top money winners. He turned pro in 1960 and played and hustled in Texas, doing things like hitting golf balls with soft drink bottles, until 1967 when he raised enough money to try the PGA tour. He placed fifth in the 1967 USGA Open but still was relatively unknown when he won the 1968 USGA Open for his first victory. He played 31 events that year, of which he won two and $132,127. His talkative, friendly manner won big galleries known as "Lee's Fleas." He has won 18 tournaments through 1975. His most astounding year was 1971 when he won five PGA events, including the USGA Open, defeating Jack Nicklaus in a play-off. He also won the British and Canadian Opens within four weeks, was named PGA Player of the Year, and AP Male Athlete of the Year, and was honored in El Paso by a crowd of 30,000 on Lee Trevino Day. Trevino also won the 1972 British Open and the Vardon Trophy in 1970, 71, 73. He was a member of the Ryder Cup team in 1969, 71, 73, 75 and played on the U.S. World Cup team in 1968, 69, 70, 71, 74 and was individual winner in 1969. Always willing to help out, he does many charity events and plays most of the year's PGA tour events. He won the 1974 World Series of Golf. The fastest ever to win $1 million on the PGA tour, he topped that figure by the end of his sixth full year. After a slump of 13 months, Trevino won the 1974 Greater New Orleans Open, the 1974 PGA Championship, and $203,442 to finish the year in fourth place. He was the No. 1 money-winner in 1970; No. 2 in 1971, 72; No. 4 in 1973, 74—winning over $200,000 per year in 1971, 72, 73, 74. He earned $134,206 in 1975, winning the Florida Citrus Open. His career earnings through 1975 were $1,398,651. He added the Colonial in early 1976, his first win in Texas.

TUFTS, JAMES WALKER B. 2/11/1835, Charlestown, Mass. D. 2/2/02, Pinehurst, N.C. Best known for the founding of Pinehurst, N.C. He developed the manufacture of soda fountain equipment in Boston. In 1891 his business consolidated with other firms to form the America Soda Fountain Co., the largest in the U.S. He purchased 5,000 acres in the North Carolina sandhills in 1895, for $1 per acre, to build a resort for people of modest means who needed the better climate. He opened the first nine holes of Pinehurst No. 1 course in 1898, the second nine holes in 1899. In December 1900 he employed Donald Ross as club pro, and in April 1901 he put on the first North and South Amateur Championship. This was followed by a North and South Open, which for many years was an annual stop for the touring pros, and a North and South Women's Amateur.

TUFTS, RICHARD SISE B. 3/16/1889, Medford, Mass. The grandson of Pinehurst's founder, he learned golf from Donald Ross and participated in running the resort from 1920-70, the last eight years as chairman. He built 40 new holes at Pinehurst and is an honorary member of the American Society of Golf Course Architects. He was active in the United States Golf Association, serving as its secretary, 1950-51; vice president, 1952-55; president, 1956-57. He was instrumental in writing the current rules of golf, and has served on more USGA committees than any other man: Green Section, Implements and Balls, Championship, Rules of Golf, Junior Championship, Handicap, and Senior Championship (serving as first chairman of the last three). He's the author of two golf books: *Principles Behind Rules of Golf* and *The Scottish Invasion.* He has been an officer of the Carolinas Golf Association, Southern Golf Association, U.S. Senior Golf Association, and American Senior Golf Association. His many honors include the USGA's Bob Jones Award in 1967 for distinguished sportsmanship; the Golf Writers'

1950 William Richardson Memorial Trophy for outstanding contributions to golf; the Atlantic Coast Sportswriters' Service to Sports Award, 1967; the American Senior G.A. Distinguished Senior Award, 1963; the Carolina Section PGA Outstanding Contribution to Golf Award, 1956; and his induction into the North Carolina and Southern Golf Associations' Halls of Fame. He was Walker Cup team non-playing captain in 1963.

TURNESA, JAMES (Jim) B. 12/9/12, Elmsford, N.Y. D. 8/27/71, Elmsford, N.Y. A member of a large golfing family, he turned pro in 1931. He won a variety of small tournaments including the 1951 Reading Open. His biggest victory was the 1952 PGA Championship; he was runner-up in 1942. In his PGA victory, Jim defeated Chick Harbert for the 1952 Championship, 1 up. In the 1942 final he was beaten by Sam Snead, 2 and 1. In 1953 he was a member of the U.S. Ryder Cup team.

TURNESA, JOSEPH (Joe) B. 1/21/01, Elmsford, N.Y. Another member of the golfing family who was a consistent money winner but who never won a national event. Joe was runner-up in the 1926 USGA Open and in the 1927 PGA Championship. He was a member of the U.S. Ryder Cup team in 1927, 29. For a time he putted one-handed. In the 1926 Open, Turnesa finished 1 stroke behind Bobby Jones, and in the 1927 PGA final he lost to Walter Hagen, 1 up.

TURNESA, WILLIAM P. (Willie) B. 1/20/14, Elmsford, N.Y. The youngest of seven golfing brothers and the only one to remain an amateur. He reached the top, too, winning the USGA Amateur in 1938, 48 and the British Amateur in 1947, a championship in which he was runner-up in 1949. He was a member of the Walker Cup team in 1947, 49, 51. Turnesa scored his 1938 Amateur victory over Pat Abbott in the final, 8 and 7, and in 1948 he defeated Ray Billows in the last round, 2 and 1. Among his many other tournament victories was the Metropolitan Amateur in 1937.

TUTHILL, JACK B. 7/14/24, Long Island, N.Y. Tuthill joined the Professional Golfers' Association in December 1960 and is the organization's current tournament director. He has also served as tournament coordinator and tournament supervisor. Prior to joining the PGA he also served as a special agent with the FBI and as a labor relations specialist in industry.

TUTWILER, EDGAR M., JR. B. 7/20/19, Mount Hope, W. Va. A consistent amateur contender who has won some events, including the 1962 Porter Cup. He was runner-up in the 1964 USGA Amateur. Tutwiler's opponent in the Amateur final was William C. Campbell, who had qualified for the championship 21 times but never won it. The two had met seven times in the West Virginia state tournaments, and Tutwiler had won six of them. This time Campbell won, 1 up. The following year the USGA switched the format of the Amateur to medal play for a period of eight years. He was a member of the Walker Cup team in 1965, 67.

UPDEGRAFF, DR. EDGAR R. B. 3/1/22, Boone, Ia. This top amateur competitor is a urologist in Tucson, Arizona. Many times a winner of the Arizona State Championship, he also won the 1957, 59 Western Amateur. He was a member of the Walker Cup team in 1963, 65, 69 and was non-playing captain in 1975. Updegraff was a member of the 1963 U.S. Americas Cup team and non-playing captain in 1967.

URZETTA, SAM B. 3/19/26, Rochester, N.Y. Urzetta had been a college basketball player and winner of N.Y. state golf tournaments when, in his third try, he won the 1950 USGA Amateur, defeating Frank Stranahan on the 39th hole. He played on the Walker Cup team in 1950, 53, and on the Americas Cup team in 1952. He turned pro in 1955 and has won some area tournaments.

VANDERBECK, MRS. CLARENCE H. B. May 1884. D. October 1935. She was the winner of the 1915 USGA Women's Amateur, defeating an English challenger, Mrs. William A. Gavin, in the final, 3 and 2. In the semifinal Mrs. Vanderbeck survived a 22-hole match to beat the rising Alexa Stirling, who won the title the next year. Mrs. Vanderbeck also won the qualifying medal. She was a consistent match player, reaching the Amateur semifinal in 1914, 15, 19, 20, 21, 23, 24. She won the Eastern in 1915, 21.

VAN DONCK, FLORY B. 6/23/12, Brussels, Belgium. Van Donck, a top international player, has won the Belgian Open five times, the Dutch Open five times, the Italian Open five times, and the Swiss and German Opens twice each. He has had other victories in Europe and South America and has represented Belgium on the Canada Cup team in 1954, 55, 56, 60. He was runner-up in the British Open in 1956, 59 and placed in the top 10 five times.

VAN WIE, VIRGINIA B. 2/9/09, Chicago, Ill. Miss Van Wie won the USGA Women's Amateur three times in a row, the fourth woman, and the last, to perform such a feat. She won in 1932, 33, 34—and then, at the top, she retired from tournament golf. She had a beautiful swing, which carried her to the finals two other years, 1928, 30. She was competing in an age of exceptionally fine players too, which only enhances her remarkable record. Both times that she lost in the final, her conqueror was Glenna Collett, and her victories in the final were over Glenna (then Mrs. Vare), Helen Hicks (the 1931 champion), and Dorothy Traung. In other matches, during her three-year reign, Miss Van Wie defeated such outstanding players as Charlotte Glutting, Mrs. Leona Pressler Cheney, British champion Enid Wilson, Edith Quier, and Rosalie Knapp. Her victory over Miss Collett in 1932 was

191

by a margin of 10 and 8. She played on the Curtis Cup teams of 1932, 34, and won the Chicago District G.A. Championship in 1926, 27, 28.

VARDON, HARRY B. 5/9/1870, Grouville, Isle of Jersey, England. D. 3/20/37, Totteridge, London, England. 5'9¼", 155. One of the greatest players in golf history and one of those most responsible for popularizing the game. As leading member of the "Great Triumvirate," with James Braid and J. H. Taylor, Vardon dominated the game in the late 19th century and early part of the 20th. He never took a lesson, but learned the game through caddying, which he started at age 7. He won six British Opens—still a record—in 1896, 98, 99, 1903, 11, 14. He was runner-up in that tournament four times, third twice, fourth once, and fifth four times. He won the USGA Open in 1900 and lost that tournament in a playoff in 1913. At age 50, in 1920, after two bouts with tuberculosis, he tied for second in the USGA Open. He was captain of Britain's first Ryder Cup team in 1921. He always wore knickerbockers and a jacket on the course, no matter what the weather. Vardon used very light clubs and was a great iron player, but a mediocre putter. He was known as a powerful, consistent, confident player. He popularized the overlapping grip, used by most golfers today and commonly known as the Vardon grip. He was a major factor in promoting golf in the U.S. through a tour in 1900 sponsored by A. G. Spalding Co., a tour during which he lost only one exhibition of dozens played. He wrote many books on golf throughout his long playing career, explaining his technique and containing photos of early sequence shots. Records on his total tournament wins do not exist, but a good guess is 62. It was reported that he once won 14 events in a row. He is honored today in the U.S. and Britain by each country's annual presentation, by their respective PGA's, of the Vardon Trophy for the lowest scoring average.

VARE, GLENNA COLLETT (Mrs. Edwin) B. 6/20/03, New Haven, Conn. One of golf's all-time greats and a dominating figure in the first third of the 20th century. She won the USGA Women's Amateur in 1922, 25, 28, 29, 30, 35—a record for USGA competitions. She was runner-up in 1931, 32 and medalist in 1921, 22, 24, 26. Mrs. Vare won 49 amateur championships in 18 years. She won 19 consecutive matches from 1928-31, another USGA record. Other victories include seven in the Eastern Women's Championship and six in the North and South. She won the French Women's Amateur in 1925 and the Canadian in 1923, 24. She was a member of the U.S. Curtis Cup team in 1932, 36, 38, 48; captain in 1934, 36, 48, 50. Perhaps her greatest match was against Joyce Wethered in the 1929 British Women's Amateur. She played the first nine in 34, was 5 up at one time, but couldn't withstand Miss Wethered's counter charge and lost, 3 and 1. In 1925 she had met Miss Wethered for the first time and lost when the English stylist shot four pars and six birdies over 10 consecutive holes. Mrs. Vare was undoubtedly the greatest golfer among American women of her period, unsurpassed at least until after World War II, when the women began turning pro and devoting all their time to the game.

VENTURI, KENNETH (Ken) B. 5/15/31, San Francisco, Cal. 6'0", 170. Venturi was runner-up in the first USGA Junior Championship in 1948. He was a member of the 1953 U.S. Walker Cup team. As an amateur, Venturi led the 1956 Masters for three rounds; he went into the final round with a 7-stroke lead but shot 80 to finish second. He turned pro shortly afterward and won 14 PGA tournaments in his career, 10 of them between 1956-60. Venturi's best year was 1964, when he won three tournaments including the USGA Open. He won the Open at Congressional C.C. in Washington, D.C., in 100-degree heat, accompanied by a doctor. Venturi shot a 70 on the final round although on the verge of heat prostration, to win by 4 shots from Tommy Jacobs. He was third place in money winnings in 1958, second in 1960, and PGA Player of the Year in 1964. Sidelined by wrist surgery during most of 1965, Ken came back to win the 1966 Lucky International. He was a member of the PGA Tournament Committee, 1960-62. In 1965 he won the Ben Hogan Award for the player who has continued to be active in golf despite a physical handicap. He rarely plays today but does some television golf commentary.

VINES, ELLSWORTH B. 9/28/11, Pasadena, Cal. One of the few athletes to succeed in two sports, Vines was one of tennis's all time greats, winning the U.S. Amateur in 1931, 32, and Wimbledon in 1932. He turned golf pro in 1942 and won five tournaments, including the 1954 California Open. He was runner-up in the 1946 All-American Open and reached the semifinal of the 1951 PGA Championship.

VOIGT, GEORGE J. B. 1894, Buffalo, N.Y. A regular amateur competitor in the 1920s and 1930s. He won the North and South Amateur in 1927, 28, 29 and played on the Walker Cup team in 1930, 32, 36. Voigt was the medalist in the 1928 USGA Amateur. The year of Bobby Jones's "Grand Slam," 1930, he had Jones two down with five to play in the British Amateur but faltered, and Jones won on the 18th hole. He was a semifinalist in the 1935 Amateur, losing to Lawson Little, the winner.

VON ELM, GEORGE B. 1901, Salt Lake City, Utah. D. 5/1/61, Pocatello, Ida. He won the 1926 USGA Amateur, defeating Bobby Jones, 2 and 1, and lost the 1931 USGA Open by 1 shot to Billy Burke in the only 72-hole playoff in U.S. Open history. Von Elm's victory over Jones in the 1926 Amateur was partial revenge for two defeats suffered at Jones's hands. Bobby beat him 9 and 8 in the 1924 final and 7 and 6 in the 1925 semifinal. In the Open of 1930 the playoff was then at 36 holes. When Von Elm and Burke were still tied, they played 36 more. George also took part in the longest overtime match in the USGA Amateur—28 holes—also in 1930, but lost it to Maurice McCarthy. Von Elm tied for third in the 1925 British Open with Walter Hagen. He won the Pacific Northwest Championship in 1921, 22, 25. He was a member of the Walker Cup team in 1926, 28, 30. He turned pro in 1930 after expressing heavy criticism of the high cost of playing tournament golf as an amateur. His professional career was less successful than his amateur.

VON NIDA, NORMAN GEORGE B. 2/14/14, Sydney, Australia. One of Australia's top all-time golfers, he won the country's Professional Championship in 1946, 48, 50, 51. A great teacher, he has worked with such pupils as Bruce Crampton, Bruce Devlin, and David Graham. Known as temperamental on the golf course, he got into a fistfight with Henry Ransom in the 1948 Rio Grande Open. He won the Australian Open in 1950, 52, 53.

VOSSLER, ERNEST (Ernie) B. 11/29/28, Fort Worth, Tex. 5'11", 175. After a brief career as a plumber, Vossler turned pro in 1954. He won the 1958 Kansas City Open, the 1959 Tijuana Open, and the 1960 Panama and Carling Opens. He was in the top 60 money winners in 1956, 57, 58, 59, 60. His best money year was 1958, when he finished 19th with $15,410. He became a club pro and has had a successful career at Southern Hills in Oklahoma. He was named Club Professional of the Year in 1967 by the PGA.

WADKINS, LANNY B. 12/5/49, Richmond, Va. 5'8½", 160. Wadkins started his golf career early, winning the 1963 National Pee Wee Championship at age 13. In 1966, at 16, he shot a 294 in the USGA Amateur, 9 strokes behind the winner. While attending Wake Forest on an Arnold Palmer golf scholarship, he had a top amateur career. In 1970 he won the USGA Amateur, five other amateur events, two collegiate tournaments, and was runner-up in the PGA's Heritage Classic. He was a member of the 1969, 71 Walker Cup teams and the 1970 World Amateur team. He was a collegiate All-American in 1970, 71. Wadkins didn't finish college, but turned pro in late 1971 and joined the tour in 1972. In 1972, he set a record for money won by a rookie with $116,616, was Rookie of the Year, and won the Sahara Invitation. He finished the year 10th in money winnings. Lanny won the Nelson and USI and $200,455 for fifth place in 1973. He had no victories in 1974, 75. His career earnings through 1975 were $397,356.

WALKER, CYRIL B. 1892, Manchester, England. D. 8/5/48, Hackensack, N.J. A dapper, fragile British professional who emigrated to the U.S. and reached a short-lived career peak when he won the 1924 USGA Open. Walker was a small man and a short hitter but he was a master at scrambling, getting up and down in 2 from off the green. His Open victory at difficult Oakland Hills came on three 74s and a 75 for 297. Bobby Jones was second, 3 shots back. This was the first Open, incidentally, in which the USGA permitted the use of the steel-shafted putter. He was personable and had many friends and a succession of club professional jobs after his Open victory, although he did not win another significant tournament. He developed drinking and health problems in later life and died in his sleep in Hackensack.

WALKER, GEORGE HERBERT B. 6/11/1874, St. Louis, Mo. D. 6/24/53, New York, N.Y. George Walker, founder of the banking and investment firm of G. H. Walker & Co. in 1900, was interested in a wide spectrum of sports and recreation with particular interest in golf. As president of the United States Golf Association in 1920 he developed the plan for amateur team matches between the United States and Great Britain and donated the International Challenge Trophy to be presented annually to the winning team. Against his wishes, this was immediately christened the Walker Cup and matches continue to be so known. Walker was also a New York State racing commissioner and, in 1925, founder and underwriter of the "new" Madison Square Garden.

WALL, ARTHUR, JR. (Art) B. 11/25/23, Honesdale, Pa. 6'0", 170. A successful touring pro in the 1950s and 1960s, Wall turned pro in 1949 and won 19 PGA tournaments, plus eight on the Caribbean tour. His best year was 1959 when he won the Crosby, Azalea, and Buick Opens, plus the Masters, where he birdied five of the last six holes. In 1959 he was the leading money winner with $53,167, the Vardon Trophy winner, and the PGA Player of the Year. He was a member of the Ryder Cup team in 1957, 59, 61. His most recent win was the 1966 Insurance City Open. He was in the top 60 money winners from 1952-64, and again in 1966, 67, 68, 71. Wall has career earnings of over $500,000. He only occasionally plays the tour today. He was a member of the PGA Tournament Committee, 1954-60. He has had 37 holes-in-one in his career. He was always an outstanding putter.

WALSH, FRANK B. 12/23/02, Chicago, Ill. Walsh was one of the great theorizers of golf. He analyzed and dissected the swing until there was not much left of it. He was a frequent contributor to the golf magazines of his day and expounded his theories at length. His best known was the "counter-clockwise" action, which closed the face of the club at the top of the swing. He even studied the effects of a wet golf glove versus a dry one, after seeing Harry Cooper dip his in a pail of water before teeing off. All this did not prevent Walsh from being a fine player. He was runner-up in the PGA Championship of 1932, losing to Olin Dutra. This was one of at least 19 times that he finished second on the PGA tour. While the pro at a New Jersey club Walsh won the state PGA twice, in 1940, 41.

WAMPLER, FREDERICK (Fred) B. 10/17/23, Bedford, Ind. Fred Wampler turned pro in 1950 and played frequently on the PGA tour in the 1950s. He won the 1954 Los Angeles Open and his best money finish was 31st in 1954.

WANAMAKER, RODMAN B. 1863. D. 3/9/28, Atlantic City, N.J. A wealthy member of the department store family who brought together the original members of the Professional Golfers' Association in January 1916, and who donated $2,580 as a purse for the first PGA Championship. Jim Barnes won it that year. Golf actually was one of his minor pursuits; his major outside interest was aviation. At his death he was head of Wanamaker's and the most heavily insured person in the world, with $6 million protection on business and family. In 1908 he had been the first individual to take out a $1 million life insurance policy.

WARD, EDWARD HARVIE B. 12/8/25, Tarboro, N.C. As a top amateur, he won the USGA Amateur in 1955, 56 and was a member of the Walker Cup team in 1953, 55, 59. He won the British Amateur in 1952, his first major international competition, and was runner-up in 1957. He won the 1948 National Collegiate, the 1948 North and South, and the 1954 Canadian Amateur; he played on the U.S. Americas Cup team in 1952, 54, 56, 58. Ward was low amateur twice in the Open and three times in the Masters. He was elected to the California Golf Hall of Fame and the North Carolina Sports Hall of Fame. He was suspended from amateur play from May 1957 to May 1958 by the USGA for accepting expenses from his employer, Ed Lowery, who had been Francis Ouimet's caddie when he won the 1913 Open. He lost interest in competitive golf after his suspension and pursued a business career. He is now back in golf, involved in teaching and promotion.

WARD, MARVIN HARVEY (Bud) B. 5/1/13, Olympia, Wash. D. 1/2/68, San Mateo, Cal. Winner of the 1939, 41 USGA Amateur Championship. He finished fourth, as an amateur, in the 1939 Open and tied for low amateur in the 1946 Open. He was a member of the Walker Cup team in 1938, 47. Ward also won the Northwest Open five times and the Western Amateur three times. He served as head pro at Peninsula C.C. until two months before his death, when his son took over the job. He died of cancer, after four operations.

WASHAM, JO ANN B. 5/24/50, Auburn, Wash. 5'3", 120. A long hitter, who graduated from Washington State University in 1972 with a degree in recreation. She turned pro and joined the LPGA tour in 1973, first winning in 1975 with the Patty Berg Classic and Portland Ladies'. The latter tournament benefits the Evans Caddie Scholarship program, and JoAnn was the second woman to ever receive such a scholarship. She finished 1975 as 12th in money with $30,950.

WATROUS, ALBERT (Al) B. 2/1/1899, Yonkers, N.Y. 5'11½", 178. Watrous had a successful career including 34 tournament victories. He won the Canadian Open in 1922 and the Western Open in 1926. He was runner-up in the 1926 British Open and played on the Ryder Cup team in 1927, 29. Watrous was a professional at the Oakland Hills C.C., Birmingham, Mich., for 37 years. An active senior player, he won the American Professional Senior Championship in 1950, 51, 57; International Senior in 1957; and PGA Quarter Century Championship in 1957, 58.

WATSON, THOMAS (Tom) B. 9/4/49, Kansas City, Mo. 5'9", 160. Watson made a fast jump from top player on the Stanford University golf team to the British Open Championship and other high professional achievements.

197

He graduated from Stanford with a degree in psychology in 1971 and joined the PGA tour the next year. He scored his first tour victory in 1974, the Western Open. That same year he led the USGA Open by 1 stroke going into the last round but finished fifth. In 1975 he won the prized British Open in a playoff, took the Byron Nelson Classic, and finally the World Series of Golf, the latter for $50,000, although it is not an official tournament. In four years as a pro he has won $390,105, in official money only.

WEAVER, BERT B. 1/13/32, Beaumont, Tex. 5'11", 185. Bert Weaver graduated from Louisiana State in 1954 and turned pro in 1956. He played the pro tour throughout the 1960s and won the 1961 Beaumont Open, the 1962 Carling, and the 1965 Jacksonville Open. He gradually went off the tour, and he now serves as a club pro in Memphis.

WEAVER, DEWITT B. 9/4/39, Danville, Ky. 5'11", 185. Dewitt Weaver turned pro in 1963 and joined the PGA tour in 1964, but lack of success sent him back to a club job for a period. He returned to the tour in 1968. One of the tour's longest hitters, he won the 1971 U.S. Match Play event, earning $76,256 for the year, and finishing in 24th place. He also won the 1972 Southern Open. His career earnings through 1975 were almost $250,000.

WEETMAN, HARRY B. 10/20/20, England. D. 7/19/72, London, England. A consistent British player, he was a member of the Ryder Cup team from 1951-63 and non-playing captain in 1965. His tournament victories include the British PGA Match Play in 1951, 58, the British Masters in 1958, and the German Open in 1957. He died after an automobile accident at the age of 51.

WEISKOPF, THOMAS (Tom) B. 11/9/42, Massillon, O. 6'3", 185. Tom Weiskopf has had a very successful career but still has not realized his enormous potential. He took up the game at age 15, and shot in the 70s a year later. He won the Western Amateur in 1963, joined the tour in 1965, and had his first win in the 1968 Andy Williams-San Diego. He has won 11 PGA events, including the 1968 Buick, the 1971 Kemper and IVB Philadelphia, and the 1972 Gleason. His best year was 1973 when he won the British Open, the Colonial, the Kemper, the IVB Philadelphia, and the Canadian Open, all in less than three months. He also won the World Series of Golf and the South African PGA that year and finished 1973 third in winnings with $245,463. Worldwide, Weiskopf won $345,000 that year. He has been in the top 20 money winners every year since 1968, and passed the million dollar earnings mark in 1974. He won the 1972 Piccadilly World Match Play and played on the 1972 World Cup team. He was a member of the Ryder Cup team in 1973, 75. In 1975 he won the Greater Greensboro and Canadian Open, defeating Jack Nicklaus in a playoff in the latter. He has tied for second in the Masters four times and was third in money winnings in 1968, 73, 75. His career earnings through 1975 were $1,224,904.

WERDEN, LINCOLN AUGUST B. 2/12/04, New York, N.Y. This veteran golf writer for the *New York Times* was the first from any newspaper to be assigned to the PGA tour on a regular basis. He was an organizer of the Golf Writers' Association of America and is a past president of that organization and of the Metropolitan Golf Writers. He was a co-founder of the Ben Hogan and Bobby Jones Awards and also of the Gold Tee Award. He was a recipient of the Richardson Award. His contributions to the game in the organizational sphere were great. A classmate of Lou Gehrig at the High School of Commerce, Werden graduated from Columbia University in 1925 and went to the *Times* in 1928. There he was the first editor of the paper's outdoors column, "Wood, Field, and Stream," and covered a great variety of sports, including figure skating, skiing, track, tennis, football, and racing. He took over the golf assignment in 1947, and covered, nationally and locally, a thousand tournaments. Retired now, Werden is the coordinator of the New York City municipal golf tournament, for the city's board of recreation and the Manufacturers Hanover Bank.

WESTLAND, ALFRED JOHN (Jack) B. 12/14/04, Everett, Wash. Westland won the USGA Amateur in 1952 at age 47, the oldest man to have done so. He won in his home district of Seattle, where he was the Republican nominee for Congress for the Second Washington District. He was elected, and he served in Congress from 1953 to 1965. He was runner-up in the 1931 USGA Amateur and won the French Amateur in 1929. The soundness of Westland's golf is shown by the fact that he reached the final of the Amateur 21 years after his first appearance there. The victor in the 1931 final was Francis Ouimet, himself winning 17 years after his first triumph in 1914. Westland won the Pacific Northwest four times, the Washington State three times. He was a member of the Walker Cup team in 1932, 34, 53, and was non-playing captain in 1961. He also served as non-playing captain of the 1954 Americas Cup team. In 1952 he was voted Metropolitan Golf Writers' Amateur of the Year. He won the U.S. Seniors' Golf Association Championship in 1962.

WETHERED, JOYCE (Lady Heathcote-Amory) B. 11/17/01, England. Considered by many as the best woman golfer of all time—with timing, a fluid swing, long hitting ability, and intense concentration. She was often compared with Bobby Jones. She won every English Ladies' Championship she entered: 1920, 21, 22, 23, 24. She won the British Women's Amateur in 1922, 24, 25, 29 and was runner-up in 1921. She represented Britain in international matches in 1921, 22, 23, 24, 25, 29. She won the Worplesdon mixed foursomes in 1922, 23, 27, 28, 31, 32, 33, 36 with various partners, including her brother Roger and writer Bernard Darwin. In 1935 she made a successful U.S. tour. In an exciting 1929 match against Glenna Collett in the British Women's final, Miss Wethered was 5 down to Collett's 34 at the end of the first nine, but played the next 18 in 73, and won on the 35th green, 3 and 1.

199

WHIGHAM, HENRY JAMES B. 12/24/1869, Tarbolton, Scotland. D. 3/17/54, New York, N.Y. The son of a well-to-do family, he attended Oxford University and was captain of the Oxford University golf team in 1892. He came to the U.S. in 1895 as a college lecturer. Whigham then won the second and third USGA Amateurs played, in 1896, 97. He married the daughter of the first U.S. Amateur champion, Charles Blair MacDonald. As a writer for the *Chicago Tribune,* he got to cover his own play in the 1897 Amateur at the Chicago C.C.—and won. He served as an overseas war correspondent in the Spanish-American War, the Boer War, the Russo-Japanese War, and the Boxer Rebellion. He became editor of *Town & Country* magazine and wrote a book, *How to Play Golf,* in 1897. He also designed the second nine holes of the Onwentsia C.C., near Chicago.

WHITE, O'NEAL (Buck) B. 2/7/11, Memphis, Tenn. Buck White did what few ever have a chance to do: he won his only PGA tour tournament in his home town, Memphis. That was in 1946, the first year the tour hit full stride again after World War II. Two years later he made his only strong bid for a national title when he tied for sixth place with Dave Douglas in the USGA Open. He was only 1 shot behind Cary Middlecoff, the winner, after three rounds but slipped to a 78 and finished 4 strokes behind.

WHITWORTH, KATHRYNNE ANN (Kathy) B. 9/22/39, Jal, N. Mex. 5'9", 140. Kathy has one of the best all-time records in women's golf. She has won more tournaments (74 through 1975) than any woman except Mickey Wright, and has won all women's major events except the USGA Women's Open, in which she was runner-up in 1971. She joined the LPGA tour in 1959 and her first big year was 1963 with eight victories. She won only one in 1964, but won eight in 1965, including the Titleholders. In 1966 she won nine, including the Titleholders, and in 1967, eight, including the LPGA Championship. She won ten in 1968; seven in 1969; two in 1970; four in 1971, including the Eve-LPGA Championship; five in 1972; seven in 1973; one in 1974, and two in 1975. Miss Whitworth was the LPGA's leading money winner in 1965, 66, 67, 68, 70, 71, 72, 73, and top all-time money winner with $576,766 through 1975. She was the winner of the Vare Trophy for the tour's lowest scoring average in 1965, 66, 67, 69, 70, 71, 72; LPGA Player of the Year in 1966, 67, 68, 69, 71, 72, 73; and Associated Press Woman Athlete of the Year in 1965, 66. In 1975 she was elected to the LPGA Hall of Fame. She was president of the LPGA Tournament Committee in 1967, 68; president of the LPGA in 1971; and vice president of the Executive Board in 1973. She holds the 72-hole LPGA scoring record of 273, scored at the 1966 Milwaukee Jaycee Open, and including a last round score of 65. A consistent player, Kathy finished high even in an off year like 1975, with two official wins and one unofficial (Colgate Triple Crown), and placing ninth on the money winners' list with $36,422. Early in 1976, Miss Whitworth scored another triumph, the Bent Tree, which she won by one shot.

WIECHERS, JAMES L. (Jim) B. 8/7/44, Oakland, Cal. 6'2", 205. Wiechers won the USGA Junior Championship in 1962. In 1966 he turned pro and joined the tour in 1967. He had moderate success on the tour, winning the 1969 West End Classic. A good short game player, he had eight finishes in the top 10 in 1973. He has won over $300,000 on the tour through 1975.

WILLIAMS, DAVID (Dave) B. 10/14/18, Randolph, Tex. Dave Williams is a golf coach at the University of Houston. He holds a master's degree in chemistry and a degree in mechanical engineering. In 25 years at Houston, Williams has coached more national championship teams than any other coach in any sport. The Houston team has won over 250 team championships—about 200 more than any other team. It has won 12 NCAA championships: 1956, 57, 58, 59, 60, 62, 64, 65, 66, 67, 69, 70; and has had seven individual champions. His 1971 team won 18 straight tournaments. He is the tournament director of the All-American Intercollegiate Invitation, the oldest 72-hole college invitation in the U.S. Top golfers coached by Williams include Homero Blancas, Jacky Cupit, Babe and Jim Hiskey, John Mahaffey, Phil Rodgers, and Kermit Zarley.

WILLING, DR. OSCAR F. B. October, 1889. An amateur player who was active in the first part of the century, winning the Northwest Amateur in 1924, 28 and the Northwest Open in 1928. In 1929 Dr. Willing went to the final round of the USGA Amateur, defeating Cyril Tolley of England and Chandler Egan along the way. He was beaten in the final by Jimmy Johnston, 4 and 3. This was the first year the Amateur was played on the Pacific Coast (Pebble Beach) and also the year Bobby Jones was upset in the first round by Johnny Goodman. Dr. Willing was a member of the U.S. Walker Cup team in 1923, 24, 30.

WILSON, ENID B. 3/15/10, Stonebroon, Derbyshire, England. One of England's top women players, Miss Wilson won the British Women's Amateur three years in a row: 1931, 32, 33. She played on the Curtis Cup team in 1932. She twice took the English Ladies' title, in 1928, 30, and was runner-up in 1927. Miss Wilson won the British Girls' Championship in 1925. In 1933 she gained the semifinal of the USGA Women's Amateur, after taking the medal with a 76, but lost to the eventual winner, Virginia Van Wie.

WILSON, LOUIS SIBBETT (Dick) B. 1/29/03, Glenside, Pa. D. 7/5/65, Delray Beach, Fla. One of the best American golf course architects. Wilson took up the profession at an early age, working with the firm of Toomey & Flynn during the 1920s. He was sometimes temperamental. He settled in Florida, the site of some of his best work, as well as his headquarters. His Florida course designs include the Doral, JDM (formerly PGA National), Bay Hill, and Pine Tree, sometimes considered his best. Others he designed include Cog Hill No. 4 and NCR in Ohio. Wilson also totally redesigned

Shinnecock Hills on Long Island, a course originally laid out by Willie Dunn in 1891.

WILSON, MARGARET JOYCE (Peggy) B. 12/28/34, Lauderdale, Miss. 5'5", 130. This high school and college (Mississippi State College for Women) basketball player and cheerleader turned to the LPGA tour in 1962 after moderate success as an amateur. She has had one victory, the 1968 Hollywood Lakes Open, and several second-place finishes. The most notable was in the 1969 USGA Women's Open, when she finished only a stroke behind Donna Caponi. She also was second in the 1965 Titleholders and the 1966 Lady Carling, and tied for second in the 1967 Milwaukee Open. When she was 15 years old Miss Wilson dreamed she was playing golf before a big gallery, and just followed her dream.

WIND, HERBERT WARREN B. 8/11/16, Brockton, Mass. One of golf's top writers, he has been on the staff of the *New Yorker* since 1962. He wrote for *Sports Illustrated,* 1954-62, and for the *New Yorker,* 1949-54. His golf books include *The Story of American Golf, The Complete Golfer, Tips from the Top* (two volumes), *Thirty Years of Championship Golf* (with Gene Sarazen), *The Greatest Game of All: My Life in Golf* (with Jack Nicklaus), *Modern Fundamentals of Golf* (with Ben Hogan), *Herbert Warren Wind's Golf Book,* and *On the Tour with Harry Sprague.* An enthusiastic golfer, Wind played in the 1950 British Amateur. He was a member of the Royal and Ancient Golf Club, director of the Yale Golf Association, a member of the USGA Museum Committee and the Bob Jones Award Committee, a member of the Metropolitan Golf Association Public Information Committee, and a member of the Oxford and Cambridge Golfing Society.

WININGER, FRANCIS G. (Bo) B. 11/16/22, Chico, Cal. D. 12/7/67, Las Vegas, Nev. 5'8", 167. A popular, personable pro who cut a debonair figure on tour during his relatively short career there. He turned pro in 1952 after playing winning golf for Texas A & M. In his first four years on the tour, he won three tournaments. In 1960, 61 he dropped off the tour to do public relations work for an oil field equipment company. He came back to win the 1962 Carling, then went on a big game safari in Africa (bagging an elephant, a rhino, and more), then returned once again to win the 1963 New Orleans Open.

WIREN, DR. GARY B. 10/5/35, Fort Dodge, Ia. Wiren turned pro in 1958. He was Golf Pro of the Year, Pacific Northwest Section, in 1971 and received the National Golf Foundation Service Award in 1972. He has been the PGA's National Director of Education since 1972. He is the author of over 40 articles on golf and two books, *Golf* and *Organizing and Conducting Junior Golf Programs.*

WOOD, CRAIG RALPH B. 11/18/01, Lake Placid, N.Y. D. 5/8/68, Palm Beach, Fla. A popular player of the 1930s and 1940s, Wood won 34 PGA tournaments during his career and had a number of almost-wins. He won the 1941 USGA Open, playing with his back in a brace, and held that title for five years, while the tournament was suspended during World War II. He also won the 1941 Masters. On the hard-luck side, Craig lost the 1939 U.S. Open to Byron Nelson in a playoff, and lost the 1935 Masters to Gene Sarazen in a playoff, caused by Sarazen's famous double eagle. Wood was a member of the Ryder Cup team in 1931, 33, 35 and was elected to the PGA Hall of Fame in 1956. He hit the longest recorded drive in major competition in the 1933 British Open, 430 yards on the fifth hole at St. Andrews, with a strong following wind. He served as pro at the Winged Foot G.C., Mamaroneck, N.Y., for many years.

WORSHAM, LEWIS (Lew) B. 10/5/17, Alta Vista, Va. Worsham turned pro in 1935 and his successful career included seven PGA tournament victories. His greatest was the 1947 USGA Open. He also won the 1953 World Championship for a $25,000 first prize, by sinking a 108-yard approach shot with a pitching wedge for an eagle 2. Worsham's victory in the Open came when Sam Snead missed a putt of about 30 inches on the final hole of a playoff, with Lew holing from about the same distance. He was the top money winner in 1953. In 1947 he was a member of the Ryder Cup team. Today he is the resident professional at the Oakmont Country Club in Oakmont, Pennsylvania, the site of many major tournaments over the years.

WRIGHT, FREDERICK J., JR. B. 1898, Watertown, Mass. D. 8/36/58, Brookline, Mass. An active amateur player from 1916, when he entered the Massachusetts Amateur for the first time. He later won the event seven times. In 1920 Wright tied with Bobby Jones for the medal in the qualifying round of the USGA Amateur. He defeated Jess Sweetser in the second round but was beaten by Jones in the third. Wright was a member of the 1923 Walker Cup team and won the 1951 Bermuda Amateur. In 1956, as a grandfather of four and employed as a Boston securities broker, he won the USGA Senior title and was runner-up in 1957. Wright died in 1958 on the 13th tee at The Country Club, Brookline, Massachusetts, during sectional qualifying for the 1958 Senior.

WRIGHT, MARY KATHRYN (Mickey) B. 2/14/35, San Diego, Cal. 5'9", 150. One of the greatest women players of all time. She won the USGA Junior Girls' Championship in 1952 and turned pro two years later. She won 82 tournaments in her career, a record, and 58 in her 10 most active years. She had at least one tournament victory a year from 1956-70, and she holds the LPGA record for the most tournament wins in a year, 14 in 1963. She won the USGA Women's Open and LPGA Championship in 1958, 61. She also won the LPGA Championship in 1960, 63; the Open in 1959, 64; and the Vare Trophy for low scoring average in 1960, 61, 62, 63, 64. Miss Wright was the Associated Press Woman Athlete of the Year in 1963, 64 and leading money winner on the LPGA tour from 1961-64. Her best overall season was 1966, with seven wins and over $40,000. She won 10 events in 1961, 10 in

1962, and 11 in 1964. She holds the LPGA 18-hole scoring record of 62, made in the last round of the 1964 Tall City Open. In 1964 she was the president of the LPGA. She's still an occasional competitor on the LPGA tour.

WYSONG, DUDLEY, JR. B. 5/15/39, McKinney, Tex. Wysong turned pro in 1963 but despite a couple of tour victories, he never made it big. His wins were the 1966 Phoenix Open and the 1967 Hawaiian. He was runner-up in the 1961 USGA Amateur and the 1966 PGA Championship. In the Amateur, Wysong defeated Joe Carr of Ireland in the semifinal, 2 up, but lost to Jack Nicklaus in the final, 8 and 6. In the 1966 PGA Championship, he was nosed out by Al Geiberger.

YANCEY, ALBERT WINSBOROUGH (Bert) B. 8/6/38, Chipley, Fla. 6'1", 190. Yancey turned pro in 1960, joined the tour in 1964, and is perhaps the tour's most avid student of the game. He cites winning the Masters as his goal. So far, he has won seven tournaments: the 1966 Azalea, Memphis, and Portland Opens; the 1967 Dallas; the 1969 Atlanta; the 1970 Crosby; and the 1972 American Golf Classic. He lost the 1968 USGA Open to Lee Trevino, although he had a 5-stroke lead going into the last 27 holes. He has been in the top fifty money winners every year from 1965-74. His career earnings through 1975 were $688,124. He attended West Point.

YATES, CHARLES RICHARDSON B. 9/9/13, Atlanta, Ga. A popular young amateur, he was well received by the British when he won the British Amateur in 1938 as a fellow townsman of Bobby Jones. Prior to that, Yates won the 1934 Intercollegiate Championship and the 1935 Western Amateur. He played on the Walker Cup team in 1936 and 1938 and was non-playing captain in 1953. He was low amateur in the Masters in 1934, 39, 40.

YOUNG, DONNA CAPONI B. 1/29/45, Detroit, Mich. Miss Young joined the LPGA tour in 1965 after being active in sports during her high school years, where she won varsity letters in seven sports. She is an outgoing, personable player and has won seven official events through 1975. She won the 1969, 70 USGA Women's Opens, the 1969 Lincoln Mercury Open, the 1970, 73 Bluegrass Invitations, and the 1975 Burdines Invitation and Lady Tara Open. She also won the 1975 Colgate European Open, an unofficial event, for the $11,000 first prize. She was voted *Golf Digest*'s Most Improved Golfer in 1969 and the *Los Angeles Times*' Woman Golfer of the Year in 1970. Her best money year was 1975 when she finished seventh on the money list with $43,291. In March 1976, Miss Young ran away with the Australian Championship, winning by 9 shots.

ZAHARIAS, MILDRED DIDRIKSON (Babe) B. 6/26/14, Port Arthur, Tex. D. 9/27/56, Galveston, Tex. One of the top female athletes of all time, very possibly the best to date. She acquired her nickname because of a childhood baseball prowess in the era of Babe Ruth. She first caught the world's attention in the 1932 Olympics when she set three records: 11.3 seconds in the 80-meter hurdles, 143 feet in the javelin, and 5'5³/₄" in the high jump. She entered her first golf tournament in November 1934 and took the medal with a 77. She won the USGA Women's Amateur in 1946, in her first try. In 1947 she became the first American woman to win the British Women's Amateur, after which she turned pro. As an amateur she won 16 consecutive tournaments from June 1946 to July 1947. She was the dominating figure on the early LPGA tour and one of the prime movers behind it. She won 31 LPGA events in eight years, almost a third of all LPGA events played in that period. Her victories as a pro include the World Championship in 1948, 49, 50, 51, the Titleholders Championship in 1950, 52, and the USGA Women's Open in 1948, 50, 54, the latter by 12 strokes, the tournament's largest winning margin, soon after a cancer operation. She used to hit 1,000 balls a day and averaged 240 yards off the tee. Her husband George was a wrestler. She was the LPGA's top money winner in 1948, 49, 50, 51 and won the Vare Trophy for her low scoring average in 1954. She was elected to the LPGA Hall of Fame in the first group of entries in 1951. She was selected by the Associated Press as Female Athlete of the Year in 1932, 45, 46, 47, 50. In 1949 the AP selected her as the Greatest Female Athlete of the Half Century. Mrs. Zaharias died of cancer after a number of operations over a three-year period.

ZARLEY, KERMIT B. 9/29/41, Seattle, Wash. 6'0", 175. The star of the University of Houston golf team, he won the NCAA Championship in 1963. He joined the PGA tour after college graduation. Zarley won the 1968 Kaiser, the 1970 Canadian Open, and the 1972 National Team Championship.

He is a regular contender and was in the top 50 money winners in 1966, 67, 68, 70, 72, 73. His career earnings through 1975 were $463,936. He has a strong religious interest and organizes Bible study groups on the tour.

ZIEGLER, LAWRENCE (Larry) B. 8/12/39, St. Louis, Mo. 6'0", 185. Ziegler turned pro in 1959 and joined the tour in 1966. He won the 1969 Michigan Classic, for which he had trouble getting his winner's check because the tournament was bankrupt. He finally received the prize money from the PGA. He won the 1975 Greater Jacksonville Open and the 1974 International Grand Prix of Morocco. Ziegler is a long hitter who is also an avid hockey fan. He sometimes works out with, and serves on the board of, the St. Louis Blues. He finished the 1974 season 27th in money winnings, and was 40th in 1975. His career earnings through 1975 were $363,400. In April 1976, he won the NBC New Orleans Open.